**Twayne's Theatrical Arts Series**

Warren French
EDITOR

# Leni Riefenstahl

Leni Riefenstahl

# Leni Riefenstahl

RENATA BERG-PAN

BOSTON

Twayne Publishers

1980

**Leni Riefenstahl**

is first published in 1980 by Twayne Publishers,
A Division of G. K. Hall & Co.

Printed on permanent/durable acid-free paper and bound
in the United States of America

*First Printing, October, 1980*

Frontispiece photo of Leni Riefenstahl at the
Munich Olympics, 1972, courtesy of
Leni Riefenstahl-Produktion

**Library of Congress Cataloging in Publication Data**

Berg-Pan, Renata.
Leni Riefenstahl

(Twayne's theatrical arts series)
Bibliography: p. 203-08
Filmography: p. 211-17
Includes index.
1. Riefenstahl, Leni.
PN1998.A3R5242   791.43′0233′0924   80-14129
ISBN 0-8057-9275-9

# Contents

# About the Author

Renata Berg-Pan was born in Hamburg, Germany, and received her post-high-school education in the United States. After studying English and comparative literature at the University of Washington, she earned a doctorate at Harvard University in 1971. As a member of the teaching staffs at the Massachusetts Institute of Technology, Harvard University, Queens College of the City University of New York, and Indiana University (Bloomington), she has taught a variety of subjects, including film theory and history, literature and philosophy, English, German, and French language and literature, as well as philosophy. Her most recent publication is *Bertolt Brecht and China*.

# Editor's Foreword

THAT THE WOMAN who has made the most original contributions as a film director should remain also filmmaking's most controversial figure is the great paradox in the history of this young art. No one can seriously deny that film directing is one of the many male-dominated professions that women have found extremely difficult to break into. We should expect that a woman who could fight her way to the top in such a jealously guarded calling would be distinguished by extraordinary talent, an extraordinary ego, and a willingness to take extraordinary risks. Certainly Leni Riefenstahl has been such a woman. Her first film successes in Dr. Arnold Fanck's mountain films involved enormous physical risks, of the kind that she still takes by becoming a scuba diver in her seventies. Her involvement with the Nazi leaders of Germany's Third Reich required even greater professional risks that in the long run have proved more crippling.

So much of what has been written about Leni Riefenstahl has been based on gossip and political speculation that her actual and potential contributions to film art have been comparatively sidetracked. The technical resourcefulness that she displayed in making *Triumph of the Will* and *Olympia*, and the unique aesthetic qualities of the finished films have been, of course, generally acknowledged. As a maker of ceremonial films, she has never had an equal; but since these films were made under the auspices of the Nazi government, not just the filmmaker herself, but the very genre has fallen under suspicion. Have other filmmakers failed to make as impressive ritualistic films because of their individual failure to achieve an inspired relationship between the content and film form; or is there indeed something about the atmosphere of an aggressive totalitarian state that alone makes such films possible? Certainly the Fascist regimes in Europe showed a unique willingness to finance such spectacles, although it should be noted that without a Riefenstahl in charge the now forgotten Italian efforts have generally been dismissed by those who have seen them as fully as boring as the ceremonials themselves are to those not passionately involved in them. To begin even to get some insight into this perplexing situation, we would have to see, for example, what someone with Riefenstahl's planning and editing skills would have made out of the *Woodstock* footage.

Probably it is impossible to write about Riefenstahl without engaging in some gossip and speculation, even some recriminations about what can perhaps most neutrally be called her obtuseness about her relationships to her sponsors. The merit of this book, we feel, is that Renata Berg-Pan has attempted insofar as possible to avoid becoming bogged down in Riefenstahl's private life and political views (or lack of them) in order to concentrate on exactly what she did bring to the screen—and what she did not.

Personally, I find the most interesting part of this book to be the detailed accounts of the mutilated and long suppressed *Tiefland* and the unrealized "Penthesilea" projects, to which Riefenstahl made her greatest emotional commitment. The fullest understanding of Riefenstahl as an artist will come, I believe, from study of her highly personal involvement in these projects rather than from her impersonal craftsmanship in *Triumph of the Will* and *Olympia*. (So strong has been her personal stamp on her work that every chapter of this book, except that on *Triumph of the Will* and possibly *Olympia* opens with a picture of her to provide a motif for the discussion.)

The more we learn about Riefenstahl, the more complex and confusing figure she becomes. New questions arise from the present study of her career. Could both she and her constant antagonist Dr. Goebbels have been so single-minded and unselfconscious as to fail to recognize the antitotalitarian tendency of *Tiefland*? How could Goebbels have continued to give even minimum support to this project at a time when military reverses were beginning to threaten the "thousand-year Reich"? Could the Nazis who killed millions have been so intimidated by one woman that they continued to pay her off to keep quiet, or were they indeed too self-deluded to recognize veiled attacks upon them? (One does recall that Picasso was able to get away with the play "Desire Trapped by the Tail" in occupied Paris.) Either alternative raises questions about the Nazi's conscious control of their own schemes and the utility of rational criticism of their actions.

The "Penthesilea" projects indicate much less ambiguously than any of Riefenstahl's completed ventures that, beyond anything else, she was a militant feminist. Feminist spokeswomen, who have varied greatly in their responses to this undeniably accomplished woman, might find evidence useful in speculating on some of their own underlying problems and aims in studying Riefenstahl's commitment—apparently the longest and most enduring of her career—to the unrealized dream of giving this myth form as a ritualistic film.

Renata Berg-Pan wisely chooses to make no final judgment of Leni Riefenstahl beyond the indisputable ones that she has remained too haughty and not self-searching enough to present herself to the world in the best light and that the development of film art has probably lost a great deal because of the obstacles placed in the way of her development after World War II for what may not be adequate reasons. (Before jumping to the conclusion, however, that Riefenstahl's troubles since 1945 have exclusively political origins, we need also to recall that such other radically original filmmakers as Orson Welles and Abel Gance have experienced similar frustrations. Rather than being exploited by the Nazis, Riefenstahl may indeed have been able to exploit them for her own purposes as she has not again been able to exploit anyone else.)

After reading Renata Berg-Pan's account, I cannot help but indulge myself in utterly useless speculation about what would have happened if someone had invited Leni Riefenstahl to stay in Hollywood when she visited in 1938? Would she have fared any better there than such welcomed refugees as Luis Buñuel and Jean Renoir? Would she have been content to out-Berkeley Busby in designing the kind of production numbers in which human bodies are reduced to components in abstract patterns, for these are indeed Hollywood's closest approximations of the most admired passages in *Triumph of the Will* and *Olympia*.

On the basis of these two Nazi documentary fantasies alone, Riefenstahl deserves a place in a series of books devoted primarily to those imaginative and inventive enough to advance the art of filmmaking; but we hope that this book will suggest also through its account of her rise through the "mountain pictures" to the creation of the visionary *The Blue Light* and of the nature of her frustrated postwar projects (consider especially the scheme proposed in 1960 for an even more "magical" *Blue Light* than the original) that the question of judging Leni Riefenstahl is a good deal more complicated than reference to only her two famous contributions to Hitler's yen to be a culture hero can suggest.

W. F.

# Preface

FRIENDS AND ACQUAINTANCES advised me against writing a book about the "Film Goddess of the Third Reich," as Leni Riefenstahl was called, among other names, during the era of the National Socialist government in Germany. They thought that the topic was too controversial, would offend too many political sensibilities, and ultimately turn against its author.

These predictions came true during the research for and the writing of this book. As long as I worked only with written or filmed sources, things were fairly easy. But I encountered difficulties as soon as I began to interview living people, check into so-called "public opinion," and approach persons involved with the Third Reich, including Riefenstahl herself. I encountered contradiction upon contradiction, had to sift through love and hate, gratitude and pain, happy and sad memories—all of which intermingled into undecipherable chaos. Those who knew and still know Leni Riefenstahl personally were careful not to say too much in praise of her, for fear, I believe, of being classed as Nazis. Authors of books and articles commenting on the high quality of her films were accused of "whitewashing" her. Everyone writing on Leni Riefenstahl feels the need, explicitly or implicitly, to justify taking up the subject. One is in a position resembling that of Ulysses when he came between the Scylla and Charybdis: One is damned if one praises Riefenstahl or if one condemns her, although in the latter instance one's chances of survival are slightly better.

The subject at hand obviously is still very much alive and hence controversial. For those who remember anything at all about the Third Reich from personal experience, it is almost impossible to view Riefenstahl's films dispassionately and exclusively as works of art. Only God, so it seems, can do that, or perhaps future critics and viewers, for whom the Third Reich is no more than a distant myth.

Moreover, not all is said and done on this subject. Leni Riefenstahl is reportedly writing or contemplating the writing of her memoirs which will undoubtedly make interesting reading and throw new light on many questions still open, although Riefenstahl's own account of her story will add fuel to the heat of the controversy surrounding her life and career. Among film critics, especially in Germany, Riefenstahl acquired a reputation as a liar after World War II. There is no question that she frequently made contradictory statements which cast doubt upon her veracity. On the other hand, those who knew her before and especially during the Third Reich frequently failed to reveal the complete truth or distorted it, and thus their testimony is also tainted. Among these is the late Dr. Arnold Fanck, Riefenstahl's mentor and "professor." The personal atmosphere surrounding the life and times of Leni Riefenstahl is fraught with jealousies, hatred, and contradiction.

Her work on celluloid, on the other hand, has a certain finality. It is for this reason that in my study I have concentrated on Riefenstahl's films rather than the gossip surrounding her person, although the latter is probably at least as interesting, if not more so. As a matter of fact, Leni Riefenstahl is one of the most adventurous, fearless, and impulsive women to have transcended the boundaries of ordinary, bourgeois, daily existence. The unusually heavy calumny and vituperation cast upon her by critics can also be traced to that fact. As for her own frequently contradictory statements, I believe that they concern only her career and relationship with the leadership of the Third Reich. It seems that Leni Riefenstahl regrets nothing and has no guilt complexes about her past. This quality she shares with many real Nazis who assumed leading positions in Germany or elsewhere in the Western world after 1945. But Riefenstahl would do herself and the rest of the world a great favor if, once and for all, she admitted that aligning herself with the National Socialists was a regrettable moral error, an error born out of a talented and ambitious artist's opportunism and good luck. So far she has failed to admit to having erred. As for her comments regarding photo-technical details and the nitty-gritty of filmmaking, Riefenstahl seems to be trustworthy and her statements could generally be confirmed by her former colleagues and assistants.

While my work here may not constitute the last word on Leni Riefenstahl and her career as a film director during the Third Reich, I hope at least that the films themselves, two of which have been hailed as great works of art, have been given the attention they deserve—attention which was not accorded them previously.

Since American as well as German foundations and academic institutions refused to support this project—probably because they found it too controversial—I had to rely mainly on the good will and hard work of individuals in a position to help me with this book. Among these is Charles Silver of the Film Department at the Museum of Modern Art in New York City. Without his assistance it would have been impossible to view the films of Riefenstahl. In fact, it would have been unthinkable to write on Riefenstahl in any other city but New York. Henry Jaworsky (formerly Heinz von Jaworsky), assistant and cameraman for two of Riefenstahl's films, gave generously of his time and provided much information otherwise unavailable to me. Gordon Hitchens, the New York journalist, gave me inestimable assistance in contacting persons in the U.S. who knew and still know Leni Riefenstahl, not all of whom wanted to be mentioned here. Eberhard Spiess of the Deutsches Institut für Filmkunde in Wiesbaden proved to be knowledgeable, punctual, interested, and most helpful during my stay at his wonderfully informal yet reliable institution. Dr. Lynne Martin of the Amerika-Haus in Frankfurt, Germany, was like a godmother to the book, providing me with physical and moral support. Frank Jones and James Lyon helped me in ways only they know, and my mother Anna Berg had to put up with me more often than she may have wished. Thanks are due also to the Archives of the Federal Republic of Germany in Koblenz, the National Archives and the Library of Congress in Washington, and the Berlin Document Center. Several distributors of films in New York, among them Phoenix Films and Janus Films, assisted me in viewing unusual prints of Riefenstahl's films. Thank you, Roland.

RENATA BERG-PAN

New York City

# Chronology

1902    Leni Riefenstahl, born Helene Berta Amalie Riefenstahl in Berlin, Germany, August 22.

1910    Begins to take dancing lessons.

1920    Appears regularly on stage as a dancer.

1926    Signs contract with Arnold Fanck to appear as dancer in *Der heilige Berg* (*The Holy Mountain*). Learns filmmaking from Arnold Fanck.

1927    Stars in *Der grosse Sprung* (*The Great Leap*), directed by Arnold Fanck.

1929    Stars in *Die weisse Hölle vom Piz Palü* (*The White Hell of Piz Palü.*) directed by W. C. Pabst and Arnold Fanck. Stars in *Das Schicksal derer von Habsburg* (*The Destiny of the Hapsburgs*), directed by Rudolf Raffé.

1930    Acts in *Stürme über dem Montblanc* (*Storms over Mont Blanc*), directed by Arnold Fanck.

1931    Establishes her own production company, Riefenstahl Films.

1932    Release of *Das blaue Licht* (*The Blue Light*), the first film she directs and in which she also stars. Meets Adolf Hitler for the first time. Wins Silver Medal at the Venice Biennial for *Das blaue Licht*.

1933    Stars with flyer Ernst Udet in *SOS Eisberg* (*SOS Iceberg*), directed by Arnold Fanck. Appointed by Hitler as "film expert to the National Socialist Party." Upon Hitler's request, films *Sieg des Glaubens* (*Victory of Faith*), about 1933 Nazi party rally. Publishes *Kampf in Schnee und Eis* (*Struggle in Snow and Ice*), autobiographical account of her films.

1934    Arranges to film *Tiefland* (*Lowlands*, released in 1954) in Spain, but is asked by Hitler to film Nazi party rally in Nuremberg that year. September 5-10, films *Triumph des Willens* (*Triumph of the Will*).

1935  March 28, premiere of *Triumph des Willens*. Directs *Tag des Freiheit (Day of Freedom)* about the German army. Publishes *Hinter den Kulissen des Reichparteitagsfilms (Behind the Scenes of the Reich Party Congress)*. May 1, awarded National Film Prize by Joseph Goebbels for *Triumph des Willens*. October 15, signs agreement to produce 1936 Summer Olympics film.

1936  June, awarded Italian Film Prize for *Triumph des Willens*. August 1—14, shoots film about the 1936 Olympic games in Berlin.

1937  July 4, awarded the Diplôme de Grand Prix for *Triumph des Willens* at the Exposition Internationale des Arts et des Techniques in Paris. Publishes *Schönheit im Olympischen Kampf (Beauty in the Olympic Struggle)*.

1938  April 20, Hitler's birthday, premiere of *Olympia I: Fest der Völker (Festival of Nations)* May 2, awarded the State Prize for the best film of the year, *Olympia*. Awarded the Polar Prize in Sweden, first prize at the International Moving Picture Festival in Venice for *Olympia*, and the *Grand Prix* in Paris for *Olympia*. November 4, arrives in New York to publicize *Olympia*.

1938  Begins preparations for shooting *Penthesilea*, based upon play by Heinrich von Kleist.

1944  Marries Peter Jacob, decorated major in the German army. March 21, sees Hitler for the last time; writes, produces, and stars in *Tiefland* (released in 1954).

1945-  Detained in various prisons and camps by Allied forces on
1948  charges of pro-Nazi activities.

1948  Receives diploma certifying award of the Gold Medal for *Olympia*, but does not receive medal.

1949-  Struggles for rehabilitation and tries to retrieve her lost films.
1953

1951  Reedits *Das blaue Licht* (released 1952). Establishes Italian version of this film.

1952  Charges that she was a Nazi dismissed by a Berlin court.

1954  Travels through Germany and Austria to promote newly finished version of *Tiefland*.

1955  Prepares to shoot mountain film *Ewige Gipfel (Eternal Summits)* in color (not completed).

1956    Begins work in Africa on *Schwarze Fracht* (*Black Cargo*), a color documentary about black slave trade, (not completed). Suffers serious car accident (possibly act of sabotage) in Northern Kenya. Makes film on the Nuba.

1957    Writes three screenplays in Spain: "Three Stars in the Mantle of the Madonna," "Light and Shade," "Dance of Death."

1958-   Tours Germany with film *Olympia*.
1959

1960    Writes a remake of *Das blaue Licht* together with two English screenwriters.

1961-   Numerous trips to Africa.
1968

1968    Publishes *Menschen wie von einem andern Stern* (*The Last of the Nuba*).

1969    Receives Gold Medal from Art Directors Club for her photography about the Nuba.

1972    Commissioned by *London Times* to photograph Olympic Games in Munich. Completes film on the Nuba in the Sudan.

1974    Attends Film Festival in Telluride, Colorado, where she is picketed by anti-Nazi groups.

1975    Learns scuba diving.

1976    Publishes *Die Nuba von Kau* (*The People of Kau*).

1978    Publishes *Korallengärten* (*Coral Gardens*), about underwater photography.

# 1

# The Life and Times of Leni Riefenstahl

## Early Years

LENI RIEFENSTAHL was born Helene Berta Amalie Riefenstahl in Berlin, on August 22, 1902. Her father, Alfred Riefenstahl, was the owner of a plumbing engineering firm. Her mother (née Scherlach), was a housewife with latent artistic talent, imagination, and great ambitions for her daughter. Riefenstahl had a brother, named Heinz, who died in World War II as a soldier in Hitler's army. During her childhood Leni Riefenstahl always had enough money to follow her dreams. Her mother supported her strongly in her inclinations, while her father, a comparatively enlightened man, wanted her to be a business woman. Thus Leni did not suffer from the usual repression of girls in a German household. No one in her family thought that she should just grow up, get married, and become a *Hausfrau*. The conflict in her family life resided in the fact that her father wished to train her in business administration, a profession for which she had no inclination, and her mother wanted to help her to fulfill her own wishes. Thus Leni Riefenstahl secretly began to take dancing lessons at the age of eight. "When I was six or seven years old, I saw *Swan Lake* in the theater, and from that moment I wanted to dance," she told the B.B.C. during a June, 1972, interview. Her father disliked her artistic ambitions and demanded that she take business courses. However, Leni and her mother were stronger than her father, and her mother managed to provide her with the desired dancing lessons behind her father's back. When Riefenstahl's father discovered that his daughter was taking these lessons, he tried to change her mind at first, but recognizing that his daughter was determined to pursue her dancing career, he decided that she should enroll in the best dancing school in Berlin and discover for herself that she had no talent.

Thus Leni Riefenstahl became a student in the famous Russian Ballet School in Berlin. After the first lesson, it was evident to her first teacher, Jutta Klammt, that her new pupil had great talent: Riefenstahl's father had miscalculated and had underestimated his daughter's talents. Instead of disinheriting her or punishing her in other ways, something not unusual in German households with strong willed daughters, her father later proudly insisted that he had supported her all along, and he allowed her to continue her lessons. This entire story speaks well for Riefenstahl's father, but it also testifies to a characteristic feature in Riefenstahl which she retained all her life: the enormous willpower and self-discipline that inspired others to support her in her endeavors.

In 1919, Riefenstahl was called upon to substitute for a well-known dancer, Anita Berber, during a performance in Berlin. Riefenstahl received only average reviews for her dancing, but she was encouraged to continue her training. Throughout her dancing career she exhibited tenacious ambition as well as truly creative abilities. "My desire was to dance alone, to dance to my own fancy," she said. "I was always different from others. I designed my own costumes, choreographed my own performances." Riefenstahl's very individualistic approach to art may have had a personal basis. She wanted to be different, to be unusual, perhaps to be noticed, and she was encouraged in her efforts. She clearly did not wish to be lost in the crowd but wanted to stand out. This tendency found expression in her later work: she wanted to do that which was unusual, and she was interested only in aspects of life that were unusual and out of the ordinary. "Whatever is purely realistic, slice-of-life, what is average, quotidian, doesn't interest me. Only the unusual, the specific, excites me. I am fascinated by what is beautiful, strong, healthy, by what is living," she told an interviewer.[1]

In her teens, Riefenstahl became interested in the forms of dance that were introduced by Isadora Duncan and other modern dancers. Like the new dancing stars, Riefenstahl had also become tired of artificial dance forms. Inspired by the art of ancient Greece, Duncan had advocated the natural use of the body, clothed in loose garments, worn by a dancer who would dance barefoot on a stage with little or no scenery or props. One of the first dancers to promote this style was Mary Wigman, who had opened her own dancing school in Berlin where Riefenstahl became one of her students.

By 1920, Riefenstahl appeared regularly on the stage as a dancer. She was noticed by well-known stage personalities all over Europe, for she appeared in the major European cities, including Munich, Berlin, Frankfurt, Prague, Zurich, and Dresden. Her mother accompanied her on her tours. Riefenstahl gradually became so popular that she could not satisfy the demand for her appearances.[2] Her dancing was also financially successful, for she earned between six and seven hundred marks for each performance (then about one hundred and fifty dollars).

In the course of her career she met Max Reinhardt, the well-known stage director. One day they happened to ride the same train, on which Riefenstahl was traveling to the Alps to act in her first film. After staring at her for a while, Reinhardt came over to her and told her how beautifully she danced. He then offered her a leading part in the new play—Heinrich von Kleist's *Penthesilea*—that he was going to produce at the Theater der Josefstadt in Vienna. "I have finally found my *Penthesilea*," Reinhardt reportedly said to Riefenstahl upon first meeting her.[3] Riefenstahl immediately set out to inform herself about Penthesilea, the queen of the legendary Amazons, of whom she had known nothing until that moment. Kleist's *Penthesilea*, composed in 1808, provided an unusual opportunity for an ambitious actress to play the title role. Rarely performed in the German theaters, Kleist's play is familiar only to students of German literature or pupils attending a German gymnasium (high school). Riefenstahl was not insensitive to the possibilities inherent in the story of Penthesilea (mentioned in Homer's *Odyssey*) and she began to read other works by Kleist, as well as works by the ancient classical writers and modern scholars concerning the queen of the Amazons. What she read struck her as curious and remarkable. From the outset she had experienced a particular feeling: "Penthesilea and I formed an indivisible entity. Each of her words, each of her expressions—I had the feeling of having already lived them myself," she confessed.[4] The story of Penthesilea remained in her mind for many years, and in the late 1930's she decided to make a film about it, thinking that only the film medium would be able to do justice to this highly dramatic and unusual story. The film project was never completed. At her meeting with Reinhardt, she promised that she would play the part of Penthesilea after she had completed her role in the film in which she was about to act. Riefenstahl failed to keep her promise. One reason was that the German film industry now began to outgrow its infancy. During Riefenstahl's teens it was generally thought that people who attended movies were only interested in cheap entertainment. An excellent example of this attitude is presented in Bertolt Brecht's short story "The Undignified Old Lady" ("Die unwürdige Greisin"). At that time, movie audiences consisted mostly of unemployed men and women who had been able to save up just enough money for a movie ticket. It was always less expensive to go to a movie than to a theater, since in Germany at least, a visit to the theater required elaborate dressing. The movie, on the other hand, could be attended by people who were shabbily dressed and who would have been turned away by the doorman of any self-respecting theater. For the poor, the movie house provided a respectable and even warm place to spend some time with their lovers. Stage directors, traditional writers, and members of the academic profession deliberately ignored the cinema as an art that was below their dignity. Leni Riefenstahl was attracted by this art form and obviously shared neither the preconceptions of the educated classes nor their prejudices against the film.

She came to know the film as a craft while still pursuing her dancing career. Her dancing experience and her training as a painter, which took place while she was also a dancer, played an important part in shaping the style of her film editing and composition.

An important person in her cinema acting and directing career, which began early in the 1920's, was Dr. Arnold Fanck, a geologist who spent his fortune on a new career of making mountain movies. Dr. Fanck, born in 1889 in Freiburg, a town in southern Germany to which he returned to live after World War II, spent a great deal of time in the mountains, skiing, climbing, enjoying the rugged grandeur of the alpine scenery, while earning a doctorate in geology at the same time. In 1920, Fanck decided to produce films. He began with short documentaries but was not happy with the results and decided to make a film about mountain people which would actually be filmed in the mountains, in contrast to most German films made up to that time, which were produced in studios.

His new genre became very successful, and among his later mountain films, *Berg des Schicksals* (*Mountain of Destiny*, 1924) was the catalyst that brought Fanck and Riefenstahl together, thus creating a team which collaborated for about a decade and produced many films, several of which are now forgotten by film historians. The almost legendary circumstances under which Fanck and Riefenstahl met are recounted in her autobiographical account of her career as an actress in Fanck's mountain films, *Kampf in Schnee und Eis* (*Struggle in Snow and Ice*). She had seriously injured her knee during one of her dance performances. Despite treatment by the best doctors in Berlin, her knee took a long time to heal and it even appeared that she would never be able to dance again. An operation was necessary, because she had a torn cartilege and bone tumor. Up to that point, Riefenstahl had seen comparatively few films, but in the course of the next few years she came to know the films of Lang, Sternberg, and Eisenstein, whose *Battleship Potemkin* she also saw.

One evening, while waiting for the street car, Riefenstahl saw an advertisement for a mountain film which was announced for screening in one of the Berlin movie theaters. The film, as it turned out, was *Mountain of Destiny*, directed by Dr. Fanck. Feeling rather low just then and needing some sort of spiritual renewal, Riefenstahl decided to see it, especially since she had never herself been in the mountains and wanted to experience them at least on film. She was so enchanted by the beauty of the mountains that she decided to leave Berlin at once and go to the Alps. She also wanted to meet the director of that film himself. Thus, though perhaps without knowing it, Riefenstahl embarked on a new adventure which led to a second career. Appearances indicate that mountains at that time represented for her a type of escape from a shattered dancing career into a pure natural environment, where problems related to civilization did not matter. This escape preserved her career as an artist and as a person, so that, at least for the time being, she survived.

Riefenstahl met Dr. Arnold Fanck through Luis Trenker. Fanck must have been fascinated by Riefenstahl, and he signed her up for his new film *Der heilige Berg* (*The Holy Mountain*, 1926), where she was to appear as a dancer. Thus Riefenstahl left the stage to appear on the screen, a choice that was not easy for her. Her injuries healed. In fact, she completely recovered and her fans expected her to return as a dancer. Contracts were offered her by producers in numerous cities in Europe. Max Reinhardt again tried to win her for the role of Penthesilea. In her *Kampf in Schnee und Eis*, she confessed that she found it difficult to make up her mind regarding which of the two careers offered her she should take. She was torn between the power of the image on the screen and the expressive power of the dance, and she did not know which of the two would be more important. A decision was finally forced upon her. It came in the form of a ruse invented by Arnold Fanck himself. He simply told her to get ready to train for a lead female role in his film *Der grosse Sprung* (*The Great Leap*, 1927). It was partly a ruse, for Riefenstahl was in love with the man with whom she was to appear in that film and with whom she was to practice and rehearse her part, i.e., Hans Schneeberger, cameraman and former world ski champion, as well as hero of World War I. "And now I can no longer turn my back on the film. It has captivated me up to the last fiber," she wrote.[5]

For a while, however, Riefenstahl tried to retain both careers. While residing in Freiburg, between films, she continued to train for her dancing career and practice dancing numbers with her pianist. But after some time she decided that it would be impossible to combine both careers. "The film is too big to tolerate the dance at the same time," she wrote.

In a way she had already made up her mind when Fanck signed her up for the film *The Holy Mountain*. The film as a form of expression for her was indeed larger and more comprehensive, with a greater future, than the dance. So she stayed. She had to learn how to ski, since that was a very important skill for a mountain film. However, she was willing to learn the required skills and did not spare herself or anyone else to acquire them. She talked Luis Trenker into going with her to Cortina d'Ambezzo to teach her how to ski. While learning this new skill, she broke a bone in her foot, as a result of which she was ordered to stay away from skiing for four weeks. Another male actor was injured also in the preparation for this film, a fact which would indicate that the film work was not without its dangers. Moreover, the weather made it impossible to continue with the shooting, and the film had to be completed at a later date.[6]

While participating in the film as an actress, Riefenstahl learned everything she could about filmmaking itself. She apparently had unbounded curiosity. Whenever Dr. Fanck gave an order, she asked for the reason and was given an answer. "He became my professor," she told an interviewer.[7] Like a good pupil, whenever not acting, she stood next to the camera learning the techniques necessary for the profession of filmmaking. She was especially interested in learning the techniques to produce darkness on film. During one of these moments a light exploded, seriously injuring one side of her face, and the doctor treating her prophesied that "Riefenstahl would never again be able to appear before the camera." However, Riefenstahl recovered from this accident within six months; her face healed, and she made the journey back to the mountains and completed her scenes in *The Holy Mountain*.

She learned most about filmmaking and directing a film during the next film in which she acted, i.e., *Der grosse Sprung (The Great Leap*, 1927). "I had to learn to ski, to climb, and by the press of circumstances, I also found myself involved with the camera work and at times I collaborated with the director's crew. I never stopped watching, observing, asking questions."[8]

Thus she learned the fundamentals of her technique of mise-en-scène from Dr. Arnold Fanck, who was an outsider in the German film industry at that time. Riefenstahl believes that perhaps for that reason she also became an outsider from the regular German film industry: "He was a savant, a geologist, besides being a photographer, who with certain other dreamers had founded a small company. I was the only girl on the crew," Riefenstahl explained.

Both Fanck and Riefenstahl had come to appreciate the beauty of the Alpine mountains by way of the camera, and this provided a strong attraction between them as well as other members of the crew: all of them loved the beautiful photographic images which were inspired by the beauty of nature.

In retrospect, critics of many persuasions have seen pre-Fascist tendencies in Fanck's mountain films. Among these the voice of Siegfried Kracauer is especially virulent. He writes: "The surge of pro-Nazi tendencies during the pre-Hitler period could not be better confirmed than by the increase and specific evolution of the

mountain films. Dr. Arnold Fanck, the uncontested father of this
species, continued along the lines he himself had developed."[9]
Ulrich Gregor, a recent West German critic, is no less vehement in
his criticism when he writes that Fanck in his mountain films "stylized, through somber melodramatic stories, the mountains into
symbols of aboriginal forces, whose beck and call man cannot
escape. Because of his fascination with the irrational, with the
phenomenon of a reality which is seen only as 'romantic,' even
cruel, because of the indexes of a supernatural power, Fanck...
belongs to the early Nazi era."[10]

In between the mountain films, Riefenstahl acted in a typical,
studio-made film called *Das Schicksal derer von Habsburg* (*The
Destiny of the Hapsburgs*, 1929)—not directed by Dr. Fanck—
dealing with the imperial family of the Austrian-Hungarian
Empire during the last phases of its existence, including World
War I, and its ultimate fall. Riefenstahl fills the minor role of the
mistress of the crown prince who loves her more than his own wife
and wants to get a divorce for her sake. Since the liaison between
the crown prince and Marie Vetsera (played by Leni Riefenstahl)
is not approved by the imperial family, the couple finally commit
suicide. This affair was the subject of the more famous French
film, *Mayerling* (1936), starring Charles Boyer, with Danielle
Darrieux as Marie Vetsera. The film shows Riefenstahl in an
untypical love triangle, in which she is one of two women wooing
the same man. Moreover, in this film she gets a whipping from her
rival, in a scene she may never have forgotten. She subsequently
made sure that she would always play the triangle the other way
round: i.e., a woman between two men.

As a woman, Riefenstahl gradually saw things differently from
Fanck and began to emancipate herself from his tutelage, thus
proving herself a good student of an excellent teacher. She came to
the conclusion that her personal sense of art was violated, because
she no longer perceived things Fanck's way, even though she acted
in his films. Asking herself how she might realize her own vision of
things and the new images that arose in her mind, she began to
plan, though subconsciously at first, her own film *Das blaue Licht*
(*The Blue Light*, 1932). The idea assumed shape only when Riefenstahl linked it with mountains. She wanted to give form to something as well as herself: "But in making this very romantic film by
instinct, without knowing exactly where I wanted to go, I also

found myself expressing the part that would be mine later. For, in a certain fashion, it was my own destiny that I had had a presentiment of and to which I had given form."[11]

The juvenile dream of idealism and purity which she realized first in *The Blue Light* persisted in her later films. "I knew that in all of my films, whatever they were, whether it concerned *Triumph of the Will*, *Olympia*, or *Tiefland*, there was . . . yes: let us say purity. Yunta was a young girl, intact and innocent, whom fear made retract at any contact with reality, with matter, with sex; and later in *Tiefland*, the character of Martha was nearly the same. But I didn't know this, I was searching. When I got somewhere, it was unconscious."

Riefenstahl has repeatedly insisted that she always was in love with beauty, especially "the form taken by beauty, and not only its exterior form, but its interior form. . . . I only know how happy it makes me when I meet good men, simple men. But it repulses me so much to find myself with false men that it is a thing to which I have never been able to give artistic form."[12]

After completing *The Blue Light* Riefenstahl was exclusively an actress only in one more film directed by Arnold Fanck, *S.O.S. Eisberg* (*S.O.S. Iceberg*, 1933), made in Greenland. This was also the last film in which she acted before the more formal establishment of links with the Third Reich which drastically changed her life.

As a result of her participation in the mountain films directed by Fanck, she had built up an image of an innocent young girl who represented idealism, love of beauty, and the clean life of the simple mountain people. She had often sacrificed her own personal comfort in order to project this image; she had suffered cold, hunger, even some degree of poverty in order to participate in films promoting this image. This image was refreshing to the German audience in the late 1920s and early 1930s, an audience which was just then being inundated with films that were emphasizing the importance of sex, greed, and "sin." It seems likely that Riefenstahl actually believed in the image of purity and harmony which she projected at that time. Perhaps she really wanted to be good—and wanted to show that her work also was good. On the other hand, the German film industry promoted a new sex wave just at the time when she was making her mountain films. Thus nude shows, hard-core pornography, and moral corruption were the major film topics. There was also a flourishing trade in drugs, prostitution, and gambling; in general, it was a period of "escapism" from the political ills of the times. The ideals projected by Riefenstahl, the actress, were unfashionable before 1933. But from 1933 on, these ideals became acceptable to an almost oppressive degree, and Riefenstahl was unable to resist the fact that all her ideals and dreams were suddenly supported by a powerful godfather, Hitler, and an entire organization, the Third Reich. The story of the life and times of Leni Riefenstahl reflects an important aspect of German history. Riefenstahl represents a poor "Gretchen" suddenly changed into the figurehead of a political establishment.

## The Third Reich

In 1933 Riefenstahl was idolized by the German people and also by Hitler, who saw her film *The Blue Light,* loved it, and asked her to make a film about the 1933 Nationalist Socialist Party Congress of 1933. It was called *Sieg des Glaubens(Victory of Faith,* 1934) and after completing it Riefenstahl thought she had fulfilled her duty to the "führer." In the summer of 1934, however, she was asked by Hitler to film the Party Congress of that year as well. The result, *Triumph des Willens (Triumph of the Will,* 1936), a film depicting the events of the 1934 Nazi party rally, is the most controversial film Riefenstahl made.

Within a very short time, Riefenstahl's ideals, her love of natural beauty, her love of purity, and her idealism which rejected conventional civilization in favor of the rugged mountains and their inhabitants, were absorbed and approved by the National Socialist regime. Henceforth, those ideals assumed very unpleasant connotations, especially in retrospect.

The German National Socialist Workers' party had come into prominence in 1930. In 1919, when Adolf Hitler joined the party in Munich as the seventh member of its executive committee, the movement only had few supporters. Hitler took charge of propaganda and public relations and became the dominant leader of the group. Under his guidance, the party soon became an important force in Bavaria, then the center of anti-Marxist, antidemocratic, and strong pronationalist forces. Bavaria also is the state with the most and highest mountains in Germany. A love for the mountains is natural for people living near them and the connection that has frequently been established between Nazism and mountain climbing may have its origins in circumstances of geography. Hitler, as we know, also loved the mountains and had a villa, called Berghof, built on top of a mountain in Berchtesgaden.

When the inflation of 1923 wiped out the savings of many middle-class citizens, they turned in increasing numbers to the Nazi movement. In November 1923, Hitler helped instigate the so-called "Beer-Hall Putsch," which was quickly suppressed by the German police. Hitler himself was arrested and served a short term of imprisonment in the Landsberg fortress where he dictated the first volume of his work *Mein Kampf* (*My Struggle*, 1929) to his deputy leader and fellow prisoner, Rudolf Hess. Leni Riefenstahl reportedly read this book in 1932 and, recommending it to one of her associates, said she was so impressed with it that she wanted to meet the writer.

Hitler's revolt failed in 1923. He later realized that political power cannot be gained by revolutionary means if the army and police remain loyal to the legitimate government. Hitler was aware that political power could be won by ballots and through "legal" methods. His tactics were now concentrated on building up a regular political party which, at the same time, should become the core of a political religion. As he was in charge of party propaganda, Hitler was able to develop a new technique of mass propaganda and mass emotionalism that was fundamentally different from the amateurish practice of other political parties in attracting the masses.

By December 1924, the party had won 900,000 votes. With the return of some degree of prosperity, however, the progress of the National Socialist party faltered. In the 1928 election, the Nationalist Socialists won only twelve seats with 810,000 votes. But these years were not wasted. Instead, they constituted a period in which a strong organization was built which could be rapidly expanded. The party's brown-shirted political army, the SA ("Sturmabteilung," meaning "Storm Division") and its black-suited elite, the SS ("Schutzstaffel," meaning "Protection Division") were increased to a size which was fearful or reassuring, depending upon which side of the political fence the observer stood. Both groups figure prominently in *Triumph of the Will*. The party's influence spread through south and west Germany.

Until 1929-1930 little impression was made in the major German state of Prussia, located in the northeast. When intensive organization in Prussia was begun, it was aided by the Great Depression, without which the party would probably never have attained power. By 1930 the Nazis could claim substantial support among several voting groups. Among these were "respectable" voters such as shopkeepers, artisans, and clerks, as well as unemployed citizens. They were drawn mostly from the bourgeois parties of the lower middle class, and from the nationalistic rightist parties. This stratum was lured on by the socialists as well as by the antisocialist ingredients of Hitler's program. The party, from the very beginning, drew its strength from the German youth. In addition, one might say by a stroke of genius on the part of Hitler, the moral as well as the financial support of influential figures in industry and big business was enlisted. These figures were attracted by the hostility of National Socialism toward organized labor and trade unions. Since Hitler was careful not to identify himself with the feudal reaction, which he fought as violently as any other party of the left, he could hold the support of the masses. The army maintained a benevolent neutrality toward a superpatriotic movement promising the restoration of the military as a powerful force.

The election of September 1930, was a landslide. The Nazis increased their representation from twelve deputies to 107, and thus they became the strongest party in the Reichstag. In the spring of 1932 Hitler ran for president in an attempt to gain control of the government by normal political methods, but was beaten by Hindenburg. Nevertheless, in July 1932, the Nazis became the largest party with 230 seats. Hitler was awarded the right to form the cabinet. Hindenburg, an elitist general and World War I hero, had a strong aversion to the "Bohemian Corporal," and in connection with a combination of opposing forces, imposed a check on the Nazi sweep to power, which turned out to be temporary, however. A political intrigue, in which Hitler and the Nationalists, led by von Papen, joined forces, was necessary to maintain the Nazi position and to force Hindenburg to call on Hitler, finally, to form the government. This Hindenburg did on January 30, 1933, the date marking the beginning of the Third Reich.

Within a short time the Nazis strengthened their grip on the nation. They outlawed the Communists and all other opposing parties. The official persecution of the Jews and their elimination from all responsible positions began. This caused an exodus of talent from Germany never before experienced. In the film industry, many talented men and women, including Lotte Eisner, Fritz Lang, Lotte Lenya, Kurt Weill, to mention only a few, left Germany. Leni Riefenstahl, however, remained, as did many others who felt comfortable with the new government. For a while it was thought that Riefenstahl was partly Jewish, and there is an anecdote indicating that Goebbels refused to be in the same room with her and publicly denounced her as Jewish.

The Nazis took additional political steps. They suppressed the labor unions and introduced compulsory labor service. The Army General Staff and the Nazi government reached an agreement whereby the nation's peacetime economy was rapidly put on a war footing. The government was centralized, and its power over all aspects of German life was increased. Hitler was given power to make laws by decree. Thus a totalitarian police state was established on a quasi-military basis.

Hitler's control did not become absolute until 1934. At first, he had to deal with the opposition from the more socialistic wing of his own party, which began to suspect that Hitler's aims were not its own. The leader of this group was Ernst Roehm, chief of staff of the SA. Roehm had increased the size of the SA from 400,000 in January 1933, to over three million by the spring of 1934. Hitler became uneasy about this new power and thought that the control of his private army was slipping away from him. Roehm now represented a threat to leadership so that Hitler moved into closer alliance with the General Staff of the "Reichswehr," the German professional army, to fight the threat. The crisis came to a head on June 30, 1934. Hitler may have thought a coup by the SA leaders was imminent. He moved quickly to arrest Roehm, whom he had shot immediately. Hundreds of others, several of them top Nazi officials, became victims of personal grudges and were also massacred during what has come to be called "The Night of the Long Knives" (this event is depicted in grisly detail in Luchino Visconti's film *The Damned*). Whatever plot existed or was imagined, it was

completely wiped out, the SA was reduced to manageable size, and
Hitler established himself as the undisputed leader of the National
Socialists. The General Staff achieved greater influence than the
surviving Nazi clique around Hitler, and a new figure, Heinrich
Himmler, came into prominence among the Nazi leaders.

On August 1, 1934, Hindenburg died and Hitler decreed that
henceforth the office of president was merged with that of chancellor and that all power was vested in himself as chancellor and
führer. Now there was no longer any serious restraining voice in
Germany capable of opposing him.

By the time of the Sixth Party Congress in September 1934,
Riefenstahl had met Hitler. The first meeting and its
circumstances, is shrouded in mystery. According to Ernst
Hanfstaengl, Riefenstahl was introduced to Hitler in 1933, because
she was a vital and attractive woman who—as he and Goebbels
hoped—might be able to bring Hitler out of his sexual isolation
and "humanize" him. Riefenstahl apparently was not averse to
being used as a woman of pleasure, for, on the evening of this
alleged first meeting with Hitler, she danced for him and, "giving
him the works," showered upon the führer a "real summer sale of
feminine charm."[14] However, like many other beautiful women
before and after her, Riefenstahl failed to please him as a woman,
or possibly, Hitler did not interest her as a man. We know now
almost with certainty that Hitler was sexually impotent and that for
this reason he liked to surround himself with beautiful women
whenever the occasion warranted it. According to Henry
Jaworsky, who occasionally traveled on trains with Riefenstahl
and thus had opportunities to converse with her at length early in
1932, Riefenstahl spoke of the führer as if she were good friends
with him and had easy access to him. She also spoke admiringly of
*Mein Kampf* and told Jaworsky to read it, a suggestion which he
rejected, being of a different political persuasion.[15] Riefenstahl herself maintains that Hitler had heard of the film *The Blue Light*,
arranged to see it, and was reportedly so fascinated by the scenery
and the visual effects that he arranged to meets its leading actress
and director.[16] Hitler, who was very fond of movies and frequently
saw at least one film a day, must surely have been aware that *The
Blue Light* had won the Silver Medal at the 1932 Venice Biennial. In
any case, in 1933 Hitler asked Riefenstahl to film the party rally of
that year. For the preceding four years, the Party Congress had

taken place in Nuremberg, and the city had become a magnificent and fitting background for these gatherings. After 1933, the Party Congress always served as a party convention at the same time and offered an official state ceremony used by Hitler for important announcements of internal and foreign policy.

It has always been a question of interest to what extent Riefenstahl's relationship to Hitler transcended professional boundaries. Numerous rumors were spread about her and her relationship with Hitler, including rumors suggesting that she was his mistress. Riefenstahl herself claims that she was not Hitler's type and that Hitler liked "cowlike" women resembling his mistress, Eva Braun. Riefenstahl herself, so she thought, was too positive and strong. From all we know about Hitler to date, this information is true. Riefenstahl has always argued that at the time of the Third Reich, she was fascinated by Hitler and that she was stunned and shocked when the extent of Nazi crimes became known to her after World War II.

Riefenstahl claims that she was interested only in artistic considerations when she accepted the commission to make the film about the Fifth Party Congress, called *Sieg des Glaubens* (*Victory of Faith*, 1933). The title of this film refers to the fact that this was the first party rally after the Nazis came to power. A rather short film, it was considered excellent when it was premiered on the night of December 2, 1933, although Riefenstahl herself does not think much of this work. She arrived in Nuremberg with no advance preparations to film a historical event that extended over several days and involved hundreds of thousands of participants at numerous locations scattered throughout the city. She was accompanied by Sepp Allgeier, Walter Frentz, and Franz Weihmayr. After the premiere of *Sieg des Glaubens*, Hitler reportedly presented a bouquet of flowers to Riefenstahl.

In the view of the *London Observer*, this film "was one long apotheosis of the Caesar spirit, in which Hitler played the role of Caesar while the troops played the role of the Roman slaves. It is certainly hoped that this film will be shown in all cinemas outside Germany, if one wishes to understand the intoxicating spirit which is moving Germany these days. . . ." On the basis of this description, we may assume that the film was almost as powerful as *Triumph of the Will*. No copy of the film is known to exist. It has been suggested that Hitler had ordered the film destroyed after the Roehm purge in 1934 had changed the Nazi hierarchy. Probably

Hitler did not want the public to be reminded of those who had "disappeared." There are also rumors that Riefenstahl is secretly keeping the film in her archives and out of the reach of publicity.

Despite the success of this film, Riefenstahl maintains that she had considerable difficulty with it and ended up with much less footage than she had wanted. Goebbels, apparently jealous of her favored position with Hitler and afraid that she was using her influence to invade what he considered his area of control, made certain that his staff did not cooperate with Riefenstahl or her film crew. Riefenstahl complained about this to Hitler: "I met with Hitler at lunchtime. The place was crowded, so he, Dr. Goebbels and I went into a small room by ourselves and had coffee. I told him what had happened. Naturally, I was excited, but I had noticed that as I talked to Hitler, Dr. Goebbel's face was very white."[17]

1934 became an important year, both for Riefenstahl and the film industry. Goebbels was appointed head of the Reich Film Association (Reichsfilmkammer), and he wasted no time in laying down the new guidelines. From now on the authorization to produce films, either professionally or for the common good, under public or private management, was by legal definition only to be permitted to members of the Reichsfilmkammer. Riefenstahl became a member of this association in 1934.

With the exception of local movie houses, by February 1, 1934, all moving picture enterprises, producers, firms which produced publicity films, associations or corporations privately or publicly directed, had to become members of the appropriate branch of the Reich Film Association, the Union of the German Moving Picture Industry, from which Jews were excluded. Goebbels even went so far as to suggest that the six American film companies doing business in Germany should dismiss their Jewish employees.[18] Many members of the German film industry who had worked with Riefenstahl were thus forced to leave the country. Asked why she herself stayed, Riefenstahl answered: "Whoever excuses himself, accuses himself" ("Wer sich entschuldigt, klagt sich an") "A Commission was proposed to me and I accepted."[19]

A new official dramatic critic was appointed by Goebbels who was to examine all manuscripts and scenarios in order to see that topics which ran counter to the spirit of the times were suppressed. All manuscript and film treatments had to be submitted to Willi

Krause, the new drama critic. Krause, however, was an artistic bungler and unqualified for the job. He had been appointed because he was a friend of Goebbels, who replaced him two years later with Hans Jürgen Nierentz.[20]

On February 16, 1934, the government passed an all-inclusive censorship bill, which in scope and severity was unprecedented anywhere in the world except for the Soviet Union. The new law contained thirty-six articles which effectively abolished artistic freedom in the German film industry. The new state assumed complete control over the creation of films. The German film industry tried to resist this new law, but those who opposed it were ousted from their positions or executed. Von Papen, for instance, denounced the new laws in a speech delivered on June 17, 1934. His speech writer was later executed. In accordance with this law, all films were prohibited which compromised important state interests or public order, offended National Socialist morals, or artistic or religious sentiments; or endangered respect for Germany abroad or her relations with foreign countries. The newly-appointed drama critic had to see every film scenario submitted by a producer and decide what was to be eliminated in the script. Once the film itself was completed, it was handed over to a censor who checked to see if the original, censored script had been followed in the final version of the film. While it is true that the "advice" of the drama critic was often ignored, so that films produced included sequences which had never been submitted for approval in script form, this law had a stifling effect upon the production of quality films. There were several loopholes in the law, and in the beginning, foreign films were not affected by it. But later, after the law had been cautiously tried out, even American films, such as the *The Trial of Mary Dugan, Voices of Spring, My Weakness, The Kid, Roman Scandals, Tarzan and His Mate, Manhattan Melodrama, Stand Up and Cheer, Baby, Take a Bow, Nana,* and *Men in White* were ultimately banned in Germany. One reason for this was the presence of Jews in the cast of foreign films. Several other foreign films, such as *Nana,* were banned on "moral" grounds.

Sensing that the German film industry was not eager to obey his new laws, Goebbels took steps to bring it into line. As early as May 1933, he called together members of SPIO (an association of German film producers) and DACHO (the official actors' and directors' association) for a series of speeches by various government functionaries. Goebbels emphasized in his speech his great admiration for the art of film, claiming that he did not understand the sudden nervousness and uncertainty in the German film industry resulting from the installation of a new government. He continued by mentioning four films which, in his opinion, should be emulated by the German film industry. These were Eisenstein's *Battleship Potemkin* (1924) for excellence as propaganda; Fritz Lang's *Nibelungen* (1925), which in his view showed modern themes in an ancient setting; *Anna Karenina* (1927) with Greta Garbo as the female lead, because it was a purely artistic film; and finally, Luis Trenker's *Der Rebell*, (1932) described by Goebbels as a perfect blend of national epic with high artistic standards.[21] The irony is that *Der Rebell* was a U.S. production (Universal Films, Producer: Joe Pasternak), something of which Goebbels was evidently unaware.

The Reich Film Association also established a film archive during this time which was dedicated on February 4, 1935, and located in Harnack House, Berlin-Dahlem. In order to eclipse the customary May 1 (Labor Day) demonstrations held in Berlin and other German cities by Communists and socialists, Goebbels began to use May 1 as the day on which awards for the best artistic achievements, including films, would be made with official pomp and circumstance. Riefenstahl received her awards for *Triumph of the Will* and *Olympia* on such occasions.

As a result of the restrictive legislation imposed upon the film industry by Goebbels, the film companies gradually began to avoid dealing with the problems of the present and produced light comedies and period pieces of dubious quality. Even Goebbels noticed that his efforts "to improve" the German film with his restrictive legislation had failed miserably by November 1934. He complained that the industry was turning out "dull, stupid, film fare."[22] The biggest film studios in Germany closed down so that the management could figure out the situation under the new regime.

Goebbels had six rating levels for films: (1) very valuable politically and artistically, (2) valuable politically and artistically, (3) valuable politically, (4) valuable artistically, (5) valuable culturally, and (6) of educational value. As a result of the laws involving the production of films, the only films that could be made, besides those that Hitler wanted produced, were totally innocuous entertainments that could hardly be related to the events during the Third Reich.

At the time when the film industry was taken over by the Nazi government, Riefenstahl was escaping again into her world of ideals, her world of beauty and melodrama. In the summer of 1934, while Germany experienced the "Night of the Long Knives" Riefenstahl was in Spain, preparing to shoot *Tiefland* (*Lowlands*, 1954). Although she had been asked by Hitler in the fall of 1933 to film the 1934 National Socialist party Congress in September 1934, she had decided to do *Tiefland*, expecting Hitler would be content to accept a replacement she had chosen for him, Walter Ruttman, who had agreed to film the 1934 party rally. When the *Tiefland* project had to be shelved because Riefenstahl was ill and had to return to Berlin, Hitler approached her again, saying that she alone had been given the assignment. Riefenstahl claims that for a moment she was really "scared of Hitler," who practically forced her to accept the assignment. Apparently annoyed at her attempt to evade the order, Hitler insisted that Riefenstahl shoot the film of the 1934 party rally. His deputy, Rudolf Hess, contacted her shortly after her return to Berlin. "I went to speak with Hitler. He was not in Berlin, so I went to Nuremberg in my car. I found him there with Speer and other people," she told the B.B.C. in 1972.

Riefenstahl tried to persuade Hitler to release her from the assignment and allow Walter Ruttmann to make the film. But Hitler convinced her that she should direct the film herself, especially after he said that she would get whatever she needed to make the film artistically successful. Thereupon Riefenstahl demanded that the film be made by her own production company rather than by the Ministry for People's Enlightenment headed by Goebbels. Hitler agreed to this request and promised that he would not interfere with the filming, thus allowing her complete freedom to make the film according to her own artistic standards. No one was allowed to see the film until it was finished. Hitler granted Riefenstahl's request for artistic and financial autonomy, and admitted that it was better for the Nazi party not to have to put up the money, considering that the party might collapse before the film was finished. In view of later developments within the party, especially the Roehm affair, Hitler's fears seem reasonable. Now there is little doubt that, whatever the mechanical and financial disguises may have been, the NSDAP actually financed the making of *Triumph of the Will.*

The Nazi party Convention of 1934 was a special event. While it was to be celebrated with the same pomp and circumstance as previous rallies, it came to be known as the "Congress of the United Nation," because in 1934 Hitler had defeated a strong opposition on the left within his own party and was especially eager to show Germany and the world a united Nazi party on film. He wished to use both the rally and the film record of it in order to win over the remaining leaderless opponents of his party and heal remaining rifts within the party.

This Nazi party congress took place from September 4 to September 10, 1934. As at all previous party congresses, masses of excited participants and spectators created the proper setting for Hitler's revelations of Nazi politics, philosophy, and culture. The party congress was imbued with a ritualism which few people were able to resist. Stagecraft, the fanatic frenzy of the masses, the banners, the marchers, shouters, and other circus elements as well as the melodrama woven into it, including Hitler's personal performances—which were miracles of physical endurance and mental alertness—all contributed to the atmosphere of mass emotionalism. This emotionalism has been compared to the religious hysteria of the fanatical Moslem crowds in the forbidden City of Mecca.[23]

By now the party rally had grown to enormous proportions and was characterized by the unanimous enthusiasm of the party members and their blind devotion to their leaders, appropriately celebrated by a gigantic demonstration in the ancient city of Nuremberg. This Second Party Congress since the seizure of power was staged on an unprecedented scale. As in all previous congresses of the National Socialist Democratic Workers party (Nationaldemokratische sozialistische Arbeiterpartei — NSDAP), there was no real discussion of problems or policies, no criticism, no voting, no decisions, only order from above and obedience from below. But there was drama, pageantry, music, marching, and oratory. Amid enormous banners and reams of bunting, thousands of standards, mountains of sausages, oceans of beer, and solemn festivities without end, the brown and black armies drilled, maneuvered, saluted and listened to the speeches. A total of

770,000 visitors descended upon the city of Nuremberg, which already had a population of 350,000, so that there was more than enough material for the crowd scenes in the film.

The fact that Riefenstahl was a woman caused her considerable difficulty in getting the best help for her camera work. At least one cameraman whose help she requested refused to work "under the artistic direction of a woman."[24] But Hitler kept his promise, and she got all the help she needed to make this film. Thus, early in 1934, Hitler assigned Albert Speer, his architect, to remodel Zeppelin Field at Nuremberg, one of the sites used for the rally. Speer intended to build a huge flight of steps topped and enclosed by a long colonnade. The overall dimensions for this were estimated at 1,300 by eighty feet. This grand reconstruction project, however, was not completed in time for the 1934 party rally. But Speer at least made sure that the buildings and grounds in Nuremberg would be in excellent condition for the event. He also designed the famous "cathedral of light" used during the rally.

Speer and Riefenstahl had met for the first time during the preparations for the sixth Nuremberg party convention. Speer was one of the few male associates who pointed out the difficulty that Riefenstahl, as a woman, encountered in establishing her authority and in gaining the support of others in making *Triumph of the Will* or other films. He remarked that as the only woman officially involved in the proceedings, she had numerous conflicts with the party organization which was soon up in arms against her. He admitted that the Nazis were by tradition antifeminist and could hardly stand the presence of this self-assured woman, especially since she knew how to bend this men's world to her purposes. There were numerous intrigues launched against her, and slanderous stories were reported to Rudolph Hess, Hitler's deputy, in order to have her ousted. These attacks ceased, however, after Riefenstahl's talents as director had been witnessed and acknowledged even by her doubters.

The party congress, always a lavish affair, reached its climax on September 7, 1934, when Hitler reviewed 85,000 party function-aries and a torch-light parade ten miles long. On September 9, he reviewed 136,000 storm troopers and SS men.

Until Hitler's advent as chancellor, Germany's leading politicians had always been educated men. They had relied on some degree of reason and *machtpolitik* in their methods. Hitler, on the other hand, knew how to instill in those with whom he came in personal contact, a fanatical devotion and the spirit of sacrifice which distinguished a political religion from a political party. Perhaps it was the "strongest inducement emanating from entirely novel and unprecedented techniques. It inaugurated the emotional mechanism of mammoth mass meetings and public demonstrations staged with consummate skill, showmanship and deep insight into the psychic lacunae of the democratic form of government based on persuasion instead of emotion."[25]

Riefenstahl's *Triumph of the Will* conveyed with great artistry what has been called Hitler's "political theology." To the members of German high society, dressed in black tie and long expensive gowns, who attended its first screening, the film projected Hitler's image of the new Germany. The premiere turned out to be a celebration of Leni Riefenstahl, who was duly honored as the director. Wearing a white fur coat when she entered the movie theater, she received applause and ovations for several minutes. After the viewing of the film, there were several curtain calls for Riefenstahl, and Hitler presented her with a huge bouquet of flowers, at the sight of which she allegedly fainted, although Riefenstahl has consistently denied that she did.

On May 1, 1935, at the newly-created Nazi "Festival of the Nation," Riefenstahl was awarded the German National Film Prize for *Triumph of the Will*. In his speech, commemorating this occasion, Goebbels referred to her work as presenting "a filmed grand vision of our führer."

In the following months, Goebbels continued to tighten his control over the film industry, gradually eliminating the loopholes that were still available to filmmakers in the censorship laws. On June 5, 1935, Goebbels established an office to control distribution of all films made in Germany, especially those intended for export. *Triumph of the Will* had his complete approval for foreign distribution. On the same day, he banned all films made before Hitler took power in which Jewish actors and actresses appeared.

On September 15, 1935, Hitler proclaimed the notorious Nuremberg Laws. These laws deprived German Jews of voting privileges, prohibited marriages between Jews and "Aryans," and disallowed all physical contact between Jews and German Aryans. A new definition of what "Jewish" meant was also proclaimed: a Jew was a person who was at least one quarter Jewish. By the end of 1935, 8,000 German Jews had committed suicide and 75,000 had emigrated ". . ., and endless numbers of others were lining up in front of foreign consulates for visas to travel abroad."[26] Riefenstahl has always been fond of pointing out that she shot *Triumph of the Will* before the promulgation of these laws. This is true, of course, although sensitive observers of the German scene must surely have known what was coming. Moreover, the editing of *Triumph of the Will* was not completed until spring, 1936. Had Riefenstahl wanted to protest the Nuremberg laws by laying down her work on *Triumph of the Will*, she would have had a chance to do so.

Riefenstahl could not have been ignorant of the new developments in Nazi Germany. Nothing in the records indicates that she took exception to the Nuremberg Laws or any other decrees, or that she decided to give up her favored position with the Nazi leadership in protest against these laws. On the other hand, there is nothing in the records indicating that she actively participated in the persecution of the Jews or took advantage of these laws to enrich herself personally, something which many others did.

Several of Riefenstahl's cameramen were Jewish or found to be Jewish under the new definition promulgated by the Nazi government. Thus Henry Jaworsky who had declined to work with her on *Triumph of the Will* but was on her crew in *The Blue Light* (1932) and *Olympia* (1938), says that when he was designated twenty-five percent "Jewish" under the new laws before World War II, he was restricted as a "specialist" for aerial cinematography ("Flugspezialist") and as such permitted to continue to work, but had to join the German army as a private. Asking Riefenstahl for help, he was told by her to lie low and try to survive because she thought the war would be lost. She also gave him the name of a person who turned out to be Ernst Udet, who helped him.[27]

Riefenstahl had abandoned all thought of continuing *Tiefland*. The success of *Triumph of the Will* propelled her into the position of a specialist in political filmmaking. Hitler came to her and requested that she make a film about Horst Wessel, the celebrated Nazi youth, who "died a hero's death" early in life. The song named after him, the well-known "Horst-Wessel-Lied," was used as the leitmotiv in *Triumph of the Will*. Horst Wessel, a pimp who died in a street brawl, only composed the first stanza of the "Horst-

Wessel-Lied." In any case, Riefenstahl refused to do the film on Horst Wessel. The Nazi officials apparently recognized that her films lent themselves admirably to their propaganda purposes and wanted to classify her as a specialist in propaganda films, an honor she respectfully declined.

Riefenstahl was also offered an opportunity to work in the Soviet Union after completing *Triumph of the Will*. She rejected this offer in the belief that she did not really feel capable of expressing herself in any other country but her own. "I didn't imagine working anywhere else. I had to live in my country. That's all," she told an interviewer.[28]

From 1935 to 1938 Riefenstahl was occupied with making *Olympia*. According to one of her collaborators, Riefenstahl took a long time to edit *Olympia*, because she wanted to make sure that it would be completed at a time when Goebbels and other Nazi officials were no longer interested in interfering with her editing work.[29]

In October 1935, she signed an agreement with the Reich Ministry of People's Enlightenment which gave her the complete rights over making the film and awarded the total sum of 1.5 million marks. When it became evident that this sum was not sufficient and she had to ask for an additional 300,000 marks, the request was granted. Riefenstahl was somewhat prodigal in the way she spent the money awarded her. However, she spent all of it on the quality of the film and though questions about her prodigality were asked no one ever accused her of embezzling any amount for personal use.[30]

Until 1936 sporting events were recorded on film only by newsreel cameramen. Only one major successful sports film had been made earlier. It was called *Wege zu Kraft und Schönheit* (*Roads to Strength and Beauty*, 1924-1925) and was produced in Germany during the silent film era. Its emphasis was on the medical and aesthetic benefits that could be derived from sports activities. Because in this film the human body was shown in the nude for the first time, it caused something of a stir among the viewing public but was highly successful. When Riefenstahl accepted the assignment to film the Olympic games, she faced many problems, which she solved with energy and skill. Henry Jaworsky has explained that "she would work a sixteen-hour day herself and then gather the whole staff around a big table later to discuss the shooting. We were tired but she was full of energy and did not care; she pounded the table, saying 'You can sleep next week.'"[31]

Although the Olympic games of 1936 took place during the first two weeks in August, Riefenstahl started taking the shots for the film several weeks before that time. She filmed a great deal of footage on location in Greece, which she visited with several cameramen. There she shot the relay marathon, which began in the small village of Olympia and ended in the Olympic stadium in Berlin where the Olympic bowl was lit with the fire from the original Olympic bowl in Olympia, Greece.

It took Riefenstahl eighteen months to edit *Olympia,* and the film was premiered on Hitler's birthday, April 20, 1938. *Olympia* was greeted with great praise by commentators and film critics, and on May 1, 1938, Goebbels awarded Riefenstahl the State Prize for the highest artistic achievement.

During the eventful year of 1938 many changes took place in Germany, as the country prepared for the war which began in 1939. The German-Italian alliance was established; the so-called Enabling Act was extended for four years; new heads were appointed for the army; and Ribbentrop became the new foreign minister, a fact indicating that the influence of the army was extended to the foreign office. In 1938 Austria was annexed. The German film industry had almost come to a standstill, however.

Production dropped and the films that were actually produced became worse, a fact of which Goebbels was acutely aware. He now moved quickly to assume control over major film companies. There were three at that time: Ufa, Tobis, both in Berlin, and Bavaria, located in Munich. Tobis was taken over by Goebbels in 1937, and in the same year the Deutsche Bank, apparently functioning as a cover for the Nazi party, bought control of Ufa and forced the resignation of all twenty directors. Goebbels installed his own directors, and thus Ufa became almost an agency of the government. A similar process was used to gain ownership over the Bavaria film company in Munich. The seizure of these film companies, however, remained a secret. Early in 1938 Goebbels established the State Academy of Film at Ufastadt-Babelsberg. Here "Aryans" could take courses in "Nazism as Parent of the New German Screen," and similar subjects.

As early as November 27, 1936, Goebbels had abolished all art criticism, announcing that this year had not brought an improvement in criticism of the arts. He prohibited "once and for all" the continuation of art criticism in its past form, claiming that the past form of criticism dated from the time of Jewish domination of the arts. He now expected that the critics would be replaced by an editor of the arts. The public would now receive reports rather than criticism of the arts in such a way that the public would be able to form its own opinion about artistic works.

Riefenstahl has claimed again and again that Goebbels obstructed her film work, and while she made *Olympia*, his obstructions made work so difficult for her that she became frustrated and decided to go abroad and even discontinue the *Olympia* project. Hitler, hearing about this, ordered Goebbels to present flowers to her in her garden so that pictures of the occasion could be distributed to counteract the rumors that Goebbels and Riefenstahl were enemies. After the war, this picture was used as evidence that Riefenstahl was friends with the top Nazi officials.

In the fall of 1938, Riefenstahl traveled to the United States, arriving in New York on November 4, 1938. She came, ostensibly, to advertise the film *Olympia* and to arrange for its American distribution. This was a very inappropriate thing to do at this time, as Riefenstahl soon found out. Called "Hitler's Honey," the "Führer's Favorite Film Maker," "Nazi Pin-up Girl," and similar names, she was snubbed by the Hollywood film industry and her visit was vigorously protested. The persecution of the Jews was no longer a secret in November 1938. In fact, five days after Riefenstahl's arrival in the United States, on November 9, 1938, the Nazis carried out the infamous "Kristallnacht" (commonly called "The Night of Broken Glass") during which all shops owned by Jews were destroyed and plundered and their owners murdered or beaten, upon order of the führer. Riefenstahl refused to believe it when she heard the news. "I did not know anything about it at the time and denied everything. I took Hitler for a great and good man."[32] The Hollywood snubbing of Riefenstahl was organized by Budd Schulberg who later, in 1946, defamed her in a very harsh article written for the *Saturday Evening Post*.

The fact that Riefenstahl went to the United States in 1938 and hoped to advertise and sell her film *Olympia* would indicate that she was politically naive. Her potential naiveté has been confirmed by many persons who knew her and maintained that Riefenstahl's devotion to her artistic concerns made her an accomplished artist, but left her ignorant of the outside world. Germany was on the brink of war and had become an enemy of many countries by the fall of 1938. Riefenstahl had spent much of her time behind cameras and in editing rooms (a total of two years in editing rooms) and possibly was unaware of world opinion against Germany. She did not realize, until it was too late, that her journey to the United States was a mistake against which nobody seems to have warned her. At any rate, the elaborate reception she received from Hitler upon her return seems to indicate that Hitler took responsibility for having sent her on her ill-fated visit to the United States. Only Walt Disney, the man whose film, *Snow White and the Seven Dwarfs*, had lost in the bid for first prize at Venice against *Olympia* in 1938, invited Riefenstahl to his studio.

After her return to Europe in January 1939, Riefenstahl began work on the film *Penthesilea*, in which she was planning to play the title role herself. She had long wanted to film this play by Kleist, although friends and associates of her argued that *Penthesilea* was not good film material. Riefenstahl disagreed and began to collect a cast, select shooting sites, and make other preparations. However, the beginning of World War II forced her to shelve this project forever.

After discarding this project she planned to film newsreels at the battlefront, in order thus to free friends and associates from military service, especially those who had not been able to find positions in the industry.

For this purpose, she arrived on September 5, 1939, at the Polish town of Konsky, where thirty-one Polish prisoners were shot in retaliation for having killed several German soldiers in defense when the Germans invaded their town. A photograph showed her on that day wearing a uniform resembling that of the SS, with a pistol in a holster. Riefenstahl rode a Mercedes-Benz driven by a Nazi soldier. She complained about the shooting incident to General Walther von Reichenau and left on the same day, thus abruptly breaking off her newsreel work. She did not expose any film at all and abandoned her newsreel work then and there.[33] However, after 1945 this incident was frequently alluded to in the press; Riefenstahl was accused of being a participant in the killing of the thirty-one Polish Jews, but a court acquitted her of the charge.

Apparently in order to escape from the horrors of war, Riefenstahl took up the *Tiefland* project again. This was a film based

upon the opera by Eugene d'Albert, which Riefenstahl had seen in
her youth in Berlin and which provided, with its sentimental drama,
an opportunity for her to escape from the horrors and difficulties
taking place in Nazi Germany. She stretched out work on this
project for the entire time of the war and beyond, failing to complete it until 1954. *Tiefland* required extensive location work and
seemed to be doomed from the beginning. Riefenstahl fell ill and
even had to direct several scenes from a stretcher. It is not clear
what else she did in Germany during the war. She continued to
admire Hitler to the very end. Thus when the German army
entered Paris in 1940, Riefenstahl wrote Hitler a letter of congratulations, indicating her admiration for his achievements.[34]

In the summer of 1944, both Riefenstahl's father and brother died
in battle. At this time she again fell ill, directed many scenes in
*Tiefland* from the stretcher, and eventually had to discontinue the
project. By now, life in wartime Germany had become extremely
difficult. Studios were closed or bombed out. Many male actors
were drafted into the army. Riefenstahl said of her brother that he
"died a hero's death in the firm belief in his führer and in Germany's
victory."[35]

Riefenstahl herself was under constant surveillance upon orders
of the führer, who, among other things, knew about a beginning
romance between Riefenstahl and Major Peter Jakob, a decorated
major, with whom Riefenstahl frequently traveled before she actually married him in 1944. The marriage was childless and ended in
divorce two years later because "love went kaputt," as Riefenstahl
expressed it.

## The Postwar Years

After the war, which ended officially with the surrender of
Germany on May 2, 1945, the German film industry was in ruins as
a result of the Allied air raids which had destroyed numerous major
buildings in Germany. Many of the pro-Nazi artists in the film
industry had fled; others faded from sight when the war ended. At
this time Riefenstahl lived in her house in Kitzbühel, an Austrian
village at the foot of the Kitzbüheler Alps. She was ousted from her
house in 1945 by American soldiers who needed it as a G.I. rest
center. Many years later she regained ownership of it. It was in this
house where the American writer, Budd Schulberg, searching for

motion pictures that could be used as evidence against German war criminals to be tried at Nuremberg, met with her and her husband. Schulberg tried, among other things, to locate the film *Victory of Faith* but Riefenstahl could not help with this or any other film material he wanted to find, since she denied any longer having any copies herself.

The German film industry was slowly beginning to produce films again. By the end of 1946 only four films had been completed in Germany. In part this small number was due to the restrictions placed on the film production by the Allied occupation forces. The Allies also determined who among the actors, actresses, directors, and other film personnel would be allowed to continue working in the film industry. They blacklisted many whom they considered Nazis. Among these was Riefenstahl.

On March 30, 1945, the Seventh Army Interrogation Center published a report based on an investigation of her by its German Intelligence Section. In general this report lists the answers Leni Riefenstahl gave her interrogators. It indicates that she did not hide her cooperation with the Nazis, including Goebbels and Hitler, but it also shows that at all times she was concerned primarily with her films rather than National Socialist politics. The report also demonstrates that Riefenstahl was an artist with a strong ego, proud of her own particular accomplishments. She appeared to be totally unconcerned about the propaganda effects her films would have on the viewer. She also was unaware of, and unconcerned about, the results that her involvement with the Nazis would bring her. She stated emphatically that she was famous long before either Goebbels or Hitler had been heard of and that she really did not need the Nazis to achieve her fame.

While several things she said contradicted certain facts, in general the American occupation authorities felt that Riefenstahl's answers to their questions gave the impression of honesty and that the "dread which she expresses about the regime and its leaders seems sincere."

Riefenstahl has always claimed that she knew nothing or next to nothing about the atrocities committed by the Nazis. She had heard of the existence of concentration camps, but she could not quite visualize what they actually were. In any case, the American authorities came to the conclusion that she was not an ambitious female who wanted to attain fame and wealth on the NSDAP bandwagon. They recognized that she was not a fanatical National Socialist who had sold her soul to the regime, but they found that "admiration for Hitler" had closed her eyes to all that this regime meant for Germany. Moreover, Hitler's protecting hand insured the continuation of her artistic activities even though the careers and lives of others in the industry had been terminated. Hitler's hand "offered protection from the political clutches, and built a dream world for her in which she could live with 'her art.'" The report concludes with the statement that Riefenstahl "never grasped and still does not grasp" the fact that, by dedicating her life to art, she has given expression to a gruesome regime and contributed to its glorification.[36]

There was no accusation coming from the British occupation forces. However, in 1952 a British newspaper, the *Daily Mirror,* featured a picture showing a train with prisoners of war being transported to Nazi concentration camps. Riefenstahl was shown in this picture, which had a caption implying that she was responsible for the transportation of the prisoners to camp. The picture was signed "Cassandra." Riefenstahl sued the newspaper and won her suit in 1956. This event, as well as subsequent ones, particularly attempts to incite public opinion against her, indicate that Riefenstahl's National Socialist past was never forgiven.

Riefenstahl was released by the American occupation authorities, because she could not be charged with any of the Nazi crimes. However, she was not issued a work permit that would have allowed her to resume her career. She fared even less well with the French occupation forces. After her arrest by the American forces in the French zone, she was turned over to the French who took her into custody and interrogated her from time to time. In 1952, after Riefenstahl had spent several years in detention camps of French and other occupational forces, the French courts ruled that her activities for the Nazis did not justify punishment.

Three years earlier, determining that Riefenstahl had been compelled by Hitler to make *Triumph of the Will* and *Olympia* and that the latter, at any rate, was intended to be a propaganda film, the German government, through the Baden-Baden State Commission, classified Riefenstahl as a "sympathizer" with the National Socialists, although it found no evidence indicating that Riefenstahl's relationship with Hitler had transcended the framework of the professional tasks given her. The classification "sympathizer" carried sufficient stigma to affect her career, despite the clearance she later received from the French courts  In 1952 the Berlin senate declared that she was "not charged" with Nazi crimes, a decision which did not go unprotested. Numerous German newspaper articles suggested she should have been charged as a participant in Nazi crimes and not be allowed to resume her work, which was legally possible for her in 1952 when she received her work permit.

After Riefenstahl was cleared by the major authorities involved in the de-Nazification process, she spent two years, from 1952 to 1954, traveling through Europe in an attempt to retrieve her films, most of which had been taken to Rome and Paris. She also began to gather together the cast and crew that she had worked with on *Tiefland*. The film was completed in 1954, but it was not successful and Riefenstahl temporarily withdrew it from circulation. In the United States it was only finally released in a 16mm version in 1979.

She planned numerous films at this time, most of which failed. She could not find distributors for her projects, because the film industry did not want to be associated with her. It was difficult for her to live down her Nazi past, and, as a matter of fact, she never succeeded in reentering the German film industry and complete a film after *Tiefland*.

When it became evident that Riefenstahl's film career in Europe was finished, she went to Africa in the mid-1950s, starting her fourth career, that of an anthropologist. She "discovered" Africa, and this continent became her new obsession. "When I am in Africa, I am a completely different person," she told an interviewer.[37] Taking photographs as a function of her interest in Africa, she sought to find a story suitable for a film that would have to be set in Africa. She found an article in a newspaper about a modern slave trade; and inspired by it, she had the Anti-Slavery Society in London send her material. According to the information thus provided, every year more than 50,000 kidnapped Africans were sold into slavery in greater Arabia. This seemed to be a great topic for a film to Riefenstahl, and thus she and a friend wrote a script for a documentary film about the slave trade. It was to be called *Black Cargo*, a title taken from a book by the same name which had just been published and to which Riefenstahl had bought the rights. It was to be partially a feature and partially a documentary film. The project had to be temporarily shelved, because on the fifth day, when she was in Kenya, her Land Rover hit a rock and fell into a dried riverbed, several hundred kilometers north of Nairobi. Riefenstahl was seriously injured and had to spend several weeks in the Nairobi hospital, but resumed the project after she had recovered. She went back on location and shot several trial scenes with her team. The principal equipment was expected to arrive on a boat via the Suez Canal. However, the war over the Suez Canal (1956) broke out just then and the ship could not pass through the Suez Canal for many months. When the boat was finally allowed to pass, the rainy season had begun, and during that time shooting was no longer possible. Moreover, the money had run out as a result of these delays. Riefenstahl flew back to Munich to persuade, with the help of one of her assistants, a distributor to advance her the money to complete the project. Upon arrival in Munich, however, she heard that her associate whose persuasive powers she needed, had fallen with his car into a ravine in Austria and was hovering between life and death in a hospital. At this point it became clear to her that the project *Black Cargo* had to be shelved forever. Possibly a successful completion of this project would have rehabilitated Leni Riefenstahl in the eyes of the film industry.

Following this "little misadventure," Riefenstahl temporarily abandoned all hope of ever making films again. She began to do what she liked; what impressed her was the life of the native Africans far away from civilization. Without necessarily wanting to make a film, she joined a scientific expedition and with that expedition found the Nuba. After the other members of the expedition returned home, she stayed on for ten additional months, traveling alone through Africa. During these travels she made numerous still photographs which she published in international magazines. Later she persuaded an American distribution company to finance a film about the Nuba of Cordofan. In the meantime she had become friends with the Mesakin Nuba tribe, having learned their language and won their confidence with the help of gifts and trinkets. The Nuba were shy about having their pictures taken, and it took her a great deal of persuasion to dispel their fears. For several reasons, Riefenstahl failed to complete the 16mm film about the Nuba by the stipulated deadline, and when she returned to the tribe in 1968-1969 in order to film supplementary material, the life of the Nuba—under the influence of civilization—had changed so drastically that she could not take anymore shots.

Photo right: Dr. Arnold Fanck
Courtesy of Deutches Institut für Filmkunde

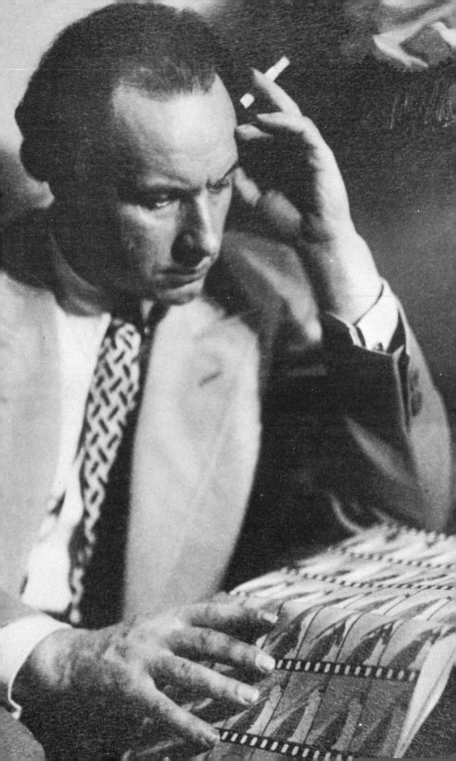

She then tried to make a film out of the material exposed up to that point, using still photography as supplementary material. The filming was not completed until 1972, and the work has never been released for public distribution. Riefenstahl has not found the time to edit the film to her satisfaction.

The life-style among the Sudanese people required a good deal of endurance on Riefenstahl's part. She was, in fact, the first European woman to be granted permission by the Sudanese government to live among the Sudanese people. In some ways, this aspect of Riefenstahl's life resembles that of the late American anthropologist Margaret Mead, who spent several years living alone among the Samoans and writing about them. Instead of writing, Riefenstahl took photographs of the Nuba. Her love for Africa was apparently inspired by Hemingway's *The Green Hills of Africa*, which she read one sleepless night in Germany during the mid-1950s. Having almost always been able to follow her inclinations and predilections at the spur of the moment, Riefenstahl, a few weeks later, flew to Africa and, in the course of some time, and as a result of her persistence and endurance, found the Nuba tribe, members of which she had accidentally discovered almost upon her first arrival in the Dark Continent. The details regarding her discovery of the Nuba of Cordofan are described in her *The Last of the Nuba*, which, like the later *The People of Kau*, features rare and fascinating pictures of a dying tribal culture. Her life among the Nuba also indicates that, at the age of sixty, Riefenstahl had lost none of her energy, hardiness, originality, curiosity, and desire for adventure that have characterized her for most of her life. Old-age homes would have no occupants if all senior citizens were like Leni Riefenstahl.

In 1969, Riefenstahl was awarded the Gold Medal from the Art Directors Club for her photography about the Nuba. While her work among the black tribes of Africa has been praised abroad, it has been heavily criticized in Germany, especially by the German news magazine *Der Spiegel* which in an 1976 article detected a relationship between Riefenstahl's alleged love of the black uniforms of the Nazi SS and the black, handsome, tall bodies of the Nuba.[38] There may be a relationship. Riefenstahl has always insisted that she likes form and structure and a sense of aesthetic drama. Possibly her predilections were partially sexual or at least erotic; that is to say, she relied on her feminine sense of the erotic

Photos left: Leni Riefenstahl among the Nuba in Central Africa
Courtesy of Leni Riefenstahl-Produktion

and chose topics, methods, and presentation in her art which appeal strongly to latent human erotic sensibilities. An underlying ingredient in her aesthetics is certainly the appeal to the erotic.

While the films about the Nuba were never released for public distribution, Riefenstahl's two books, *The Last of the Nuba* (1974) and especially *The People of Kau* (1976), contain photographs that demonstrate the willingness of the Nuba population to undergo suffering in order to produce what its members conceive of as beautiful bodies. In many ways the Nuba are "undemocratic." They have decided that evidences of fighting, suffering pain, getting mutilated in a battle with knives are worth saving as visible testimony to their style of life and to the values of their society, and Riefenstahl has caught the spirit of their aesthetic. Here, as always, she celebrates whatever is young, strong, and beautiful. Her two books on the Nuba have been hailed by critics as contributions not only to photography but also to anthropology, establishing Riefenstahl as a photographic Margaret Mead.

In 1972 Riefenstahl, commissioned by the *London Times*, covered the Munich Olympic Games as a photographer. She also received intermittent assignments, such as covering the lives of rock singer Mick Jagger and his wife, Bianca, in photo essays, assignments that kept her financially afloat.

Finally, in 1975, she embarked on her fifth career. After working as a ballet dancer, movie actress, film director, and anthropologist, she became a scuba diver, again in connection with her photographic work. She describes the details leading to this new profession in the opening chapters of her most recent book, *Coral Gardens* (1978). While on vacation in Kenya, on the Indian Ocean she participated in a scuba diving course offered by the hotel at which she was staying. She lied about her age, which at that time, 1975, was seventy-three and was accepted for the strenuous diving course, among whose participants she was, though looking twenty years younger than her age, by far the oldest member. Riefenstahl spent several months learning how to dive, liked what she saw underwater, and decided to turn it into photography. Anyone who has seen the glories of the underwater world through diving glasses will fully believe that Riefenstahl was "hypnotized" by the exotic colors, shapes, and movements she discovered while diving into the tropical seas. Many of the pictures she took appeared in international magazines and in her *Coral Gardens*.

Her recent career would seem to indicate that Riefenstahl has turned her back on politics and decided to spend the last years of her life contemplating and photographing pure form in corals, fish, and other manifestations of the beauty of nature. However, the world has not forgiven her for her past association with the National Socialist regime. She is still picketed when she appears at film festivals, as at Telluride, Colorado, in August 1974, for example. Her life is often in danger when public attention is called to her films, especially *Triumph of the Will* and *Olympia*. Because of protests from Berlin's Jewish community, *Olympia* was eventually withdrawn from the Berlin 1972 film festival.

Even in her troubled days, however, Riefenstahl always has had friends and admirers. Thus, in 1959, Joseph von Sternberg, director of *The Blue Angel*, offered her his arm in order to lead her to an official reception in the Doge Palace in Rome, in the course of which she was able to screen her *Olympia* during a late showing. A Jewish judge offered his name by way of supporting her as a moral witness during one of the many trials to which she had to submit herself after World War II. Similar gestures of help and support have been offered her throughout her years of despair.[39] Even the Hollywood film industry, which had snubbed her in 1938 and which was represented at the Telluride film festival, has gradually begun to admit that there should be a separation between politics and film art and that, judged only on her work in film, Riefenstahl was a great artist. Nevertheless, it appears certain that Riefenstahl will remain a controversial figure until the end of her days. For thirteen years of association with the Third Reich, she has been punished with thirty years of ostracism.

# 2

## Struggle in Snow and Ice: Dr. Fanck's Mountain Films

IN NOVEMBER 1920, the light went out in a small movie house in Freiburg, Germany. No one in the audience expected much from a film that would be premiered in Freiburg. Berlin had always been the center of the cinema industry in Germany. The best films were made and usually first shown in Berlin. Moreover, what kind of plot could be expected from a mountain film in which nature was the protagonist? *Das Wunder des Schneeschuhs (The Miracle of the Ski*, 1920) had practically no plot beyond the portrayal of the activities of expert skiers, whose boldness and skill, whose determination in the struggle against snow and ice awakened feverish suspense in the audience. Two idealists, the ethnologist Dr. Tauern and the geologist, Dr. Fanck, had invested their entire fortune in this venture.[1] That night the history of the German film was expanded to include a new genre: the mountain film.

In the following year, Dr. Fanck returned with a new film: *Im Kampf mit dem Berge (Struggling With the Mountain*, 1921), again presenting a nature drama. It unfolded 13,800 feet above sea level and took place far above the clouds but lacked the elegance and lightness of the previous film. *Im Kampf mit dem Berge* was monumental and heavy-handed. There were no fun and games among the skiers, and no humor provided comic relief as in *Miracle on Skis*. This film showed a struggle with rapacious glacier gaps, with steep mountain walls and deep crevices.

The two mountain lovers from Freiburg surpassed themselves in each of the succeeding films, giving the impression that their third film, *Fuchsjagd im Engadin (Fox Hunt in the Engadine*, 1922), was the ultimate in daring, beauty, and strength, showing impossible feats of mountain climbing and courage. Yet the real dangers and frequent near-fatal accidents that accompanied the making of these films were almost invisible to viewers who only saw the

55

beauty of the mountains, the clouds, the sunlight refracted by the pulverized snow, and the physical beauty of the skiers. Dr. Fanck's autobiography shows that men and women in his films broke bones, had painful flesh wounds, and contracted illnesses resulting from overexposure to the hard climatic conditions. They also had to carry their own camera equipment, weighing several tons.[2]

These films contributed to the sudden popularity of skiing in Europe during the 1920s. Soon Fanck and Tauern were working on another mountain film which would surpass the three preceding works. The fourth film, called *Berg des Schicksals* (*Mountain of Destiny*, 1922), could not be surpassed, so it seemed to the critics, as the pinnacle of alpine film art. No film had ever shown with the same finesse as this one the floating clouds, the way in which the clouds fell apart and drifted around rocks, almost like ghosts, and how a thunderstorm rages among the mountains.

The plot of this film was based upon the first ascent of the Guglia del Diavolo in the Brenta mountains by the Italian mountaineer Carbarie, and it tells the following story. The best climber in the Tyrolean mountains cannot stand the thought that the Guglia has never been conquered by man, and he tries several times to do it himself while his wife and his child wait below in fear, totally uncomprehending the passion that forces him to seek such dangerous activities. His mother, however, is proud of his iron will. He dies on the mountain, and years later his son, now grown, wants to climb the same mountain, but he had promised his mother not to do so. His ambitious girlfriend is disappointed by his apparent cowardice and, spurred on when she sees two "strangers" climb the mountain, she tries an ascent herself. She fails and gets lost on a cliff, unable to go any further. Her friend, the mountaineer, climbs up to save her, with the blessing of his mother, and succeeds. The description of this film in the German film journal *Illustrierter Film Kurier* refers to the "character-building" challenge that the mountain provides and the ambition and passion it instills in certain people.[3]

It is not surprising that Riefenstahl was excited by this film, where a young girl was shown to be more ambitious than a man. It was this film which by her own admission became also her mountain of destiny. She saw it advertised on a poster—the first such advertisement Fanck had used for his films—while recovering from an injured knee suffered during one of her dancing numbers, and went to see it. The film received good reviews and was described as "culturally valuable." The label "culturally valuable" made it difficult for Dr. Fanck to find a distributor; but after he coined the word "nature feature film" to describe his work, the problem was easier to solve. Fanck rented the movie theater at Nollendorf Platz in Berlin, and for four months showed *Berg des Schicksals* to a sold-out house.

At the end of 1926, Fanck surprised the film world with his new movie, *Der heilige Berg* (*The Holy Mountain*), in which Riefenstahl made her debut as a film actress. Other participants were Luis Trenker, Hans Schneeberger, Hannes Schneider, Ernst Petersen and Sepp Allgeier, the latter being a photographer with whom Riefenstahl later worked on her own films. Among these wonderful men, there appeared, to the surprise of reviewers, an exciting new woman: "The young dancer Leni Riefenstahl, an almost improbably fragile being, animated by the most sophisticated rhythms, not only a dancer, but also an actress who contributes a great deal of soul," one wrote.[4] The plot presents Diotima (Riefenstahl) with two suitors. She seems to prefer one, Vigo, while the other one (played by Luis Trenker) gets jealous. During the ascent of a steep mountain wall, the jealousy between the two men breaks out into the open and Vigo, in the process of a quarrel, falls off, held only by the rope tied to his friend and rival, who after some deliberations, decides to save him. However, the friend freezes to death. Not wishing to cut the rope and drop the body of his frozen friend merely to save himself, the other man also freezes to death. Before he dies, however, he has a dream in which he leads his bride, Diotima, into the crystal beauty of the holy mountain in order to marry her at an altar made of snow and ice. This film was Fanck's first international success. According to him, he and his crew provided most of the financing, and it later earned one million marks, but the proceeds went into the coffers of UFA.[5] Riefenstahl's role involved presenting a dance for which she had become famous in her earlier career, i.e., "Dance at the Sea." In *Der heilige Berg*, Fanck had his dancer symbolize the ocean (Woman) and the mountain (Man).[6]

These mountain films dealt with more than a struggle against snow and ice. In *Der heilige Berg*, at any rate, Riefenstahl appears to enjoy the love and admiration bestowed upon her by the male actors. Fanck writes that one evening he saw Luis Trenker on his

knees before Leni Riefenstahl so that Fanck himself felt called
upon to "retire discreetly." During the shooting of this film, Fanck
made sure that he spent his nights on a different floor in the house
where the crew stayed from the floor on which Riefenstahl,
Trenker and photographer Hans Schneeberger slept. The jealousy
between Trenker and Schneeberger over Riefenstahl, in fact, gave
Fanck the idea for the plot. Riefenstahl was engaged to both of
these men at different times, though she did not marry either.[7] The
relationship between her and Luis Trenker developed into mutual
hatred and ugly calumny after the war.

In *Der heilige Berg*, nature is no longer presented as the only
protagonist but serves as a starting point and backdrop for a human
drama. In many ways Fanck surpassed himself again, this time by
developing a new style. *Der heilige Berg* features several wonderful
heroes who had to learn to master their fiery instincts. Riefenstahl's
acting in the film was not viewed without criticism, and one commentator called her an "oily goat." This expression inspired the next
film made by Fanck.

While Riefenstahl had to do little else but dance and ski in *Der
heilige Berg*, things were different in Fanck's next movie. One day
he asked her to read a script which was to be the basis for a film
comedy, *Der grosse Sprung* (*The Great Leap*, 1927). Riefenstahl
read the script several times. Fanck had selected her to play the
principal part. However, she confessed that she would not be able
to muster up the physical endurance necessary for the part. Fanck
refused to accept her excuse and simply said: "Leni, you will now
travel with Floh [i.e., nickname for Hans Schneeberger] into the
Dolomites. Let him teach you mountain climbing, especially with
bare feet. To pass the exam on your climbing ability, climb up to
the Vajolett Mountains and rehearse your love scene with him up
there, since he is simultaneously your youthful lover, who has to get
rid of his great shyness in the same way in which you have to lose
your sensitivity in the soles of your feet." It is thus that Riefenstahl
became a bold mountain climber (*K*, 36).

The film, copies of which are no longer available, presents a
grotesque comedy showing Riefenstahl as a goat girl, Gita, who is
herding her flock. Gita lives in her alpine cabin. A wealthy businessman with his servant arrives for vacation in Gita's village and falls in
love with Gita, much to the chagrin of another suitor. The wealthy
man wishes to talk to Gita and arrives at her cabin in a tuxedo,

holding a bouquet of flowers. However, Gita, as usual, is sitting on top of a mountain and invites her suitor to come up there and join her. He finally succeeds and the rest of the film consists of situation comedy scenes reminiscent of Buster Keaton and Charlie Chaplin films. Wearing a miniskirt, bolero jackets and knee-boots, and romping with her goats through this rather enjoyable film comedy, Riefenstahl makes an excellent partner for Hans Schneeberger, who plays the out-of-town suitor. *Der grosse Sprung* combines a variety of ideas and sequences rarely seen on the German screen in the 1920s.

Fanck invented many new cinematic techniques and special effects for this film. The acrobatic skills and skiing expertise necessary for some of these special effects were truly breathtaking and confirm Riefenstahl's statements that the mountain films demanded enormous feats of physical endurance and skill (*K*, 36ff.).

The best and most famous of the mountain films directed by Fanck in which Riefenstahl acted was undoubtedly *Die weisse Hölle vom Piz Palü* (*The White Hell of Piz Palü*, 1929). The Piz Palü, a mountain well-known among alpinists which can be scaled only by well-trained mountaineers, is the real hero of this film and dominates it even in scenes where the dramatic flying stunts of Ernst Udet seem to represent modern heroism in action. In this film Riefenstahl's achievements of physical endurance and skill surpassed all previous ones accomplished by women in Fanck-directed films. Fanck succeeded in harmonizing the moods of his actors with the environment and demonstrated that the mountains managed to cast a spell over humans in a way which hypnotizes them. Riefenstahl repeatedly confessed that the mountains exercised enormous power over her psyche. This power, of which she became aware only as a result of the film medium, enabled her to endure the great difficulties involved in making mountain films. "The difference between our mountain films and those made by other directors," she explained, in a BBC interview in 1972, "is that Dr. Fanck never wanted to use a double, didn't use tricks. He wanted everything to be real. Sometimes the scenes were so real, like the time I was buried in an avalanche, that the critics in Berlin wrote that it can't be true, that it was faked in a studio."

The script of *Die weisse Hölle vom Piz Palü* was authored by both Fanck and Ladislaus Vajda. G. W. Pabst, the famous director

(*Joyless Street, The Threepenny Opera, Pandora's Box*) also
participated in the project and directed several scenes in the film.
According to one participant, "it was a wonderful picture. The
original was shot on location in Switzerland, and it was terribly
cold in the mountains in the winter. Most of the cast and the crew
came down with pneumonia." Apparently, Pabst and Fanck both
had a sadistic drive and they all froze. All night long the crew drank
hot wine and punch just to keep breathing. Riefenstahl was
evidently wonderful. In this film she was driving herself as hard as
anybody and often more. She worked day and night.
Schneeberger was in love with her and she with him and they were
an excellent team. She would work extremely hard, harder than
anyone else. Even Pabst had to admire her. He said, "It is terrible.
What a woman."[8]

*Die weisse Hölle vom Piz Palü* was sponsored by Universal
productions, the American firm headed by Carl Laemmle. Harry
Sokal, who was once engaged to Riefenstahl but later had a falling-
out with her, was the producer.[9] According to Fanck, Sokal became
very rich with this film.

The story of *Die weisse Hölle vom Pitz Palü* is rather sentimental,
even though Pabst probably reduced the sentimentality to a minimum. As a character, Riefenstahl is again shown as a woman
between two men, something which by now had become a cliche.
She also took it up as a theme in two of the films she directed later.
Maria and Hans Brand, mountaineers and skiers, are spending their
honeymoon in a cabin on Piz Palü. Here they meet Dr. Johannes
Krafft, who had spent his honeymoon in exactly the same cabin
two years earlier and who had lost his wife, Maria, in an avalanche
at that time. He has returned to continue looking for Maria, an
activity in which he has been engaged for the past two years and as
a result of which he is now called "the ghost of Piz Palü." Maria
Brand (played by Riefenstahl) not only has the same first name as
Krafft's wife but even looks like her. Krafft tells the honeymooning
couple details regarding Maria's death, and it is during the
narrative which is shown in flashback scenes that the most
impressive photography can be witnessed. A mountain guide
appears in the cabin, warning the three people that warm winds
are expected and that the ice will soon come roaring down from
Piz Palü. He warns the travelers to stay off the mountain. At night,
the three people all share one mattress, with Maria sleeping in the

middle. Hans Brand, noticing a certain attraction between Krafft and Maria, gets jealous. Despite the warnings of the guide, the three go off the next morning to climb the mountain on skis. The simmering tension between the two men, of which Maria is the cause, comes to the surface when Hans Brand insists on taking the lead during this climb, which until then Krafft had held. As a result of an avalanche, Hans loses his foothold, slips down the mountain, and remains hanging on an ice wall. Krafft manages to get the half-frozen Hans back up again, and he himself then slides down the mountain and breaks his leg, but finally joins the other two and all three sit down on a narrow ledge, watching the snow and ice come down all around them. Hans is severely injured. While they are trapped on the ledge, another group of mountaineers is swept away by the avalanche, and in a village below all able-bodied men are alerted and requested to participate in the search for the bodies. At this point a plane begins to look for the Krafft party, the members of which are almost frozen before they are spotted. Krafft takes off his last jacket, gives it to Hans Brand and is shown to be wearing only a thin shirt. Hans and Maria Brand are finally saved but Krafft has disappeared before the rescue crew arrives, leaving a note behind which reads: "Dear old Christian [the name of the guide], 'don't try to find me. Save the others. I have gone to *her.*'" The final shot of the film shows a ghostlike figure, Dr. Krafft, sitting in an ice cave, holding watch over Piz Palü. There is one scene which has become fairly famous. This is a sequence with the caption "Pygmies climbing up the mountain," showing members of the rescue party as tiny spots on the huge white mountain, which is described as a giant "roaring defiance" and which actually is the hero and winner in this struggle between man and nature. The photography is breathtaking. Until this film, very few movies had shown the interior of glacier caves. *Die weisse Hölle vom Piz Palü* contains many shots of unearthly beauty, exhibiting the mysterious world underneath glaciers, with ice crystals reflecting the search lights.

The difficulty involved in taking shots of the glacier interiors is described by Fanck himself. To begin with, during the month of March, when most of the shots were taken, it was difficult to find a crevice that was not covered with snow and could reflect the light of the torches, an effect Fanck wanted to achieve. Only one shot could be taken every night, because of the safety precautions and technical problems involved in the making of excellent photography. Taking shots of avalanches was no less difficult. Occasionally it was necessary to use dynamite so that an avalanche could be produced during the right time of day when sunlight would be properly reflected in the snow powder. For once, Fanck admits, dolls had to be used in shots of an avalanche because his actors would surely have lost their lives if he had allowed them to be buried by millions of tons of snow.

It seems, however, that the world was not very grateful to Fanck and his crew for undergoing these difficulties in order to obtain rare and beautiful pictures. The German press, at any rate, did not believe in the authenticity of this work and maintained that it was done in a studio. This reaction depressed Fanck and his crew enormously. Occasionally Fanck did use trick photography in order to show through the camera what in reality would never have happened, but he never used it to falsify physical skills and achievements that were not really possible. Moreover, in *Die weisse Hölle vom Piz Palü*, the flying stunts of Udet provided proof—not only in theory but also in practice—that stranded mountaineers could be saved by planes.

Clearly, all participants in the film, including the actors and photographers, needed real courage. Riefenstahl had genuine fears that she would be devoured by a crevice underneath the snow and wrote that this film required the most difficult, the wildest, and the most dangerous struggle against nature which she had ever fought (*K*, 42). This is confirmed by Fanck, who describes in detail how Riefenstahl was literally blown away by the strong winds raging on Piz Palü and could be retrieved only with great difficulty. She was treated like any male colleague and not spared any of the hardships that everyone else had to endure.

Most of the shots were taken at the foot of the Morteratsch Glacier—in the area of the Bernina Alps where the grandiose shape of the Piz Palü rises to almost 12,000 feet, with three summits which are eternally covered by ice.

The complete film was very well-received by the movie industry and critics, although many still refused to believe that the scenes shot at the risk of the participants' lives were made on location. Critics also wrote that *Die weisse Hölle vom Piz Palü* triumphed over anything that had ever been created on film and that probably nothing like it would ever be created again. It also finally brought

Photo right: Model of the ice cave in Fanck's *Der heilige Berg*

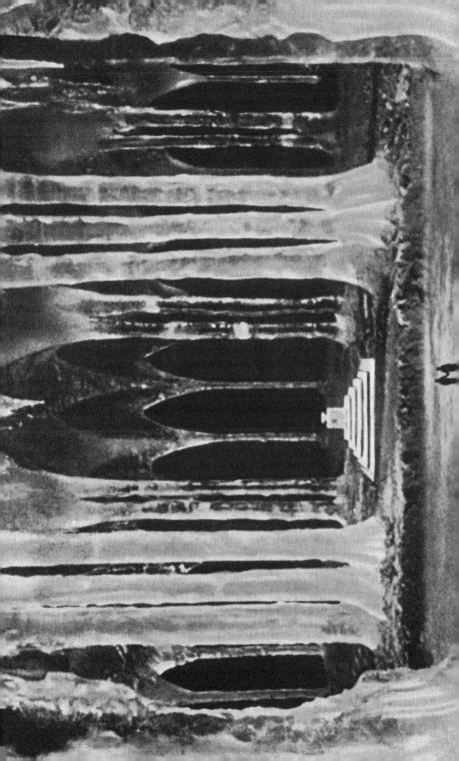

Riefenstahl to the attention of the American movie audiences with whom she became a favorite. *Die weisse Hölle vom Piz Palü* was, in fact, the first German film shown at the Roxy Theater in New York City. In Germany the film ran in the largest movie house, the UFA Palast in Berlin, for eleven weeks with four screenings per day, and it earned UFA a total of 274,000 marks. Fanck, however, had sold the rights to it for 25,000 marks before making it and never saw a penny of the box office receipts. In retrospect, and from the point of view of modern film art, it was perhaps not worth the effort to make a film whose photography is so fantastic that the real dangers and achievements of the crew do not appear to be credible, but the making of *Die weisse Hölle vom Piz Palü* symbolizes the powerful attraction which the mountain itself had for all members of the film crew. Riefenstahl herself repeatedly confessed that she was psychologically dependent on the mountains and could never resist their spell (*K*, p. 9ff.).

After *Die weisse Hölle vom Piz Palü* was completed, Riefenstahl again worked as an actress under the direction of Arnold Fanck. The new film was called *Stürme über dem Mont Blanc* (*Storms Over Mont Blanc* or *Avalanche*, 1930). This was her first sound film. (The first major sound film produced in Germany was *Der blaue Engel* [*The Blue Angel*, 1929], directed by Joseph von Sternberg.) Riefenstahl does not have a beautiful speaking voice. Her very pronounced Berlin accent with its nasal intonation can be disturbing to a listener. However, due to the technical devices used In *Stürme über dem Mont Blanc* she managed to bridge the gap between silent and sound film with comparative ease. But she seems to have realized that with the advent of the sound film, her career as an actress was in jeopardy, to say the least, and it was after this film that she gradually made herself independent and looked for a chance to be her own director. In the few sound films, primarily those directed by her, where she does appear as an actress, she speaks very little. In the entire film *The Blue Light*, for instance, she speaks just a few dozen words. In *Stürme über dem Mont Blanc*, Riefenstahl again plays the only woman. The same film crew that had always worked with Fanck and Riefenstahl— Hans Schneeberger, Richard Angst, and Sepp Allgeier—also participated. The members all had to climb up the 15,000 feet Mont Blanc, and again the main features that Fanck exhibited in the silent films appear—the huge mountain masses, clouds, fog,

Photo left: Leni Riefenstahl struggling with rocks, snow, and ice during the filming of one of her mountain films.
Courtesy of Leni Riefenstahl-Produktion

thunderstorms, flashes of lightning, the sun. Originally Fanck had wanted to title this film "Above the Clouds," and, in fact, the majestic cloud display is the main feature of this film which has a rather sentimental story. It has been pointed out by Kracauer that the opening sequence of the *Triumph of the Will* showed very similar cloud masses which surrounded Hitler's airplane on its flight to Nuremberg. Kracauer sees in this the "ultimate fusion of the mountain cult and the Hitler cult."[10]

Fanck created impressive sound effects to supplement truly magnificent photography by using fragments of music by Bach and Beethoven. In the film a radio abandoned on Mont Blanc intermittently penetrates the roaring noises produced by the storm, thus making the sounds of the mountains appear to be almost superhuman and hence especially gruesome. The difficulties involved in making this film were even greater than those in previous Fanck films. The crew was 13,800 feet above ocean level and working, cooking, breathing, sustaining the cold— at this height everything became more difficult and exhaustion soon set in.

Riefenstahl here plays an astronomy student, the daughter of a semiretired astronomer, who accidentally meets the weather reporter living alone on top of Mont Blanc. This reporter is her father's friend, and on Christmas eve the two men and the young woman celebrate together. The young woman's father dies in the thin air and Hella (Leni Riefenstahl) and the weather reporter fall in love without telling each other about it. They part, and Hella goes back to her job at the observatory further down the mountain, while the weather reporter stays with his radio transmitter on Mont Blanc, the highest point in Europe. The weather reporter loses his mittens, his hands freeze, his fire goes out, and he is near death. Hella finally rescues him with the help of an airplane (flown by Ernst Udet), and the film ends with the implication that the two will stay together. Especially interesting and new for the genre is the use of the radio transmitter and the effects created with it, including the sounds of Beethoven's music played on an organ. The main theme of this film is that Mont Blanc, because of its height and despite its forbidding grandeur, has created special bonds between people who live far apart. Riefenstahl again plays a woman between two men in a dramatic triangle.

A lesser known film in which Riefenstahl acted under the direction of Fanck was *Der weisse Rausch (The White Frenzy,*

1931), another work picturing the horrors and beauties of mountains. Its cast, in addition to Riefenstahl, included Hannes Schneider, Guzzi Lantschner, Walter Riml, Rudi Matt, and others, as well as fifty ski champions. The plot is very simple. Three people (two men and one woman) come to the Alps to learn how to ski. The strange positions that beginning skiers develop provide many occasions for laughter. Most of the photography deals with skiers in action. There is a lot of situation comedy, showing skiers falling down, trapped on craggy mountain tops, and in impossibly convoluted positions.

After completing *Das blaue Licht* (*The Blue Light*, 1932) a mountain film which she directed herself (to be discussed in chapter 3), Riefenstahl starred one more time under Fanck's direction. In 1933 she participated in an adventurous expedition to Greenland in order to film *S.O.S. Eisberg* (*S.O.S. Iceberg*, 1933). This film was made under the auspices of the Danish government. It was co-produced by Arnold Fanck, Ernst Sorge of Deutsche Film, and American producer Carl Laemmle of Universal. According to Riefenstahl, Dr. Fanck could not find an actress who could take the role of the female lead because it required great physical effort, something to which Riefenstahl had become accustomed by that time.[11] Fanck had wanted Elly Beihorn, a German woman pilot, to participate as an actress, but the Americans wanted Riefenstahl, who was not a pilot and hence not suitable for the film. Riefenstahl finally came to Fanck "bawling" and begging him not to deprive her of the twenty thousand dollars she could earn by acting in this film. Fanck, "remembering how much hardship she had endured in his films," finally gave in and signed up Riefenstahl, to the detriment of the film, in his opinion.

The unusual difficulties in making such a film at that time are illustrated by the fact that an American director, who had just gone to Greenland to shoot a film with his own boat and 120 crew members, had returned with only nineteen survivors. Fanck, relying on what he had learned through his alpine experiences, decided to take on the assignment anyway, and, as it turned out, because of the generosity of the American film company, his crew lived like kings in Greenland, despite the many dangers they had to endure.

The plot of *S.O.S. Iceberg* involves an arctic researcher, Dr. Karl Lorenz, who has been lost in the icy wilds of Greenland. According to the program notes of the *Illustrierter Film Kurier,* a Danish scientific expedition to Greenland is prematurely discontinued after one of its members, Dr. Karl Lorenz, becomes lost—and is thought to have died.[12] Upon further investigation by members of the scientific academic community, however, it is believed that Dr. Lorenz is still alive; thus, a new expedition, including Hella Lorenz, the wife of Dr. Lorenz (played by Leni Riefenstahl), starts out in search of him. After many months of superhuman difficulties, during which most of the members of the expedition perish, Dr. Lorenz, long believed to be dead, is found and, together with his wife and close associate, is saved by a fearless pilot (played by Ernst Udet). Riefenstahl's activities, among other things, involved difficult flying stunts. In addition there is a great deal of suspense as well as beautiful photography of the icy desert and its hardy inhabitants, the bears and Eskimos, so that even today the film (distributed by Universal) offers the viewer exciting entertainment.

As usual in Fanck-directed films, the shooting required a great deal of courage of the crew members, and the dangers in which the cast found itself were quite real: Fanck and several associates almost died making the film. Ernst Udet, who had already participated in *Die weisse Hölle vom Piz Palü*, was again a pilot in this film. At one point his engine lost power and crashed into the base of an iceberg. He was rescued by Eskimos. Within a few minutes after Udet was brought ashore, the iceberg, upon which the crew had set up its camera equipment, broke up. Half of the iceberg crumbled into pieces, carrying the men and their equipment into the water. The production unit ship almost capsized. Eskimos in their kayaks and members of the ship's crew in motorboats rescued the men and two women of the unit, although most of the sound equipment was destroyed. The boats of the crew were frequently squashed between icebergs, crew members were isolated, almost starved to death, and lost in the white wilderness. According to Fanck, the whole project was saved from total failure only because of the camaraderie among the crew members.

*S.O.S. Iceberg* did not draw good reviews, despite Riefenstahl's daring participation. In fact, the Americans, who had sponsored *S.O.S. Iceberg*, were disappointed, because the film did not have enough sensational scenes and too little plot. American audiences did not appreciate that which was real and possible, nor did they appreciate the beauties of nature exhibited in the film. In fact, an American version, directed by Tay Garnett, produced simul-

Photo right: *S.O.S. Iceberg*; Eskimos in kayaks against background of glaciers and iceberg
Courtesy of Deutsches Institut für Filmkunde

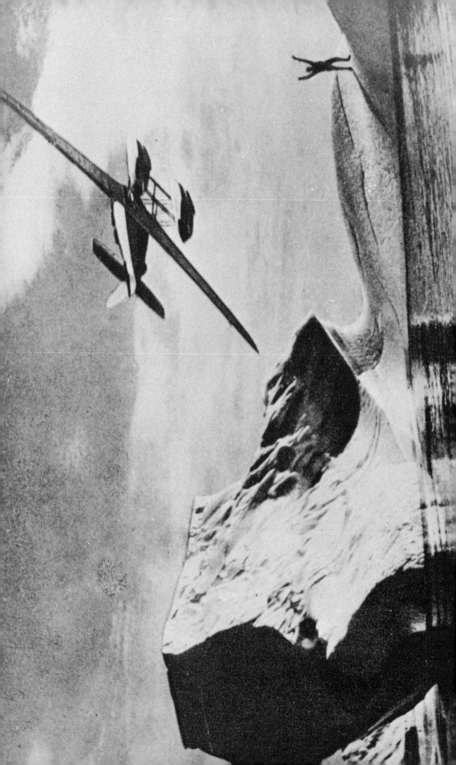

taneously with the Fanck-directed film, was and still is distributed by Universal. Certain scenes for both films were shot in the Bernina Alps and in the SOFA Studio in Berlin. An artificial iceberg, moreover, was constructed in the European Alps, so that the hazards endured by the actors could be minimized. Neither Arnold Fanck nor Leni Riefenstahl referred to this fact. The German critics found the film too sensational and blamed the Americans for wanting "to see and experience something in return for their money, just as in their Magazine stories."[13] Yet *S.O.S. Iceberg* gives expression to a theme which had become typical of Fanck's previous mountain films, namely, a sense of yearning in the Northern man for an experience in the world of white silence, for heroic camaraderie which unites the men in their struggle against nature under harsh conditions. In fact, to one commentator, the men participating in the film appeared to present "a panorama of Vikings," where Riefenstahl herself "fitted right in." Her acting has been described as "economical, rational, almost masculine."[14]

Riefenstahl herself described the conditions surrounding the making of this film. She emphasized that the difficulties of the struggle against nature attracted her as well as those with whom she worked. She repeatedly had the urge to go back into the white silences of Greenland but apparently never did. *S.O.S. Iceberg* contains many characteristics typical of Fanck's alpine mountain films. It exhibits qualities such as heroic endurance, camaraderie, a genuine love for unspoiled and dangerous natural sights which test human strength and survival, all qualities which are not found in everybody but which distinguish some people from others. This fact had made it possible for several critics to maintain that these films show "incipient fascism"; it has been suggested that the "surge of pro-Nazi tendencies during the pre-Hitler period could not better be confirmed than by the increase and specific evolution of the mountain films." The irony, of course, is that *S.O.S. Iceberg* was produced by Paul Kohner, who is Jewish.

In general, the argument goes as follows. Mountain films present a drama between man and his enemy, the mountain. Heroic qualities, such as courage, hardiness, self-sacrifice, pride, and endurance, have to be developed in man to conquer his enemy, the mountain. In fact, the very idea of conquest can be thought of as containing Fascist tendencies. In other words, any man in any mountain film will always be distinguished from the common

Photo left: *S.O.S. Iceberg*; a plane to the rescue of stranded crew member
Courtesy of Deutsches Institut für Filmkunde

herd. Moreover, mountain films usually show a conflict between civilization, seen as bad, versus nature, seen as good; and in German mountain films, the spectator is happy if nature wins out. This may be considered Fascist. Thus wilderness, purity, that which is untouched and perhaps primitive is seen as good, and—so the argument goes—this contains Fascist implications. The men and women in these films worship nature, and perhaps the insistence on showing a certain human camaraderie among the participants, and perhaps the emphasis on slightly superhuman qualities, such as endurance, courage, love of danger, tend to create a myth about the superiority of man. Considering that mountain climbers are of many nationalities and that mountain climbing is not an exclusively Teutonic activity, this argument is not particularly convincing. It implies, of course, an indirect definition of fascism: fascism is the glorification of man's fight against nature. It would be beyond the scope of this book to attempt its own detailed definition of fascism, or to analyze the merits of the one stated.

With the exception of *Die weisse Hölle vom Piz Palü*, the films which show Riefenstahl in her struggle against snow and ice have not survived as great documents of film art, although *S.O.S. Iceberg* stills enjoys a limited popularity.

After 1938, Fanck could not find employment in the German film industry. In fact, he was already somewhat unpopular with the Nazi regime after 1934, because he had sued a film company which had not paid him the promised fee and had won his suit, something which Goebbels did not like. Fanck never received the promised payment. It has been argued by critics that Fanck was fascinated by irrational forces, that his films show a reality which is "romantic, yes, even cruel," and that his films contain intimations of supernatural powers. "The step from this mythology to the adoration of power is a small one, and exhibited in the career of Fanck's student, Leni Riefenstahl," according to at least one German film historian.[15]

# 3

## The Eternal Feminine
## as the *Femme Fatale:*
## *The Blue Light*

### Production

BY 1931 LENI RIEFENSTAHL had established herself as a star, who was world famous, beautiful, and self-assured, and knew filmmaking before and behind the camera. She now broke away from Arnold Fanck, from whom she had learned a lot about filmmaking, as she had decided to make a film of her own. "I set about seeking a thread, a theme, a style in the realm of legend," she explained. "Something that might allow me to give free reign to my juvenile sense of romanticism and the beautiful image."[1] In her autobiography, she wrote that she visualized the story of the blue light, and that she put it together as a result of the impressions she had gathered while wandering through the mountains (*K*, 67). The idea which she finally selected had occurred to her while she was still a dancer. One of her acts was called "The Blue Flower," after a symbol of German romanticism that represents a quest for something which in beauty and excitement transcends the ordinary circumstances of human life. The blue flower is a leitmotiv in one of the most famous pieces of German romantic literature, Novalis' *Heinrich von Ofterdingen* (1802). It is a symbol of the infinite, and whoever sets out in search of the blue flower knows that he will never really find it because it represents a human dream. When Riefenstahl combined the theme of her dancing act with the beauty and hazards of the mountains, the result was the initial script for the first film which she directed herself.

"Dr. Fanck has always made beautiful images, which often produced fairy-tale effects, because of his use of back lighting, the snow, the ice, and the glittering effects, as well as the blossoms, etc., but the actions were realistic," Riefenstahl told an interviewer.[2]

71

Riefenstahl felt, however, that for realistic actions one needs realistic images and that, if she wanted to present beautiful images, something she liked to do, she should also show an action which comes from the world of fairies, from a legend or ballad, where the motif of the image is a precondition. In other words, she insisted that form and content have to coincide—that fairy-tales require fantastic photographic settings and that realistic scenery requires realistic plot and action. In her view, Fanck had succeeded in presenting realistic scenery and perhaps some realistic action, but she wanted to produce films with unrealistic action, i.e., a fairy-tale or ballad, presented in unrealistic cinematic images. Her film *The Blue Light* was to be the vehicle for this aesthetic philosophy. She went on to argue that during a normal event, when someone saves somebody else or when someone flies, that is to say, when something realistic happens, there could be sunshine, but there could also be bad weather, as is also the case in real life. "The idea that it would be good if form and content were identical led to the idea that in order to show such images, I should write a ballad, a fairy-tale, or a legend. That was the reason, and for that reason I wrote *The Blue Light* because the legend challenges one to show it in unusual images," Riefenstahl told Herman Weigel. Commenting further on her ideas for the film, she said that later in 1960 she wanted to turn it into the style of a ballet and that it was to be a fairy-tale which would be danced, photographed in color, and reminiscent of the story of *The Red Shoes*.

Originally Riefenstahl had not been eager to direct this film herself. She told one interviewer that she found it difficult to get started as a director, but that she wanted to play Yunta according to her own vision. She wanted to play in a film where *the woman* is the most important figure—not *the mountain* as had been the case in all the Fanck-directed films in which she had acted. In Fanck's films the woman had always been in the background. "I wanted a good part, and since I did not get it, I had to write it myself," Riefenstahl also confessed.

Having learned all of Fanck's techniques, having made friends with his best cameramen, his actors and actresses, his financial advisors, Riefenstahl borrowed many members from Fanck's production unit in order to make this film: cameraman Hans Schneeberger, who had worked with her on *Die weisse Hölle vom Piz Palü*; production manager Walter Traut, who later supervised production activities in all of Riefenstahl's films; and camera assistant Jaworsky, who tells us that "salary was rock-bottom minimum." "Low budget productions and no unions involved, but everyone in the company was in the same situation. We all loved what she did," he continued. He worked for ten dollars a month plus expenses, and he supplemented his own income from additional articles he wrote for film journals. It seems that most participants in *The Blue Light* had agreed to work without salary. Guzzi Lantschner, Alpine expert and world champion skier, also agreed to participate in the film. Riefenstahl had some difficulty getting the money. In *Kampf in Schnee und Eis* she tells us that she earned part of the money in the film *Weisser Rausch* (1931), for which she received a salary in the winter months of 1931. In addition, Sokal, "though a clever, careful businessman," had sufficient confidence in her abilities to finance *The Blue Light* with a sum of 50,000 marks (*K*, 68-69). In fact, she directed the film herself because she could not pay another director. It was not easy to make this film. "And boy, eight hours climbing up the mountain, before we did a shot, with everything on our backs—no cable cars and that nonsense," Jaworski remembered.[3]

The participants had to be idealists to work like this; they had to love it. Béla Balázs, one of the leaders of the German avant-garde, a well-known author at that time, and also a Marxist and a Soviet citizen, helped Riefenstahl with the scenario. In fact, he supervised the shooting, and his influence is noticeable everywhere in the film. "I was very lucky that he could take off three or four weeks to be present and in control for the most important scenes in which I acted," Riefenstahl recalled.[4]

Riefenstahl was in charge of the production and originated many of the techniques that made this film an outstanding success. Other filmmakers copied her innovations. Part of *The Blue Light* was shot on negative film material which was new at that time. It was infrared film negative. Infrared means that the film is especially sensitive to the red part of the spectrum so that one has to put a very heavy red filter in front of the camera lens to get a distortion that excludes all blue. In other words, the sky becomes all black, and things come out as if they were shot in moonlight. Part of *The Blue Light* was shot with this technique, especially sections where moonlight had to be shown. For admirers of the lovely moonlit nights shown in this film, it may be a sobering realization to know that this footage was actually shot in the day-time, with a clear blue sky, although the film comes out black. This technique was Riefenstahl's own idea. One day, while she was in the mountains with her crew, she said to her director of photography, Hans Schneeberger, who was also an old friend and lover: "Put in the green filter, together with the red filter." Schneeberger protested, arguing that the result would be no picture at all. However, there was a picture with a new and unexpected effect, namely, the green leaves came out like white leaves, as if illuminated with moonlight. Later on, scientists were able to explain with a new theory what Riefenstahl had accomplished merely on the basis of her intuition—and while ignorant of the "scientific" basis of the light effect. Agfa Film designed a special film stock for Riefenstahl which had a high green and red sensitivity and a low blue speed. In part this new film was used for *The Blue Light*, and the result was the mystical twilight atmosphere characterizing most of the photography in the film. In her zeal to create this mystical atmosphere, Riefenstahl forgot reality completely. According to Jaworsky, she and the crew received letters from viewers after the film had been completed. In several scenes the moon in *The Blue Light* rises on the left and sets on the right, from the point of view of the spectator. This implies that the moon rises in the west and sets in the east. However, in the northern hemisphere, the moon actually rises in the east and sets in the west. Riefenstahl, however, had photographed the sun, shot so it is set in reverse at one frame per second, and as a result of the special filters, she created the impression that the heavenly body seen in the film was the moon. A simple reversal of the film would have solved this problem, of course.[5] Even in the 1952 version the moon still moves west to east.

Dr. Fanck, to whom Riefenstahl showed a copy of the script before she filmed it, told her that it would be impossible to infuse the desired mysticism into Yunta's climbing of Monte Cristallo unless Riefenstahl had a large studio and a lot of money and provided that she did not use outside arc lights. "Dr. Fanck was very pessimistic," she recalled. "I didn't give up . . . , however, and after three days I got the idea that if I make the mountain full of fog and she [Yunta] climbs through this fog, it will add the unrealistic effect that I want. The problem was how to do it. I decided to use smoke bombs, but we had to wait until it was not too stormy. The smoke bombs were very successful. They put the whole mountain in 'fog.'"

Riefenstahl was able to keep her crew working smoothly together. Despite her beauty and evidently her willingness to bestow her feminine favors upon several of the men with whom she was working, no jealousies visibly marred her work. In fact, it seems that the erotic excitement infusing the shooting carried over to the excitement of the film itself. About her staff Riefenstahl said:

> In the selection of a staff I always had to have the feeling that we would find each other sympathetic so that we would be able to go through thick and thin together. Throughout the entire three months of shooting, there were never any bad moods, any nagging or even dissatisfaction. It was really ideal togetherness. We were just like a family of eight. Everything was paid out of a common pot. Everyone tried to spend as little as possible to keep the pot alive as long as possible. If anyone had torn shoes or needed anything urgently, it was paid from the pot. I myself abstained from any personal purchases for fourteen months. (*K*, 69)

Work began in July, 1931, in the Tessin, a section in Switzerland, where she lived with her film crew in a small village, called Foroglio, which featured a waterfall. During the first four weeks, their team consisted of six persons, later to be expanded to eight, and it was financed most sparingly. The crew members did not have to pay hotel bills, since there was no hotel in the village. There was no pub either. According to Riefenstahl, "the entire village consisted of nine adults, a few children, two cows, ten sheep, and several cats." Most of the houses were empty, because several years earlier many inhabitants had emigrated to the United States. Everyone on Riefenstahl's team had his own house, his bed, a bowl for washing, and this was all they needed. There was no one pushing the team to hasten their work, no film company was urging them on, and so, without undue haste, they were able to discuss the shooting in great detail

The most difficult part seems to have been persuading the peasants of the mountain area to participate in this film. Riefenstahl had been looking for the right kind of faces for a long time. Finally she discovered them in front of a church in a small village called Sorentino: "I tried to start a conversation with several among them. I failed, however. When I talked to them, they turned their backs on me, and their faces were not exactly friendly. Taking long strides, they finally left the churchyard. Occasionally I managed to take an unobserved camera shot" (*K*, 70).

The innkeeper of the village told Riefenstahl something about the inhabitants. He doubted that she would succeed in getting them to participate in the film. But Riefenstahl did not give up hope and remained in the village for several days in order to familiarize herself with the peasants. She walked through the streets, said hello to the people, stood in front of their houses, and spoke to their children. All of this took a while, because the houses were placed far apart. However, she was deeply attracted by the looks of these villagers who possessed "heads that appeared to be drawn by Dürer." She finally succeeded in overcoming the peasants' hesitancy when she invited one of them to have a glass of wine with her. To her surprise, he accepted, and after that the ice was broken. It seems that a little wine had to be on hand throughout the shooting of *The Blue Light* in order to overcome the villagers' resistance. In any case, it took Riefenstahl most of the summer of 1931 to win the confidence of the people of the Sarn Valley.

Often her team managed to shoot only for a few minutes per day, because of the need for a certain angle of the sun in order to get the desired light refraction in the waterfall. Film sections were developed immediately afterward so that the team could determine if the mood was suitably caught on film. Every member of the crew had a copy of the script which Riefenstahl had written with the cooperation of Béla Balázs. In the evening, the members of the crew all sat by the fire and discussed the scenes. Everyone offered his opinion, and no one worked separately on a special assignment. Instead, all worked together on the entire film. For four weeks they shot every day, and the first 9,000 feet were sent to Berlin for development. While waiting for the results, Riefenstahl received a telegram from Dr. Fanck saying, "Congratulations—the photography is indescribably beautiful—images like these have never been seen before" (*K*, 74).

However, later, when Riefenstahl, still somewhat unsure of herself, had sent Fanck sections of the edited film, he had taken it all apart and she found it lying on his floor when she visited him. She took home the exposed film material and started all over again. "This experience made me so critical toward my own work that I ruthlessly left out everything that produced only length or monotony, no matter how much I liked the shot itself."[6]

The crew began to shoot in July, but the principal actor, playing Vigo, Mathias Wieman, did not arrive until the beginning of August, when the team traveled to the Brenta Dolomites in order to shoot the climbing scenes taking place in front of the mountain hut, with the Crozza (called "Monte Cristallo" in the film) in the background. Most of the scenes were shot in Val-Balona. The crew lived only on cheese and bread.

Riefenstahl ordered a small generator truck from Vienna in order to illuminate the village homes, the huts, and the church, all of which appeared in the film. The initial interior scenes involving the local peasants were taken at Runkelstein Castle. The peasants were allegedly descendants of the Visigoths, and Riefenstahl liked the stark and clear lines of their faces and their proud bearing. In the beginning the peasants refused to be photographed. Diplomatic skill, tact, and small bribes were necessary to win their confidence, and this provided a good lesson for Riefenstahl, who put to good use what she had learned about winning reticent people when she made her film about the Nuba several decades later.

There were numerous difficulties to overcome even after the peasants had agreed to act in the film. In one instance, they had to be driven by car to a location, but since many of them had never seen an automobile, they refused to enter that "infernal" machine. After several weeks of shooting, Riefenstahl, on the last day, had to photograph a big festival—the party at the end of the film, after the villagers had been able to get the crystals from the mountain. The crew members were exhausted; Riefenstahl herself could hardly stand up any longer because fatigue and hunger had weakened her and she felt absolutely miserable. Yet the film script called for a merry festival with dancing and singing. The peasants were lying in various corners, on the floor, snoring, but the scene of the festival gave no clue that it was filmed under these circumstances. Somehow Riefenstahl managed to pull her team together for a gay, loud scene, in which the peasants celebrated the rape of Monte Cristallo.

Riefenstahl herself confesses that for her the editing was the best part of making a film. In the editing process she feels most creative, not dependent upon other circumstances, but able to impose her vision upon the filmed material. "I do not want to leave my editing room at all," she wrote. "I would actually like to sleep here" (*K*, 78). Finally, thousands of rolls of film were transformed into *The Blue Light*.

## Analysis

The analysis of this film is based upon the 1952 version which is
quite different from the original release print. The original
negative was lost as a result of the war, and the dubbed negative,
together with the other film material, was confiscated by the
French and transported to Paris. Since Riefenstahl had shot each
picture two or three times, she had material available in addition to
that which went into the film. This material, however, had been
confiscated by the Americans, who returned it to Riefenstahl in
1950. Members of the German and Italian film industry were
interested in a new edition of the film, and in 1952 Riefenstahl
made a new copy of the remaining material.

The original version was premiered on March 24, 1932, in the Ufa
Palast, Berlin, and the program notes of the German film journal
*Illustrierter Film Kurier* refer to the steep rocks, deep crevices,
dense fogs, and numerous romantic landscapes in the Dolomites:
"An inaccessible field of crystals lies in the mountains, upon which
a blue light of magic beauty shines. In its strangeness, it lures on
while terrifying at the same time the tough and stubborn peasants
of the Sarn Valley."

Only one person derives unalloyed pleasure from the beauty of
this light, namely, a stranger by the name of Yunta, a semicivilized
young Italian girl who scales the heights of the mountains with the
infallibility of a somnambulist. Every time a full moon shines on
these crystals, an accident occurs and climbers fall to their death.
Yunta is identified as a witch, persecuted, and almost stoned to
death, because she is thought to possess supernatural powers. She
is saved by a German painter, whose romantic feeling for nature
has brought him to this region. He falls in love with the girl and
wants to make her rich and respected; and, using a new trail up the
mountains, he opens the way to the hitherto inaccessible crystals
which are now exploited by the villagers. But Yunta—for whom
wealth is useless—is deeply saddened by the rape of the beautiful
shiny crystals, of whose magic power she is now deprived, and she
plunges into the abyss.

Riefenstahl commented: "Yunta was happy with the blue light.
It was a symbol to her, an ideal. Vigo was a good man, but he was
a realistic person. He didn't try to understand her idealism. When her
ideal was destroyed, Yunta no longer wanted to live. I have seen

this in life very often. People who love beauty and have an ideal, when they must face the realistic world, they are broken."[7] "The story of the girl and that village," Riefenstahl confessed to another interviewer, "is nearly the story of my life, but I didn't know that until later."[8]

In the original version, there was a frame to the story of *The Blue Light* that is not part of the 1952 edition of the film. According to Riefenstahl, the original film began with a shot of the village of Santa Maria, including a soundtrack featuring the noise of cars honking, as part of the background to the beauty of the location of Santa Maria. A newly married couple on their honeymoon is about to enter an inn. A number of children are playing around the inn, offering little pieces of crystal for sale. One little girl carries a picture in her hand, a picture of Yunta, apparently the patron saint of Santa Maria. The young woman takes the picture, enters the inn, and comes into an empty room. This room contains a strange atmosphere, somber and stark, the same kind of atmosphere pervading the film whenever the peasants enter it. The same picture of Yunta is also in this room. The innkeeper arrives and the woman asks him, "Who is Yunta?" because the name Yunta always appeared beneath this picture. The innkeeper replies, "Bring the book," and a little boy runs off and returns with a book, the same book appearing on the screen of the 1952 version of the film, showing a picture of Yunta as the patron saint. From here the film proceeds as in the 1952 version but it ends in a scene where Yunta's head is superimposed upon the head of the newly married young woman. We then see the young woman stand and watch the waterfall, presumably thinking about Yunta.

According to Riefenstahl, the voices in the 1952 version were newly dubbed and a lot of changes had to be made from the orginal version. With the exception of the voices of Riefenstahl and Mathias Wieman (Vigo), nearly all the voices had to be dubbed by new speakers, since the original actors were no longer available.

The music was also newly composed, albeit by the same composer, Giuseppe Becce, and Riefenstahl herself told an interviewer that in her opinion the second composition was better than the first.[9]

*The Blue Light* deals with far-reaching conflicts in human life. The conflict here is a clash between the world of dreams and world of reality. The world of dreams is represented by Yunta, who finds her way to the grotto with the crystals only while actually sleepwalking, and who, when she wakes up and finds her dream destroyed, falls to her death. The world of reality, on the other hand, is represented by the villagers, whose somber, hard faces dominate this film at least as much as the mountains and who realize the monetary value of the crystals, but are otherwise totally unencumbered by an appreciation of the beauty of nature and a desire to save this treasure. Clearly, they are not environmentalists. The crystals, although they are beautiful, represent a prospective source of wealth as well as a real source of danger for them. The villagers civilize nature by raping it. In a larger context, this conflict also shows a battle between civilization—seen as evil— and nature—seen as good. The mountains, the fog, the waterfalls, and Yunta, the heroine, represent nature. The theme, showing the conflict between destructive civilization and the untouched beauty of nature, pervades nearly all German mountain films. Critics have claimed, therefore, that the *The Blue Light*, as well as all German mountain films, are Fascist (see the preceding chapter). Kracauer, in his well-known book, writes that "this mountain girl conforms to a political regime which relies on intuition, worships nature and cultivates myths."[10] There is no mention of any political regime in *The Blue Light*; and although intuition does, indeed, play an important part in the film, that alone certainly would not make it a Fascist work.

The connection between German romanticism and *The Blue Light*, which has been noticed by many commentators, takes many forms. "The blue flower" mentioned by Riefenstahl represents a vision of the romantic writer Novalis in his *Heinrich von Ofterdingen*. It is, moreover, a very complex symbol. Like Yunta, who literally can only find the crystals in her sleepwalking activities, so Heinrich only sees the "blue flower" in his dreams.

There are other similarities between *The Blue Light* and the novella *Heinrich von Ofterdingen*. Those passages, in which Heinrich is dreaming, could especially serve as captions for the *The Blue Light* because they seem to comment on the scenes so vigorously. In chapter 1 of *Heinrich von Ofterdingen*, for example, we find the following: "He approached the grotto, which trembled and wavered with incredible colors. The walls of the cave were covered with a liquid substance which was not hot, but cold—and which was transformed into a soft bluish color."

Throughout the novella there are references to light, to jewels, and to scenes that speak openly of crystals. Novalis, like Riefenstahl, was also concerned with the conflict of dreams versus reality in his work. However, Novalis never separates the two worlds; and in the last section of the first part of his *Heinrich von Ofterdingen* he presents a wild intermingling of fantasy and reality, giving us a detailed description of his favorite world—the world of twilight. Often, in fact, Heinrich comments on the beauty of the light that is established between day and night: "Who would not like to walk in the twilight, when the night is refracted by the day, and when daylight is refracted into deeper shadows and colors." Novalis goes on to show that dream and reality join in a mystical union, which is not accessible to pragmatic reason, as becomes clear toward the end of the novella, which represents an apotheosis of the union between dream and reality.

Riefenstahl may not have known *Heinrich von Ofterdingen* as a literary work of art. But as a German it would have been impossible for her to be oblivious to the legend of the blue flower, which has become a symbol of the German romantic movement in general and appears in numerous poems, essays, and paintings referring to the romantic era. That one of Riefenstahl's dance numbers should be called "The Blue Flower" is not surprising at all. The mysticism infusing Novalis's novel was transformed by Riefenstahl into a strange, mystical atmosphere.

Cinematically, this mysticism is expressed in three ways in Riefenstahl's work. First, she creates an atmosphere of doom and impending disaster by the use of dissolves and the concentration of the camera upon uncanny shapes in the natural environment. Second, she deliberately uses fog whenever Yunta is climbing up the mountain peak to the grotto with the crystals, which she does only at night. Third, she creates a sense of tension as a result of her carefully developed close-ups. Naturally, the mysticism in *The Blue Light* is entirely nonverbal. Much of the time the film is steeped in a kind of chiaroscuro, a cinematic twilight, which was much used in the performing arts in Germany during the 1920s, notably by Max Reinhardt on the stage and by the expressionist film directors like Robert Wiene (*The Cabinet of Dr. Caligári*) and Fritz Lang. "And the ghosts, which had haunted the German Romantics, revived like the shades of Hades after draughts of blood," writes Lotte Eisner in *The Haunted Screen*.[11] The inborn

German liking for chiaroscuro and shadow found an ideal artistic outlet in the cinema, and visions nourished by moods of vague and troubled yearning could have found no more apt mode of expression "at once concrete and unreal," Eisner continues.[12] In fact, she claims that the romantic mysticism is something characterizing the Germans more than any other nation. Thus Riefenstahl's desire to create mysticism in the film continues a German tradition which experienced something of a rebirth during the years of the expressionist film.

In its predilection for romantic mysticism, *The Blue Light* relies heavily for its effects on the intermingling of light and shadow, constantly juxtaposing one with the other and thus contributing to the mood of doom that appeals to obscure fears and exhibits a strange beauty. The mountains, occupying large spaces on the screen, lend themselves well to the powerful interplay between light and shadow. In *Heinrich von Ofterdingen*, on the other hand, there was very little sense of fear and doom. In general, Heinrich's dreams were pleasant and his fantasies were always better than the realities, or at least as good. In her film, Riefenstahl frequently shows jagged trees, with uncanny branch formations, projected against the black sky. She is, in effect, projecting the superstitions of the villagers of Santa Maria upon the screen, borrowing forms she may have seen in *The Cabinet of Dr. Caligári* or Murnau's *Faust*.

Sequence 1:

The film, set evidently in the eighteenth century, opens with a shot of Yunta sitting on a rock on top of a ragged mountain peak, attacked by heavy snow and ice storms, while looking intently at a piece of crystal. From time to time the camera shifts, showing Yunta surrounded by waterfalls, or rocks in the shadow of other mountains, thus relating her to the beauty of this wild rugged mountain terrain, over which she presides, as if she were the queen. She is clearly the sole inhabitant of this wilderness, looking down from her heights on civilization below. Thus the conflict between nature and civilization is immediately established in the beginning of the film, and the values are suitably distinguished. Yunta, the queen of the mountains, pure, unspoiled, and majestic, by association with the mountains, looks down upon the narrow winding road on which a new guest from the cities, Vigo, arrives in a coach. This arrival scene is strangely reminiscent of one of the early scenes in Murnau's *Nosferatu*. In both films, the doors of the coach close as if by an invisible hand and the new arrival fails to understand the language of the local people. He is simply left standing by the driver who takes off without any further greeting. In *The Blue Light* a local villager speaking a German dialect, which Vigo can understand, approaches him in order to welcome him at the inn. The mood of gloom and danger is introduced with the next shot, showing a craggy mountain cave, halfway in shadow, featuring several crucifixes, erected there "in the memory of the boys who died climbing Mount Cristallo." At this moment Yunta, looking now like a simple Gypsy girl, passes the two men, and a mystical relationship between her and the crucifixes, or rather those they commemorate, is thus established. The camera focuses on her ragged clothes, her shy and simple demeanor, and immediately afterward upon the village priest who crosses himself upon seeing her, thus making clear that she is an outcast; in any case, she is not welcome.

The camera shifts to the interior of the simple village church, showing the peasants praying, indicating that this is a special day. This quiet, somber interior is contrasted with the next series of shots showing Yunta passing the village, which is populated by merchants, among whom there is a fat man intent upon buying crystals from the villagers. Here the close-ups, which are the overriding feature of the film, begin. The wrinkled and somber faces of the village elders, sitting on benches around a tree, speak volumes, and they establish an atmosphere of sobriety and doom, mostly carried by their silent glances. The new arrival is affected by the somber mood and, sipping his wine, observes, "You are not very merry around here," whereupon he is told that a full moon is expected tonight which means that at least one young man in the village of Santa Maria will die. "A curse lies upon us," the innkeeper says. The curse is emphatically accentuated by the somber faces of the other villagers, whose furtive glances communicate their fear and superstition to the viewer. It is in scenes like this that the influence of Béla Balász becomes very noticeable. In his well-known work, *Theory of the Film*, he devotes several pages to the art of the close-up. The close-up, he argues, was especially meaningful during the days of the silent film: "Close-ups radiate a tender human attitude in the contemplation of hidden things, a delicate solicitude, a gentle bending over the intimacies of life-in-the-miniature, a warm sensibility. Good close-ups are lyrical; it is the heart, not the eye, that has perceived them."[13] According to Jaworsky, a member of the film crew for *The Blue Light*, Balász's influence on the film is very strong.

The enormous tension between the villagers, the innkeeper, Vigo the painter, and Yunta the Gypsy girl is communicated primarily through close-ups. The film seems to consist entirely of furtive glances, expressing the tension, hostility, fears, and superstitions of the villagers and Yunta's awareness of their feeling toward her. "Close-ups are the pictures expressing the poetic sensibility of the director," Balázs wrote. "They show the faces of things and those expressions of them which are significant because they are reflected expressions of our subconscious feelings. . . . It is much easier to lie in words than with the face and the film has proved it beyond doubt."[14] The entire conflict between Yunta, the innocent mountain girl, and the villagers, who are greedy and eminently corruptible, despite their overbearing self-righteousness, is made visible in these close-ups. A new dimension, almost untenable and difficult to grasp, manifests itself in their faces, their long stares, their glinting eyes, which speak what Balázs called their "poetic soliloquys and their manifestations of mental, not physical loneliness."

The genuine, hard, strongly cut faces of these villagers of the Sarn Valley lent themselves well for this approach to the language of the close-up. Riefenstahl chose these people precisely because she found their faces beautiful. Balázs theorizes: "For beauty is what we like—we know of no other beauty—and this human experience is not something independent, but a function changing with races, epochs, and cultures. Beauty is a subjective experience of human consciousness, brought about by objective reality; it has its own laws, but those laws are the universal laws of consciousness and to that extent of course not purely subjective."[15] The beauty of the peasants' faces speaks a strong language; there is very little dialogue; and thus the language of the physiognomies is especially powerful. This fits the environment well enough, for the peasants are singularly taciturn. It takes only a few words of the innkeeper to communicate to Vigo that his youngest son had also died in his attempt to search for the mystery of the blue light. Because of the taciturn nature of this film, much guessing has to be done by the viewer. The first sequence of the film concludes with intimations of the erotic attraction which Yunta holds for the males of this village. Because she is mystically linked with the blue light, the susceptibility of the young males in the village for the lure of the blue light is inevitably also linked with Yunta, who thus becomes the proverbial *femme fatale*.

Her special attraction for the males is also expressed through close-ups. Tonio, the son of the innkeeper, is sexually attracted to Yunta, who is, if not unaware of her attraction, at least shyly afraid of male aggressiveness and avoids it by staying away from all contact with men. Tonio's passion is communicated through the sudden gleam in his eyes, his furtive glances at Yunta, and later, by his attempt to waylay her in a dark barn. Tonio is attracted and repelled at the same time. He is attracted by the uncontrollable nature of Yunta's existence. She will not be possessed. He is attracted by the danger which she represents because of her mystical association with the blue light.

The sequence closes with additional examples of Yunta's outcast status. The children follow her, call her names (in Italian), throw her basket down, a basket filled with berries but hiding a crystal. A fat tourist who attempts to take the crystal from her—realizing that she would not be protected from this theft by the villagers—is bitten in the hand. The other villagers merely stare at her in disgust and with profound disapproval. "What do you have against her," Vigo asks the innkeeper. "Why can only this young woman climb up the mountain, while our boys fall to their deaths? Yunta, that cursed witch!" is the answer, and that establishes Yunta's position in the village once and for all. The next shot shows Yunta running through lovely mountain forests, across meadows, and finally we see her arriving at a mountain cabin where she rests, breathing heavily. Thus the queen of the mountains must run away from civilization. Now the camera cuts to the innkeeper and Vigo the painter, who are talking about the deaths of those who had been mysteriously lured by the blue light.

Sequence 2:

In this sequence of images the presentiments of the previous shots find their realization. It shows the night of the full moon and the fears and superstitions of the villagers. It is dominated by the mysterious blue light and indirectly by Yunta, who is mystically associated with the blue light. With the help of dissolves, Riefenstahl here indicates the passage of time from day to night and uses her chance to relate the murky fears in the villagers—and in the viewers—as a result of this special night of a full moon. A presentiment of disaster is also indicated through the dissolves used here. The next scene is somberly humorous. The village of Santa Maria is preparing for this night. The moon slowly rises behind the mountains. A strange feeling of uneasiness overcomes everyone in the village, including Vigo, who is gripped with fear also. He is first tempted to open his window and watch the moon rise, but he then decides to close it. Now follows a series of truly superb shots, full of murky mysticism but beautiful nevertheless. The camera again takes close-ups, this time of the rapt faces of young boys and men, who stare up at the moon, waiting, enchanted, for the rays to produce the seductive blue light. Old faces are visible behind windows, closing shutters, locking doors. Tonio's father locks the door to his son's room and pockets the key, thus giving expression to the power of the expected blue light. The women are clearly immune to the magic emanating from the blue light. Only young men are susceptible to it, and this emphasizes the erotic element in the attraction. Yunta is also watching the blue light from her mountain hut. Suddenly a dog barks, a window shutter is violently opened, and a young man, Livio, is seen running out into the empty street: Yunta's next victim, according to cinematic language. The camera moves back to her, sitting, in rapt attention watching the moon, and waiting for the blue light to shine forth. This scene again emphasizes that somehow the young men are in pursuit of that which is beautiful. But unlike Yunta, they want to possess what is beautiful, and hence they are destroyed. Yunta thus represents the ineluctable beauty of nature, its dangers and mysteries, and thus her role as a witch is not entirely unwarranted. She presides over her mountain cave containing the crystals, and she seems to be the force protecting it from rape.

Sequence 3:

It is daylight and the camera focuses on four men carrying a stetcher, with the body of the latest victim of Monte Cristallo, the blue light, and Yunta. The latter is ambling through the street, picking up an apple from the ground, following the group with the stretcher. The stretcher, presumably carrying the body of Livio, is placed in front of his mother. Shots of villagers pursuing their various activities. This gives Riefenstahl an excellent opportunity for candid close-ups of the villagers, spinning, staring at Yunta, watching the body. When Yunta passes the group, Livio's mother looks up, raises her fist, and shouts in Italian, "That is her fault!" whereupon the villagers grab pitchforks, rocks, and other weapons, and begin to pursue Yunta through the village. When she is almost surrounded by her enemies, Vigo, observing the entire scene from the window, jumps down and places himself between Yunta and her pursuers. He argues with the men, especially Tonio, who is carrying a big stick, and while the villagers listen to him, Yunta takes a rock and throws it in Tonio's face. Tonio is not really displeased, despite the pain this causes him. It shows that Yunta can be wicked. The next shots show her running up the mountains to her little cabin which she inhabits with Guzzi, a young friend and companion, with whom she has a relationship with erotic overtones.

Vigo, the outsider, has helped Yunta, another outsider. Yunta disappears into the mountains, and Riefenstahl uses this opportunity to show the glamour and splendid beauty of the Dolomites in bright summer weather. Speaking Italian and weeping intermittently, Yunta tells Guzzi her story. Relying again on on her lyrical close-ups, Riefenstahl conveys the erotic tension between Guzzi and Yunta. The underlying contradictions become visible in close-ups when Vigo, the painter and Yunta's protector, comes up the mountain and is noticed by Guzzi. He is still far away and Yunta, playing seductress, secretly meets him halfway up the mountain, wishing to surprise him and lure him on. She hides behind the bushes in such a way that her beautiful face is reflected in a small lake below, although the rest of her body is not visible. Vigo has to pass this lake on the way up to the hut. She drops the half-eaten apple on the ground. When Vigo discovers her reflection in the lake, he also finds the apple, and properly seduced, he intensifies his search for Yunta. The entire scene is a seduction scene, but without the overt sexual overtones familiar to the modern moviegoer. In fact, the subtlety of the scene, despite the many well-known symbols from traditional literature, is typical of the silent films of the 1920s where sexuality is rarely overt but usually implied and indirect. In the seduction scene here we have the symbols of feminine seductiveness, the apple, feminine beauty—indirectly expressed in the reflection and therefore made even more beautiful because more elusive. Vigo cannot resist the lure, and calling Yunta's name, he hears a rustling in the bushes, mysterious sounds reach his ears, as if the voices of nature were humming to him, and without actually meeting Yunta, he finally makes his way into the hut up the mountain where he is greeted with considerable jealousy by Guzzi, who immediately senses in Vigo a competitor for Yunta's affections. Yunta, who wears a tight-fitting blouse, partially unbuttoned, enters some time after Vigo has arrived, and proves herself to be a courteous hostess, although shy and withdrawn. Again the close-ups of the faces give away the underlying tension between Yunta, Vigo, and Guzzi, a triangle of the kind in which Yunta often seems to be involved. The two men are silently fighting over her. This is a common scene, almost a cliché, in Riefenstahl's early films, the effect of which is in part due to the fact that her early films are either silent films or films that were made in the beginning of the sound era, when close-ups were particularly expressive in order to make up for the absence of sound. While triangular sexual situations like the one between Guzzi, Yunta, and Vigo are not uncommon in dramatic works— after all, they provided excellent dramatic suspense—Riefenstahl's editing increases tension to a very high degree, and this makes the final film a true expression of her vision. It is possible that Riefenstahl saw herself as the *femme fatale* in real life but decided to transform this vision or dream into art rather than living it in reality. There is a great deal of tacit erotic tension in these scenes. As a result of the close-ups which frequently concentrate on the eyes, an almost unbearable suspense is created resulting from the strong attraction, like a magnetic field, of the forces between men and women. Thus, this film can be described as a study in the cinematic representation of tacit, nonverbal, and invisible forms of erotic love.

Vigo departs, after having conceded that it is "so beautiful up here, I do not want to leave," whereupon the camera swiftly moves to another couple, Tonio and Lucia. Tonio is ploughing the fields and Lucia offers him grapes. However, Tonio is not interested in the madonnalike beauty and saintly goodness of Lucia. Riefenstahl tells us that she had looked for this face for a long time. Then the film cuts to an interior scene, where a band of musicians is playing for a dance. Vigo sits down and a series of close-ups of the villagers' faces follows, radiating disapproval presumably because Vigo had helped Yunta escape their anger earlier that day. Lucia again wishes to approach Tonio, but it is clear that Tonio is only thinking of Yunta and the blue light.

Sequence 4:

This sequence takes place high up in the mountains and contains scenes of the Dolomites of breathtaking beauty. It begins with Yunta sitting high up on a promontory, Guzzi leaning sleepily against her. She watches Vigo, who comes up the mountain, armed with sticks of bread, cheese, canvas, and a paint brush. Yunta likes him but not in the erotic sense. She sees in Vigo only her savior, not her lover. They cannot communicate, because they do not understand each other's language. Yunta looks absolutely ravishing with her slit skirt and handsome bosom. She and Vigo tell each other the words for cheese and bread in Italian.

Vigo sleeps on hay with a blanket, like Guzzi and Yunta. During the day he makes himself useful by cutting wood, and thus this mountain idyll is complete. The beauty of the mountains inspires Vigo to spend much of his time painting, calling Yunta his "rock witch" (i.e., "Steinhexe"). Vigo is so content in the mountains that he insists that he will not return to the people in the valley, thus reinforcing the thematic conflict between nature and civilization. Yunta is not listening to this piece of information, being totally engrossed in the contemplation of a large piece of crystal, evidently from the grotto on Monte Cristallo. Vigo contemplates Yunta's beauty and self-absorption and he becomes passionate, walking toward Yunta, embracing and ardently kissing her. But Yunta, sensing danger in Vigo's ardor, pulls away, afraid and shy. She represents the totally unspoiled, innocent child of nature. Guzzi, the shepherd boy, observes the scene in silent anger, and the erotic tensions between the two men become evident again, but Yunta appears to be totally unresponsive to Eros. Vigo, after this scene, seems to be awakening from a dream he had forgotten himself. Yunta's relationship to the blue light becomes clear again. In order to remain beautiful she is to be untouched, undisturbed by civilization, here represented by Vigo. In the same sense, the blue light is beautiful only because it is inaccessible to the greed and even to the eyes of men. Yunta represents someone who will never belong to any one man. Totally aware of her special status, she allows no one to touch her. Thus she has established another link with the blue light that shines from the grotto and is only accessible to her.

The shadows are getting longer and darker. Dusk has set in, and the twilight gives Riefenstahl another opportunity to show her cinematic ability, capturing the mood with her camera. The stark, sparse, barely furnished interiors, contrasted with the serious, rough-hewn faces, again create a mood of impending doom. The bell strikes midnight, and again the moon slowly crosses the sky until its rays hit the crystals. Tonio is now married to Lucia, and his father looks into the room to ascertain that he is indeed with beautiful Lucia, whom he does not love. A few minutes later, Tonio, apparently having poisoned her, bolts out of the window, rushes up to Monte Cristallo, fatefully attracted by the blue light that is casting its sheen over the village.

The cutting here conveys the passing of time, indicated in the succeeding shots which show the ever-growing shadows. This cutting method reinforces the sense of disaster; and though we have no indication at all of what day of the month it is, Riefenstahl's cutting tells us that on this night there will be a full moon with its concomitant beauties and dangers. It is a dark night, and the moon, up in the sky, is partially concealed by mountains and roof tops. Much of the effect in this sequence stems from Riefenstahl's cutting technique, which juxtaposes the two couples, Tony and Lucia, on the one hand, and Vigo and Yunta, on the other, with the result that Yunta's special attraction for males becomes even more obvious. The moon is swimming behind chimneys. There are strange formations of branches and trees, with the moon in the background, as in a surrealist painting.

At the hut, Vigo appears to be in deep despair, because he finds it impossible to express his love for Yunta. His head leans against a post and despairingly he looks at Yunta. She awakens, under the influence of the beautiful rays emanating from the blue light shining through the door of her hut. The strange light causes restlessness in susceptible sleepers, so Vigo finally leaves the hut to cool his heavy head outside. Unknown to Vigo, Yunta also comes out of the hut, but she walks away, toward the steep rock, leading straight to the source of the blue light.

Watching Yunta climb up the mountain, Vigo, stunned, follows her. There follows a shot of the steep mountain crag against the sky, giving an indication that it might take supernatural powers to climb that ridge, something that the superstitious peasants of Santa Maria had always believed, anyway. They had even considered the blue light a mysterious and wild power. In the course of the following scenes it becomes clear that the blue light is simply due to a natural phenomenon caused by the way in which the rays of the full moon hit the crystals. The clouds now enshrining the mountain appear to accentuate the supernatural abilities behind Yunta's uncanny climbing skills; she is now in a true chiaroscuro—in shadow and light—between day and night.

Now a drama ensues. We see Yunta climbing up Monte Cristallo, followed by the two men who love her and are drawn to the dangerous light by her; she thus represents the "eternal feminine" who is literally drawing the men upward. She never looks down—that is her secret—and hence she never worries about falling. Ideologically interpreted, this means, of course, that Yunta is inconsiderate of the weaker members of the human species; she does not look back and wait for them, but climbs up and up and up. The result is that the man whose love for her is illegitimate, as it were (Tonio), eventually loses his grip on the mountain, her domain, and falls to his death. Vigo, on the other hand, who is legitimately in love with her, finds a new, easier path to the crystals. But he also does not measure up to her; by finding an easier path, he is shown to be a compromiser, a "realist." A very beautiful scene in the film in this sequence, unforgettable to anyone who has seen it, is the arrival of Vigo at the grotto. He observes Yunta sitting in the grotto like a queen of the mountain treasure, photographed in profile, as a shadow against the sky and kneeling in appreciation of the crystal beauty she beholds. From Riefenstahl's lyrical close-ups we know that Vigo realizes that Yunta is untouchable. She is "das ewig Weibliche, das zieht uns hinan"("the eternal feminine drawing us upward"—a famous quote from Goethe's *Faust*). When Yunta becomes aware that Vigo has discovered her secret, she utters a cry.

While this false movement wakes up Yunta from her trance, it also reveals that Vigo, despite his rationalism, is a kind of romantic hero who is capable of surprise and love and also susceptible to beauty. Yunta cries out when she sees Vigo. She covers her eyes, as if wishing that she had never seen him. At this moment the rock

upon which Tonio had been hanging breaks off and Tonio falls to
his death. This scene thus demonstrates that the two men pursuing
Yunta fare quite differently: one truly loves her and is rewarded
while the other, wishing to violate her, falls. As a result, Yunta truly
appears to be a witch to the viewer, pleasing those who love her
and killing those who wish to destroy her. She represents the
mystique of the mountain: whoever wishes to conquer it will die,
and whoever wishes to understand and love it, will live. This is a
dream, of course. It is an environmentalist's dream. It is the dream
of someone who wishes to preserve the beauty of nature as both a
threat and a source of pleasure. Yunta, as the entire film implies, is
the goddess of the blue light, and as such, in effect untouchable,
like a thing of ineffable beauty.

Sequence 6:

The camera shifts to Vigo and Yunta who have safely returned to
the cabin. Vigo leaves Yunta's cabin in order to alert the villagers,
inviting them to exploit the crystals. Speaking to Yunta, he says,
"These crystals are a danger for you. That is a treasure we must
get." Yunta, not understanding a word he says, wants him to stay
with her: "Resta aqui," she replies. The scene shifts and we get to
witness the bell tower in the village of Santa Maria. The villagers
gather on the church square, talking animatedly and happily.
Everybody is suddenly all happiness and smiles and Vigo is the
center of attention, hovering over a plan which indicates how the
villagers could gain access to the grotto of the blue light. March
music sets in, and the next scene shows the villagers carrying huge
baskets of crystals from Monte Cristallo. There follows a shot of
the grotto, and we see the villagers hammering away at the crystals
which are thrown into huge baskets and carried down the
mountain. The focus shifts to an inn where the villagers are happily
dancing, in a way we never saw them before. Vigo is the hero of
this party. He wants to leave, however, because he has an
appointment with Yunta that evening, but he is held back by the
villagers, now exceptionally sociable, because they have made so
much money as a result of the crystals. The peasants seem to be
very ugly in this sequence, exhibiting tooth gaps when they smile,
and appearing rather crazy. They try to hold Vigo back. The
innkeeper, whose son was a competitor of Vigo, looks through the

window at the party; he is disconsolate, remembering the death of Tonio. Now there follows a shot of Yunta walking along her favorite mountain path and noticing that crystals are lying on the ground. Fearful that something might have happened to her favorite spot on the mountain, she climbs to the grotto, where she finds nothing but a piece of rock. The somber mood conveyed by the photography of the totally bare cave, where not even one piece of crystal is left to adorn the stark, grey, and now lifeless rock, is stunning. At this point the film could serve as an example in favor of environmental protection. The modern viewer is as stunned as Yunta at the rapacity of the villagers, who have failed to leave even one piece behind.

Dejected, Yunta descends and, no longer wanting to live, falls to her death. But in true Riefenstahl fashion, she lands on a lovely meadow, looking as beautiful as ever. She appears uninjured—not one drop of blood flows from her mouth—and she thus joins the mountain flowers that Vigo discovers, together with Yunta, when he once again tries to climb to the mountain hut. Instead of finding a happy and rich Yunta, he sees a dead body, as beautiful and appropriate to the mountains as the flowers surrounding it. For Vigo, then, the road to hell was paved with good intentions.

Now the scene shifts to the village, and we see again the image of the patron saint, Yunta, imprinted upon the cover of a leather-bound book, containing the story introduced in the beginning of the film: "This is the story of Yunta, whom the village treated so unfairly and who brought such wealth upon the village." Despite its sentimental story, the film has an inescapable effect upon the modern moviegoer. Its main theme is stated with genuine cinematic skill.

## Reception

*The Blue Light* enjoyed a modest commercial success in Germany, although it was favorably received by German critics. It became a great success in France and England. In fact, it played for fifty months at the Rialto Theater in London. Riefenstahl received telegrams from Hollywood and other parts of the world, congratulating her on her success. In the May 19, 1934 issue a *New Yorker* reviewer described *The Blue Light* as "a little dip into the eerie, touched off with a good deal of romantic beauty of

background."He called it "especially satisfying." "This Fräulein
Riefenstahl must love her mountains and have done a good deal of
hiking and prying about the Tyrolean Alps and the Dolomites to
know them as well as this movie indicates she does. I should
imagine it would require a steady and energetic course in
mountain-climbing, under all conditions, in daylight, and at nighttime to know how to photograph them so continually in their most
telling moments." The same reviewer found that the film provided
great comfort as a tonic of landscape alone. The *New York Sun*
(May 9, 1934) called it "one of the most pictorial films of the year.
Leni Riefenstahl, author, director, and star—is an expert climber as
well as a handsome woman." In the *New York Herald Tribune* a
reviewer wrote, ". . . for sheer pictorial beauty, the film is perhaps
unexcelled. Told with absorbing intensity. . . . How flawlessly this
girl, who plays the lead and also wrote and directed it, accomplished her task." The film won a silver medal at the Venice Film
Festival. Not all commentators were as enthusiastic about *The Blue
Light* as the Americans. It has variously been described as a film
with a "Wagnerian atmosphere," as a typically "Teutonic mountain
film," as a film containing the seeds of fascism, and as a work
"steeped in Weltweh and Himmelssehnsuch á la Novalis and Tieck."

Siegfried Kracauer, who may not have seen the film or
apparently misunderstood it, wrote that "while the peasants are
merely related to the soil, Yunta is a true incarnation of elemental

powers, strikingly confirmed as such by the circumstance of her death. She dies when sober reasoning has explained, and thus destroyed, the legend of the blue light. With the glow of the crystals her very soul is taken away...this mountain girl conforms to a political regime which relies on intuition, worships nature and cultivates myths. To be sure, at the end the village rejoices in its fortune and the myth seems defeated, but this rational solution is treated in such a summary way that it enhances rather than reduces Yunta's significance." Lotte Eisner finds *The Blue Light* a cheap imitation of Fanck's mountain film techniques. She objects to Riefenstahl's studio effect used when photographing the crystals in the cave and finds that the "freshness and spontaneity of the open-air shots are marred by the over-perfect, over-smooth shots." In her opinion Riefenstahl excelled in filming in the studio only whenever the climbs were too difficult or the acrobatics too dangerous; they were made in "landscapes of salt and white powder –representing snow and ice."[16] Eisner's judgment is incorrect. Riefenstahl had genuine mountain crystals brought in from various local museums and other places in order to provide certain scenes with genuine natural beauty. Several of the grotto scenes were in fact shot in a studio in Berlin. Jaworsky tells us that the glittering beauty of the crystal-studded grotto up in the mountains is due to the shiny remnants of bottles and other glass pieces obtained from a glass factory. However, the climbing scenes themselves appear to have been exclusively shot on location. Ulrich Gregor and Enno Patalas, German critics of the left, find that *The Blue Light* consists of little more than a meager plot which is used as a pretext to steep the mountain world of the Dolomites into a mystical twilight, for the production of which Riefenstahl had to invent all kinds of cinematic tricks.[17] Another reviewer, in 1934, called it a highly fascinating fantasy. Al Miller, the spokesman for the Telluride Film Festival, in 1974 referred to *The Blue Light* as a film that assumes "a high place in the Nazi hierarchy."

Upon its re-creation in 1952, the film was described by German critics as representing "early romanticism" and as undeserving of the label "artistically valuable," which had been bestowed upon it in 1932. It was accused of exhibiting dramatic motivation which was unclear. However, in general, the film can be described as a successful work of art.

Photo top left: Riefenstahl teaching a Sarn Valley peasant how to act in *The Blue Light*
Courtesy of Deutsches Institut für Filmkunde

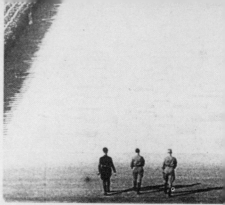
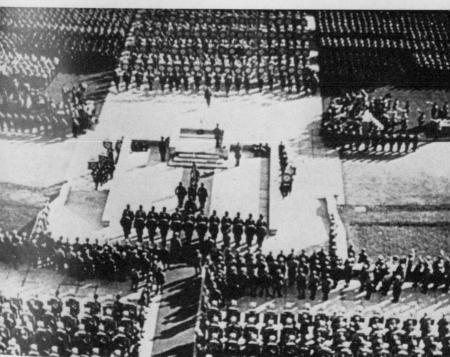

96–100 *Triumph of the Will* (*Triumph des Willens*), 1935. Leni Riefenstahl.

# 4

## Artistic Configurations of a Mass Rally: *Triumph of the Will*

### Production

IN 1934 HITLER requested that Leni Riefenstahl film the party rally of that year. She had already filmed the party rally of 1933, a work now lost, called *Sieg des Glaubens* (*Victory of Faith*). In 1934 she was reluctant to assume the new assignment, because she had plans to shoot *Tiefland* in Spain. In order to resolve the conflict, she enlisted the help of her friend, director Walter Ruttman, a Communist, whom she considered an expert in documentary films, to shoot this film. He liked the assignment, was willing to accept it, and Riefenstahl left for Spain in June, 1934, to shoot *Tiefland*. During the shooting she fell ill, spent several weeks in the hospital, and temporarily abandoned the project. Ruttman filmed only the prologue, and even that footage is now lost. On the basis of a description of his material in the German film journal *Lichtbildbühne* (September 12, 1934) Ruttman had shot a montage of various aspects of German history covering the twenty years preceding Hitler's ascent to power: World War I, the Treaty of Versailles, unemployment and unspeakable misery were shown floating past the inner eye of the führer. Toward the end of the prologue, Ruttman showed Hitler, seized by the sheer power of his will, writing *Mein Kampf*, which is viewed as a symbol of the rise of the National Socialist party. With the help of trick photography indicating the collapse of the German stock market and creating the inflation of 1923, Ruttman approached the problem from a Marxist perspective, i.e., he tried to show the economic circumstances behind Hitler's rise to power, something which Riefenstahl left out entirely in her film. On the basis of what we know, it appears that Ruttman, though a Communist, was not hostile to Hitler and that he, like many other Germans, saw in him a man

97

capable of helping Germany out of its misery. Riefenstahl disliked Ruttman's work and described it as "chaos." "He evoked the historical by use of headlines and such. You cannot create with paper in that way. . . . He tried to shoot great heroic shots from underneath—you know, like Eisenstein. . . . I could not use a meter."[1]

When she returned to Berlin in August 1934, Hitler's deputy, Rudolph Hess, contacted her and told her that she, not Ruttman, had been asked to make the film about the 1934 party rally and that she was expected to fulfill the assignment. The fact is that Ruttman had intended to make the film a history of the Nazi party, something which the Nazis did not like. They made genuinely historical films of the rise of the Nazi party—*S.A. Mann Brandt, Hitlerjunge Quex,* and *Hans Westmar*—only in 1933. Riefenstahl's style was more to the liking of the leaders of the Nazi party than Ruttman's, although, or perhaps because, Riefenstahl did not "know what is SS and what is SA. I don't know what is important and what is not important."[2] She pointed out that Goebbels, head of the German film industry, did not like her, but Hitler reassured her that he had ordered Goebbels to cooperate.

It is no wonder that Hitler wanted a first-rate filmmaker to direct the film of the party rally, having insisted several years earlier that he wanted to "exploit the film as an instrument of propaganda in such a way that the audience will be clearly aware that . . . they are going to see a political film. It nauseates me when I find political propaganda hiding under the cloak of art. Let it be either art or politics."[3] For a politician, this comment is somewhat unexpected, yet similar views were expressed by Goebbels in a speech made on the birthday of Horst Wessel in 1933.[4]

Realizing that she could not evade the assignment, Riefenstahl now demanded that the film be made by her own company rather than by the Ministry for People's Enlightenment and Propaganda. Hitler agreed to this demand and promised not to interfere with the filming; he granted her complete freedom to make the film as she desired. Riefenstahl acknowledges in one of the major titles of the film itself that it was, in fact, made by order of the führer. Although ostensibly UFA financed and distributed *Triumph of the Will* there is little doubt that the Nazi party (NSDAP) actually provided the funds as well as the setting and every facility possible for unimpeded film recording of the event.

Riefenstahl said that it was a very "cheap film." According to her testimony, she "had only 280,000 marks. [$110,000 in 1934]. I had only two cameras at my disposal. . . . I had to make many tests, improvise many things."[5] She also claimed that she had only two weeks to plan the filming of the event. This seems to be contradictory to a statement in her own brochure, *Hinter den Kulissen des Reichsparteitagsfilms* (*Behind the Scenes of the Reichs Party Congress Film*, 1934), where she admits that she began preparations for it in the spring preceding the party convention. However, there is evidence that the brochure was ghostwritten by Ernst Jaeger.

On many occasions after the shooting of the film during inter-views and in other contexts, Riefenstahl complained that numerous obstacles were placed in her way; however, in *Hinter den Kulissen des Reichparteitagsfilms*, which is a reliable source of information about many background details regarding the film, she gratefully acknowledged cooperation between the authorities and the film crew.[7] The book, moreover, contains numerous statements demonstrating that Riefenstahl was much more in support of the Nazi party than she later pretended to be.

The title of the film was suggested by Hitler himself.[8] The film was produced by Leni Riefenstahl Studio Film, and it is registered in that name in the archives at Koblenz in Germany. The crew consisted of 172 persons, broken down into the following: ten technical staff, thirty-six cameramen and assistants, nine aerial photographers, seventeen newsreel men, twelve newsreel crew from Tibs Company, seventeen lighting men, two still photographers, twenty-six drivers, thirty-seven watchmen and security personnel, four labor service workers, and two office assistants. They used twenty-two chauffeur-driven cars. The cameramen were under the direction of Sepp Allgeier, who was cameraman in several of Fanck's and Riefenstahl's earlier films. The camera crew used thirty cameras and were dressed as SA men so that they would not be noticeable in the crowd. Although there are at least twelve sequences in the film where the wary spectator can detect the cameras at work, in general the crew working in the film is very well disguised.[9]

Contrary to certain allegations, especially those made by Albert Speer, the 1934 party convention was not staged solely for

Riefenstahl's cameras. Speer writes in his *Inside the Third Reich* that several scenes had to be reshot because Riefenstahl did not like them. Riefenstahl claims that nothing in the film was staged, nor was any part of the film reshot in a studio. Only several sound effects were made in the studio.[10] The Party Rally was an annual event and it was staged for cameras to the extent that political events are planned with cameras and press people in mind. Nevertheless, Hitler, knowing the importance of producing an interesting film about the event of 1934, helped a great deal in the planning of it.

The crew worked around the clock for seven days and nights. According to Riefenstahl each cameraman was his own director, because there were no means of central communication with production headquarters. "This was a basic rule as we worked," Riefenstahl writes. "Let no man get bogged down with unimportant details. But leave nothing out! Go after the real events as if possessed. There can be no stop and no impossible. Everything that happens must be caught like a blitz intuitively.'[11]

Riefenstahl trusted the intuitive judgment of that personnel she had carefully selected for the shooting of this film. In her own estimation, however, fifty percent of the completed film is composed of footage from Allgeier's own camera.

The guiding idea for Riefenstahl was that the film had to be composed, like newsreels, of swiftly moving images. Moreover, she was innovative and full of ideas in the preparation of the film. Thus, she had pits dug before the speakers' platform, tracks laid so that her cameramen could make traveling shots, and elevators built so that filming could be done above the million and a half people attending the rally. She also arranged to have cameramen aboard a dirigible for aerial shots. All these devices contributed to the kind of cinematic energy which characterizes this film as well as her other films. Riefenstahl recorded sixty-one hours of film from every imaginable angle, from rooftops, windows, gutters, and eye-level, and from a variety of moving devices, including automobiles, fire-truck ladders, dirigibles, airplanes, and roller skates, as well as conventional camera dollies. The variety in the visual quality of the film derives primarily from these different angles and from the use of different speeds in black and white film stock. Although there are many intimate shots in the film, few people acknowledge the presence of cameras.

The main purpose of the film, from the point of view of Hitler and the Nazi party, was to show to the German people the solidarity of the Nazi party and to present to pretelevision German audiences the new Nazi leadership. This purpose was brilliantly accomplished.

Riefenstahl edited the film herself, reducing it from sixty-one to a little more than two hours. "In my cutting room, it was the most difficult work of my life," she said, describing the task that took at least five months to fulfill. "I was eighteen hours per day and night in the cutting room thinking how I can make the film interesting," she told a B.B.C. interviewer in 1972. She also explained that she did not care much about chronological accuracy on the screen and that she intuitively tried to find a unifying way to edit the film in a way which would progressively take the viewer from act to act and from impression to impression. The film was premiered on March 28, 1935. No Nazi official had seen the film before its first official screening. Riefenstahl compares the process of editing to dancing, insisting that she had learned much about artistic shape from her early training as a ballet dancer. The completed film was a realization of her own vision. The sound, with the exception of the speeches, was synchronized in the studio in only three days. Since she had no extensive magnetic recording equipment, and since the production was physically very difficult, Riefenstahl could not use direct sound. The speeches were recorded exactly at the time they were delivered, although they were excerpted. The only exception is the speech by Streicher which had to be partly redone, because of initial technical difficulties. The sound track is a mixture of speeches, music, and cheers from the crowd, but its special effect stems from Herbert Windt's compositions. Windt also wrote the music for *Olympia* and *Tiefland*. The crowd sounds were created in part by Windt and Riefenstahl with the assistance of some friends. Since the cameras used for the film were running at different speeds, from eighteen frames to twenty-four frames per second, the difficulty involved in synchronizing the music with the variable speeds of the footage contributed by the cameramen was considerable. In order to solve this problem in the long parade scene (scene 11), Riefenstahl herself conducted the studio orchestra to match the tempo of the music to the rhythm of the marching troops. In order to create a score of great variety, Windt combined a few Wagnerian themes with several pseudo-Wagnerian heroic phrases and German folksongs and march music, as well as party anthems. Especially effective is the use of the well-known, somber war song, "I Once Had a Comrade" ("Ich hatt einen Kameraden"), which is very moving and slow, together with the more militant and energetic "Horst Wessel Lied" ("Die Fahne hoch"), which was the official anthem of the Nazi party. The contribution of the music to the overall effect of the film has been largely disregarded by critics, especially non-German critics. The fact is, however, that the influence of the music upon the pysche of the viewers, especially German viewers, is at least as strong as the influence of the cinematic images.

Many commentators feel that fear grips them whenever they watch the film. It is true that it manages to evoke very strong feelings in the spectator, including a sense of fear; but it also produces a sense of hope and optimism, depending upon the political position of the viewer with respect to the Third Reich. The sense of hope and optimism played into the hands of the National Socialists.[12] Even though Hitler liked the film when he saw it on March 28, 1934, during its premiere at the Ufa-Palast am Zoo in Berlin, it was not generally successful with the German public, which preferred to see entertainment movies; and it was not used very widely specifically as propaganda. It is true that people came to see it and that in the larger cities it had some success. But there were complaints, mostly from Nazi officials, who objected that the film was too artistic. Others complained that they or their organizations were not sufficiently represented. This shows that Riefenstahl was not concerned with pleasing the petty tastes of the political powers, but instead followed artistic principles which did, nevertheless, play into the hands of those powers. Most important, however, is that the film was actually financed by political interests.

The general impression about Germany conveyed by the film is discipline, unity, vitality—all of it spearheaded by Adolf Hitler, the führer. However, can we say that a viewer, upon seeing the film could be inspired to become a Nazi? Is that why *Triumph of the Will* has been called "dangerous," the "work of an Evil Genius," and other names? It seems that the epithets were thought of only after the evil power of the Third Reich became truly apparent, namely, from 1935 on, long after the film had actually been shot. The hypnotizing seance of the film worked only for Germans, though by no means for all of them, not for other nations. When *Triumph of the Will* was shown in England, for instance, it was sometimes screened together with an anti-*Triumph of the Will* film, which made Hitler appear ridiculous and broke the spell of the führer.

The typically German elements are the music and the language, both of which contribute considerably to the power of the film. Yet it is doubtful that *Triumph of the Will* is as seductive and dangerous as has often been maintained. It is only and primarily in retrospect that the modern spectator sees the dangers in the film, for behind the führer and the masses surrounding him, which he controls like an animal tamer, there are always the victims. The smoke of the torches derives, in part, from the gas chambers. For a person with knowledge of the history of the case, behind the columns of neatly marching youths there is the macabre parade of prisoners of Stalingrad. Behind the triumph there is, for the modern viewer, also the defeat. Yet, *Triumph of the Will* is not the holocaust itself. "It is only the window through which one can look into the gullet of the monster. The monster is still resting in a demonic balance, shortly before its fatal leap."[13] Perhaps only God can view *Triumph of the Will* objectively.

Goebbels, who according to Riefenstahl, was very much opposed to her making *Triumph of the Will*, praised the film and awarded it the National Film Prize during the Festival of the Nation, held on May 1, 1935. The question arises at this point, why Leni Riefenstahl, who to all appearances protested vigorously to the assignment of shooting *Triumph of the Will*, was so upset about the fact that Goebbels objected to her directing it? Should she not have been pleased? Riefenstahl also received the "Diplôme de Grand Prix" in France on July 4, 1937, at the Exposition Internationale des Art et des Techniques in Paris. Her appearance to receive the award was protested by French workers.

## Analysis

It has become customary to divide the film into twelve sequences in order to make possible the analysis of the two hour and twenty minute work.[14] It has been observed by several other commentators that this film is above all an achievement of editing rather than photography. The editing is responsible for its liveliness and the absence of the monotony usually accompanying political conventions. Editing, however, implies selection, and selection inevitably means emphasis and distortion. As a result of Riefenstahl's editing, three themes emerge. These are the deification of Hitler, the solidarity between the German people and the Nazi party brought about by Hitler and his leadership, and, finally, the promise and hope for a future glorious Germany. All this is not to say that Hitler was perceived as God by everybody, that the solidarity between the Nazis and the German people existed, and that the Germans all had new hope for the future. Rather, Riefenstahl implied this in the film, and the spectator can hardly escape the impression conveyed by her editing.

The most interesting aspect is perhaps the deification of Hitler. He is neither Chaplin's "great dictator" nor a spitting demon. He is neither ridiculous nor horrifying. One cannot even say that this man is completely unpleasant. There is something about his personality, a kind of glamour, which resembles a degree of harmlessness and good-naturedness. Today we know more about his inner thoughts and actual deeds than he revealed then. But during this time, many people—by no means all Germans—seem to have followed him like the Pied Piper himself. He speaks like a true demagogue. He is also a pedagogue and teaches with his raised index finger. Sometimes he behaves like a film star, smiling and happy. Occasionally he is shown as a saint, his arms clasped in front of his chest. He succeeds in evoking every kind of reaction he wants to. He has built into his behavior a large number of conditioned reflexes. He steers with impulses from his podium, arouses applause, accepts it, calms it down again with his hand, quiets down the storm. There are moments in his speech, especially the final speech, when the speaker is forced to stop. For one second we detect a glint in his eye; it brightens up and remains that way for almost a second and a half. Hitler is smiling to himself. It is a self-satisfied smile, but not very simple. It hides not only the joys of power but also the feeling that his dream has finally become reality, that he is the chosen one, that everyone is following him. The crowded hall, the storms of applause, the ecstasy of the masses—all appear to justify him. Yet his speeches also refer to limitations, to a sect, a group of carefully chosen members, who, together with the führer, are glad about their election and hover over all those others who have not yet received their spiritual baptism. All this is visible in Riefenstahl's film. The director gives artistic expression to a heroic, undemocratic conception of life here. She seems to say that harmony is beautiful, that only the perfect form is beautiful, that only whatever is superhuman is beautiful. While this idea may not be reprehensible in itself, it becomes uncomfortable to the viewer because it is associated with the implication that the beautiful and heroic can be found only in

Germany. From later works of Riefenstahl we know that this is not what she actually means to say. For instance, in her uncompleted film, *The Nuba*, she also shows heroically beautiful people. They are not blonde or white. They are dark and African. This would indicate that Riefenstahl not only believes in but tries to show a concept of beauty which transcends individual nations and races.

In addition to demonstrating party unity and displaying civilian and military strength, the film gives a record of many groups from colorful peasants representing the oldest German traditions in dress and music, to the youngest boys representing the hope of the future. It is interesting to note that there were women in various Nazi activities, but they are rarely seen in the film, and Riefenstahl does not seem to like women, as indicated by the fact that they are rarely seen in this or any other Riefenstahl film. She plays the only prominent women's roles in her films herself.

The film has movement and avoids the tedium of the processions at party conventions. This movement may be interpreted as a "metaphor for progress," giving the general impression of discipline, unity and vitality, all controlled and directed by Hitler, the führer.[15]

## Scene 1

*Triumph of the Will* opens with a dark screen, a moment lasting 63 seconds and creating suspense and drama. The musical overture establishes a heroic mood, and the first images of the eagle and the swastika, symbols of the Nazi party, are seen. A narrative comment begins, underscored with an orchestral version of the official Nazi anthem, the "Horst Wessel Lied" ("Die Fahne hoch"),[16] which becomes the leitmotiv of the film, mixed with the sounds of an airplane engine, and we see a plane in the clouds. At this point we read the words on the screen: "Twenty years after the outbreak of the war, sixteen years after Germany's crucifixion, nineteen months after the commencement of the German renaissance, Adolf Hitler flew to Nuremberg again to review the columns of his faithful adherents."[17] The plane, evidently Hitler's, again is visible against the clouds, and shots of it in the air over the city are intercut with aerial shots of the procession of the marchers into the city.[18]

In a few minutes, the impression of solitary power, of isolated strength, of the uncanny mystery of the führer of the Nazi party is shown as a result of this sequence. The emotional impact of

*Triumph of the Will* is based on three items, which are not necessarily felt in the same way by non-German viewers. These are the collective, emotional excitement of the crowd, the elite secret party of their leaders, and the use of nonverbal as well as verbal technique including music, pageantry, lighting, and color.

Among the visual symbols, Hitler is most prominent. Although he was not beautiful or even imposing, he was a superb demagogue who knew that repetition, acting, and shouting were more influential in swaying the crowds than common sense. It matters little that *Triumph of the Will* has not been synchronized in other languages, because Germans viewing the film frequently fail to make sense of the speeches that are delivered by Hitler and the other politicians on the screen. The powerful impression stems partly from the noise made by the speakers; the speeches, when listened to for the first time, provide a nonrational experience.

Following the opening sequence in which Hitler is cinematically associated with the eagle, the clouds, and the gods, there is a brief montage showing him for the first time, as he steps from his airplane. His car and the accompanying motorcade move quickly through the city streets lined with cheering crowds, and all the excitement is focused on him, thus establishing a link between the cheering Germans and their führer, and gives credence to the sentence which later appears: "Ein Reich, Ein Volk, Ein Führer," ("One Empire, One People, One Leader"). A number of cinematic devices are used to reinforce the messianic presence of the leader, such as the capturing of the sun as it is refracted in the upraised palm of Hitler's hand, or the scene where Hitler's car stops so that he can accept a gift of flowers offered by a little girl who is held up by her mother; or in the scene where a cat seems to stop licking itself when the führer passes. This sequence ends with Hitler appearing on the balcony of the Hotel Deutscher Hof.

The first scene had established Hitler as "a man above men as well as a man among men."[19] It shows that he is a leader whose power is vested both in his personal popularity and in the combined strength of his faithful troops.

Scene 2

This scene begins with shots of banners and flags fluttering from standards on nearby buildings. We see a band concert being played in front of Hitler's hotel, Deutscher Hof. Crowds listening to the band and cheering Hitler have to be pushed back. The flags are frequently transparent, and we see buildings and people through them. It is evening. The events are lit up by torches, and in the dim light we recognize the conductor, the band, and the troops that gently restrain the surging crowds as they listen to the music, while the Nazi officials stand on the hotel balcony and survey the scene.

Scene 3

The scene establishes a mood of peace and tranquillity, showing the first moment of early morning, when there are no people about. The towers of the old town emerge dimly on the screen, and the background music, from the "Meistersinger von Nuremberg," act 3, is the hymn "Awake: The dawn of the day draws near." The camera pans across rooftops, a curtain is drawn back, a window opens, flags and banners flutter gently in the breeze. A camera mounted on a slowly moving boat on the Pegnitz River records further views of the city. Melodies from Wagner's music, mixed with the sounds of the chimes from nearby church towers close the scene.

Now a new sequence begins with a dissolve from the bell tower into an aerial view of the tent city which was built to house the troops and the workers visiting Nuremberg for the rally. The sound changes from the preceding calm. We see thousands of men leave their tents where they slept on straw—as candid shots of the interiors reveal. The men move around the grounds in the early morning light. The camera rests on these attractive, healthy men, who, naked to the waist, begin to wash up for the day, shaving and helping each other, while singing well-known, cheerful German folksongs.

The vitality and activity shown in this scene is underscored by the brightness of the rising sun, in contrast to the quiet dimness of scene 2, attesting to Riefenstahl's ability to create visual variety. The men sing while they work, something very typical among organized groups in German public life until the arrival of the so-called "economic miracle." They prepare breakfast, accompanied by cheers and shouts of friends and companions.

After the meal, the camera shifts to show youthful games, which express a consistently high note of joviality, accompanied by a mix of songs, shouts, and cheers. The editing of this sequence results in a sense of energy and optimism, giving the viewer the impression that life in the camp consists of joy, fun, and friendship under Hitler's rule. Whether intentional or not, the scene further promotes the impression that Germany's youth stands solidly behind Hitler. It should be pointed out that scenes like this were very common in German public life long before Hitler's time and for at least ten years after. Germany had many youth groups, such as the Boy Scouts and sport associations like the Deutscher Turnerbund, which frequently staged conventions and meetings characterized by scenes similar to the one shown here. Thus, while the political import of this particular scene is ominous in retrospect, its like is by no means an uncommon feature in German public life.

The camera in this third sequence then moves to a man playing a concertina leading a group of men, women, and children, dressed in traditional regional costumes from various German provinces, emphasizing once more the idea that Hitler has the support of the entire German people.[20] These happy people mingle with their musicians as they approach the city with their flower garlands and harvest offerings. Hitler then reviews a group of young flagbearers and reinforces the seriousness of the moment by shaking hands with each of them, thus again showing how close he is to the people. Now entering a large open touring car, he heads a motorcade of party officials. The spectators, including us, also participate as part of the crowd looking at the leader.

Scene 4

This scene shows the opening congress of delegates, but the speeches accompanying it halt the rhythm of the film that was established in the previous sequences. Now we hear what could have become real, though static, propaganda. However, the propaganda value disappears because the speeches blend into the film as a whole, making them almost impossible to understand upon first hearing. Once separated from the context and analyzed, the speeches are as empty as most political speeches. They are rambling, vague, overblown, and distinctly nonhumorous. They contain no disturbing ideas, nor do they indicate the evil which was to come as a result of the Nazi party policies hinted at in some of them. They are by far the most tedious part of the film, and we listen to them only because Riefenstahl intercuts them with many interesting shots that underscore, emphasize, or elaborate the speeches.

The first speaker is Rudolf Hess, deputy leader of the Nazi party, wearing the uniform of a storm trooper. Shots of Hess are intercut with shots of the listening crowd, of party insignia, of eagles and swastikas and individual faces, and of a large sign at the end of the the hall which reads "Alles für Deutschland" ("Everything for Germany").

Only an edited version of Hess's speech can be presented here.[21] He begins by declaring the Sixth Party Congress open and follows with a brief commemoration of the late president of the Reich, Field Marshall Hindenburg. He continues by welcoming the representatives of foreign countries and representatives of Germany's military forces. He greets the führer and points out how much he means to Germany, saying in effect that the führer is Germany, and that Germany will attain her aim, that is to say, become the homeland of all Germans in the world, thanks to the leadership of the führer. This sentence is followed by loud applause. He ends his speech with the Nazi greeting, "Sieg Heil," repeating it twice.

Hess's speech is followed by those of other Nazi leaders, beginning with a Bavarian district leader ("Gauleiter"), who merely reads Hitler's proclamation, saying that "no revolution could last forever without leading to total anarchy. Just as the world cannot exist on wars, nations cannot exist on revolutions. There is nothing great on this earth that has ruled the world for millenia and was created in decades. The highest tree has had the longest period of growth. What has withstood centuries will also need centuries to become strong."

Ten more party leaders are heard, each being introduced by a title which "fires" on his name and then dissolves into a close-up shot of the speaker.

The speakers are Alfred Rosenberg, Reich leader of Foreign Policy Office and commissioner for supervision of Ideological Education of the NSDAP, who was also the author of the well-known book expounding Nazi party mythology, i.e., *The Myth of the 20th Century*. He is followed by Otto Dietrich, Reich press chief; Fritz Todt, general inspector for the German Road System;

Fritz Reinhardt, head of the Official NSDAP School of Orators; Walter Darré, Reich minister of agriculture; Julius Streicher, publisher of *The Stormtrooper* ("Der Stürmer") and district leader ("Gauleiter") of Franconia (Franken); Robert Ley, leader of the Reich Labor Front; Hans Frank, Reich minister of justice; Paul Joseph Goebbels, Reich minister of propaganda; Konstantin Hierl, leader of the Reich Labor Service.

The scene, during which all of these politicians give their speeches, is lengthy, and, more than any other, tends to distort reality. To begin with, the speeches are compiled from various meetings and not just from the opening session, as the film implies. Moreover, these are only excerpts and thus unfaithful representations of the real oratory. Finally, the speeches emphasize the future; they emphasize progress and unity but leave out aspects which do not fit into this theme.

Rosenberg announces, "It is our unshakable belief in ourselves, it is our hope for today's special youth, who tempestuously charging forward, will one day be called upon to continue the efforts begun in the stormy years of the 1918 Munich Revolution, an event which gripped all of Germany, and the historical importance of which is already being embodied today by the entire German nation."

Dietrich claims that truth is the foundation on which the power of the press is based. Todt speaks about the autobahn system which had been begun under Hitler's leadership. Reinhardt refers to the reconstruction which is in progress everywhere, and he speaks of the new values that are created, of new activity in Germany. Darré speaks in support of the farmers who are the backbone of Germany's economic welfare. Streicher, the next speaker, utters only one sentence, but it serves to show his function as an anti-Semite, for he insists that a nation that does not value its racial purity will perish. Ley, whose speech follows next, insists that the German worker should be made a proud citizen enjoying equal rights with the rest of the nation. Frank proclaims generalities about the National Socialist state of "order, freedom and law," obviously a travesty in view of the facts we now know.

Goebbels speaks of the flame of "our enthusiasm" which he hopes will never die. He also says that while it would be all right to have a power based upon guns, he nevertheless thought it would be better and more gratifying to win the hearts of a nation and keep them. Hierl, speaking with a south German accent, briefly states that he is awaiting the order of the führer regarding general labor service conscription.

These speeches emphasize one main theme: the beginning of a new, better time for Germany, something which in Nazi lingo has frequently been described as "Aufbruch." It was the expression of hope and joy that Riefenstahl emphasized in her editing of the speeches. That this hope and joy would turn into misery and death for millions of people was not shown in the film. But in the flush of the Nazis' early triumph, a sense of unity, solidarity, and great expectations for things to come is the overriding theme.

## Scene 5

In this scene Riefenstahl presents us with a huge outdoor rally involving members of the Labor Service on the Zeppelinwiese in Nuremberg. Opening with a continued and immensely impressive close-up of the Labor Service flag, the film shows Hitler ascending a raised platform amid huge applause. Since Hitler was rather short (5'8"), he almost always spoke from raised structures so as to increase his height. Hierl, the labor representative, addressed Hitler: "My führer! Heil workers!" The workers answer: "Heil, my führer!" The leaders of the workers then tells them to present their shovels and to stand "at ease." Like a group of soldiers, with shovels instead of guns, they stand at attention first and later at ease, though there is no apparent difference to the common eye. They are arranged in military discipline and a ceremony of loyalty now follows. We see shots of Hitler and Hierl watching the demonstration, intercut with shots of the workers. Candid close-ups reveal that the hands of the workers are tightly folded over their shovels. The leader addresses the workers and they answer in unison. The workers say: "Here we stand; we are ready to carry Germany into a new era. Germany!" The leader then speaks: "Comrade, where are you from?" Worker: "From Friesenland." Leader: "And you?" Worker: "From Pomerania, and from Königsberg. From Silesia, from the seaside, from the Black Forest, from Dresden, from the Danube, from the Rhine, and from the Saar."

In the succeeding passages, the leader and the two workers, alternating words and phrases, say that they represent "one empire, one people, one leader," that they are all working together in the bogs, quarries, in the sandpits, and in the dikes of the North

Sea. They "plant trees . . ., build roads from village to village, from town to town," creating new acreage for the farmer. Fields and forests, acres and bread will be created for Germany. Flags are lowered to the ground in honor of those who died in World War I, and the leader says that "we did not stand in the trenches, nor did we stand under the drumfire of the grenades, and, nevertheless, we are soldiers, with our hammers, axes, shovels, hoes and spades—we are the young troops of the Reich." They end by singing "Wir sind die Männer vom Bauernstand" ("We are the Men of the Farms"). The emphasis on the military nature of an unmilitary group of people is typical of this and other scenes in the film. While a band playing the melody of "I had a Comrade"—a well-known German military song telling the story of how a soldier died in the war, the flags are dipped, one after another, and the workers, recalling previous famous battle scenes, such as Langemark, Tannenberg, Liège, Verdun, and others, conclude the scene with "Comrades, by Red Front and reaction killed. . . . you are not dead, you are alive—in Germany."[22]

This scene emphasizes a motif that has been reiterated throughout the film, a motif that has been used again and again in all contexts, at all times, by most governments, to incite young people to war. It is the idea that an individual death leads to the greater glory of Germany (or whatever nation it may be). Perhaps many men seeing this film would be inspired to kill other men; perhaps a mother, sending her son to war, would do so with considerably more enthusiasm as a result of scenes of this kind, and in this respect the film may, in fact, have been fatal to many people. Now Hitler speaks to the workers, and while he does so, we see him from various angles, from a distance, and in close-ups. There are shots intercut with the listening workers, close-ups of belts, insignia, and flags, with the result that the listener manages to remain attentive to Hitler's speech which he would not have done otherwise. Hitler frequently falls into his Austrian dialect (i.e., he rolls his r's, voices unvoiced s sounds, etc.), and raises his fist on several occasions in order to give his words more emphasis. Pointing out that the men of the Labor Service appear before him for the first time, he reminds them that they represent a great idea, namely, the concept that labor will now be as highly respected as any other form of labor, he says that a worker has to be a member of his community

Photo right: Hitler addressing the S.A. in *Triumph of the Will*
Courtesy of Deutsches Institut für Filmkunde

first before this community, meaning Germany, can join the community of nations. This is a thinly disguised threat that a German had better follow the National Socialist movement, a theme Hitler has been stressing in all of his speeches during the party convention. he ends this speech with a general reminder that the workers are serving Germany which is proud of her "sons marching in your ranks."

At the end of this speech, the workers, singing "We are work soldiers,"[23] march toward the camera as if going to work after having been inspired by their leader.

Scene 6

This scene shows the nighttime rally of the storm troopers, and is accompanied by the sound track featuring the melody of "Volk ans Gewehr" ("People, take your guns!"). The camera records torches, flags, and the storm troopers who are frequently seen in silhouette in the smoky light. They are contrasted with their leader, Lutze, who appears in the spotlight. The shadowy background, almost a chiaroscuro, provides highly dramatic material for the camera. Lutze, speaking to the troopers in his falsetto voice, says "that he marched as a storm trooper in the very beginning of the movement" and points out that he is still "here today," a storm trooper, fighting loyally for the führer. Lutz's remarks are a reminder that he was not killed in the massacre of SA leader Roehm and his followers. "Comrades! Many of you who are here tonight know me from those first years of our movement when I marched with you in your rank and file as an SA man. I am as much of an SA man now as I was then. We SA men have known only one thing: fidelity to, and fighting for the führer." After his speech there is huge applause. Now follows a large display of aerial fireworks, bonfires, pinwheels, and flaming torches, providing a pleasant relief from the tedium of the speeches in the previous scenes. Lutze and his fellow SA men watch the display. Other storm troopers are shown singing, chanting, laughing, and throwing wood onto the fires. The overall mood is that of gaiety and restlessness, but the setting is dim, despite the blazing bonfires and the smoking torches—and this chiaroscuro appears to be a perfect setting for the storm troopers whose tasks in the Reich were usually carried out under the cover of night. The scene preserves a record of the rally and establishes a contrast to the next scene, where the dark, smoky mystique of the SA rally "reinforces the men's blood brotherhood and suggests their mythic origins in fire."[24]

Scene 7

This scene reiterates the idea that there is mass support for the führer. We now see a sunlit youth rally with young boys who are fresh and apparently uninitiated into the Nazi party cult, boys who know nothing of smoke, fire, purges, or girls. For there are no girls anywhere in sight. The boys start out drumming away happily. As in the previous, male-dominated scenes, there is no reference to sex here, no reference to feminine beauty, or to relationships between the sexes. This is clearly a solemn world. It is a pure macho world, unencumbered by the "eternal feminine." The only beauty visible is that of steel, drums, guns, and flags. The only idol worth looking at for the young boys seems to be the führer. It is a world which blissfully ignores women, except when they are spectators. In this respect Riefenstahl showed the reality as the Nazis represented it, namely, as a world where women participated marginally, at most, as passive spectators. It has been argued that Riefenstahl's film does not show reality as it is. Quite aside from the fact that reality is a difficult thing to argue about, most works of art make no pretension to representing a universal concept of reality. Leni Riefenstahl's film shows a number of things that were quite real: the position of women in Nazi Germany and the nationwide adolation of the führer were quite real. Riefenstahl's principle of beauty, moreover, was based upon eliminating all that which did not fit into her intuitive sense of beauty, and the eliminated elements included women, Jews, and misformed persons.[25] She thus imitated in her life the philosophy of the authoritarian state in which she lived and worked. While she did not go so far as to show only blonde Germans (she told the truth in showing brown-haired as well as blonde ones, a true reflection of the racial makeup of the German people),[26] she exhibited no deformed faces or bodies and almost no women and girls as part of the convention. Her world is a male world dominated by steel and willpower. Who would ever deny that this is one reality which reigned in Germany from 1933 to 1945? *Triumph of the Will* shows a certain kind of reality as it existed then, overcast by Riefenstahl's own interpretation of it. She simply internalized the values of a male-dominated world, although she herself was female.[27] From that point of view she was, indeed, an opportunist, as has been charged by many of even her well-meaning critics. She followed the majority, accepted the status quo and offered no resistance.

The scene of the Hitler Youth which follows shows a number of her political prejudices. Here we witness a huge daytime rally of the Hitler Youth groups in the vast Nuremberg Youth Stadium. Its participants are mostly fresh, well-scrubbed boys of the youth forces. Hitler's entry into the stadium is recorded in montage, capturing the excitement and anticipation in the crowd, which bristles with activity as Hitler receives the ovations and welcomes the crowd. Baldur von Shirach, leader of the Hitler Youth, introduces Hitler, saying: "My führer,...we experience the hour that makes us happy and proud...a young people is facing you...that does not know class or caste...you are the example demonstrating the greatest unselfishness in the nation, this young generation wants to be unselfish too...you embody the concept of fidelity for us, we want to be faithful, too."

Hitler then speaks, addressing the crowds with the words, "My German Youth," going on first to remind them of the previous rally, where they were also present, telling them that they were only one segment of German society. He then tells the Youth that it has become the united nation of Germany. He wants them to educate themselves for this united nation of Germany. They have to practice obedience as well as heroism. They must be peace-loving as well as courageous. They have to harden themselves while they are young. There will be deprivations, but they have to accept them. Germany will live on in them, and they will hold up the banner when he and others shall "pass away." He believes that their minds are filled with the same spirit that dominates "us." During this speech there is constant applause and raising of arms among his audience. Hitler himself puts his hands on his heart in acknowledgment of the recognition awarded him. While he speaks here, or on other occasions, he always wears a military uniform. He ends his speech with the dramatic sentence that "we know that Germany is before us, within us, and behind us."

Throughout the speech Hitler never smiles, while emphasizing the theme that those who stand in the stadium are only a small segment of the mass who stand outside, all over Germany. The

Youth surrounding him seem to surge in on him, applauding enthusiastically, waving their arms. They appear to be as stern as Hitler himself, something that strikes the viewer as totally unnatural, although it projects the idea that they are hypnotized by the overall solemnity of the occasion and by their leader. The individual faces shown by the camera are rapt in attention, almost as if beyond themselves, imbued with a higher idea. Applauding Hitler, they finally give him an enthusiastic good-bye.

## Scene 8

This sequence is very brief. Its content was to become the theme of Riefenstahl's short *Tag der Freiheit* (*Day of Freedom*), a separate film spun off from *Triumph of the Will*, which I will discuss elsewhere. The episode shows Hitler, Goering, and other military officials grouped on a platform, reviewing the infantry and cavalry.

## Scene 9

Here the cameras are fixed on a vast outdoor rally held early in the evening. The assembly is attended by 180,000 party members and 250,000 spectators, and it singles out only Hitler as an individual. The men—and again hardly any women are shown in this sequence—are frequently obscured by the flags they carry and by the 21,000 party standards representing more than 700,000 party functionaries gathered from all over Germany. By means of a specially constructed stage and the podium, Hitler is placed apart from his immediate entourage and, more important, high above the crowd, looking down upon all Germany at his feet. His one arm is constantly stretched out by way of the well-known Nazi greeting. The camera occasionally rests upon an ivy-draped swastika. People in this sequence have become decorative items, arranged in architectural patterns, which are stunningly beautiful as forms in themselves, reminding the viewer of ballet choreographies, where the individuals are also lost in large patterns. Scenes of this kind have previously appeared in German films, notably in Fritz Lang's *Die Nibelungen* and *Metropolis*. They attest to Riefenstahl's own training as a ballet dancer and her creative abilities as a choreographer. However, scenes of this kind also constitute a very German predilection, having been used in numerous German rallies, including rallies which were not preeminently political, such as the large, organized Turnfeste (gymnastics festival), Boy Scout gatherings, and similar events. Thus, arranging people into larger patterns has always been a favorite German pastime, and Riefenstahl continues a tradition which was at least one hundred years old.

We may assume that many participants in the huge rally were not pained by the fact that here they figured merely as cogs in a big wheel and were reduced to patterns. The serious and rapt expression on the faces of the participants captured by the camera would seem to indicate that for them it was exciting to give themselves up to a total idea, symbolized in the architectural and choreographical design.

The contrast between this beautifully arranged mass of people on the one hand, and Hitler's godlike presence on the other, is a theme in this scene. The controlling images are the recurrent shots of a huge eagle designed by Albert Speer, the swastika, and the forest of flags. Now Hitler, standing out from this huge rally, speaks again. From his high platform, with hands folded in front of him, he refers to the preceding party congress of 1933, the first after the Nazi party gained control of Germany in January 1933. He points out that this rally is much larger, having 200,000 men assembled who were "summoned by nothing but the command of their hearts, nothing but the command of their loyalty." Insisting in the next section of the speech that "our people's great misery . . . moved us, united us in battle," he goes on to deny that such a "huge thing" as this rally was possible only at the command of the state. He begins to shout: "It is not the state that commands us, but we that command the state." At this point a glamorous chiaroscuro shot of the rally plus the architectural eagle in the back, illuminated by lights from below, the so-called "cathedral of light," projects a glorified version of the state that supports Hitler's words. The führer now shouts: "It is not the state that has created us, but we are creating the state." He goes on to praise the movement to which everyone is allegedly devoting his strength, indirectly admonishing everyone present to remain loyal to it, maintaining that "the Lord" has created Germany, thus implying that he has been called on by the same Lord to lead this nation.[28] The musical score here contains a well-known theme from Wagner's *Tristan and Isolde*.

Hitler ends this dramatic speech by reminding his listeners that they should "think only of Germany, the Nation, the Reich, and our German people," ending with a three-fold "Sieg-Heil!" The speech is followed by a sequence showing soldiers carrying torches and marching in.

The camera, moving from its position on tracks below and to the side of the podium, records Hitler's speech in a series of shots looking up at him, shots from behind, and close-ups, as well as medium and long shots. These shots are intercut with shots of faces of the flagbearers and the listening audience. The crowd appears to be lost in the vastness of the architectural setting and the haze produced by the smoking torches. The 200,000 men marching in the stadium come to our consciousness only as a mass, not as individuals.

In this memorable scene Hitler, the man, is advanced to an even higher level than in the previous scenes, so that it appears that he has become lord of the creation at his feet, receiving the adolation of his people, to whom he has descended. The camera coverage of Hitler is intimate, recording rare and barely noticeable smiles, his nervous excited manner of speech, yet always careful to avoid showing the real man behind the official image. Stern, implacable, somewhat forbidding, Hitler remains the führer, creating his own image, shaping his own portrait before the camera. While Riefenstahl's cameramen recorded a variety of Hitler's moods, from grave seriousness to occasional moments of what might even be called charm, he nevertheless is presented as a state portrait. His physical shortness and unprepossessing looks are never dwelled upon but disguised and glossed over with the help of several special structural devices established at the rallies. Shots of Hitler never reveal his unprepossessing features. Thus we rarely see his full figure, since in most shots he is shown from the waist up, sitting or standing on cars, surrounded by people, partly covered by the structures of the podium or the microphone. Moreover, most shots of him are taken from below, always making him the center of attention and admiration, and enlarging the importance of his leadership. In reality, Hitler had few duties at the party rally. He usually arrived by plane, observed the events, and spoke to his supporters. Yet Riefenstahl presents him as if descending from unknown heights, delivering holy words, and inspiring his people with his will, something reflected in the title of the film.

Scene 10

Introduced by solemn Wagner-like music, this scene begins with the impressive outdoor memorial service and military review in the vast Luitpold arena. This is probably the scene which viewers of the film remember most vividly, because it is, in fact, a masterpiece in cinematic and structural contrasts.[29] The disciplined organization of the vast masses into squares, rows, and other rectangular configurations is highly dramatic, and it is made even more so, because it is contrasted with three lonely figures— Hitler, Himmler, and Lutze—walking on a wide aisle to the war memorial where they are supposedly laying a wreath. Until now the film had been done within a relatively limited camera frame, something like a portrait. The entire hierarchy of Nazi leadership is now made structurally visible. The leader is raised above his men, the men are raised above the boys, and all of them have been raised above the peasant, workers, and especially the women, all spectators of Nazi glory. Yet this scene at the cenotaph is a massive demonstration of the living, disciplined strength of the Nazi party. The impression of discipline derives from the rectangular shapes into which the troops and participants are arranged, who, when they actually move, are allowed to form circles. Almost one million men are marching or standing as if they were a single force. With this background of discipline and order as the backdrop, the three men are seen walking down the wide road, away from the camera, and toward the cenotaph. They salute the monument with outstretched arms, in Nazi fashion, while the camera also focuses on the fire that is burning in several small bowls surrounding the cenotaph and which gives the scene an air of intense solemnity. The presence of Himmler and Lutze, leaders of the SS and the SA, means that party unity, especially in view of the recent massacres within the ranks of the SA, is to be stressed now.[30]

The restraint of the photography and editing match the simplicity and solemnity of the ceremony.[31] The action of the first part of the scene is static, and Riefenstahl had to call on all of her creative abilities to use the camera dramatically, in order to bring interest into the scene. The war memorial is a simple, heavy structure. After the wreath-laying ceremony, Hitler reviews the panorama of his troops as they march toward the podium, go up the steps on both sides, as well as around and behind it. A total of

97,000 men from the SA and 11,000 members from the SS were involved in this parade, and their mass movement is recorded by the camera from many angles. Thousands of men carry their flags, standards, and insignia in solemn motion, photographed through a telephoto lens. Hitler, stern and erect, with arms clasped across his chest, reviews the long and impressive lines of soldiers, storm troopers, and bands. The variety of the photography indicates the extensive planning involved in the placement and operation of the cameras. Numerous low-level shots of goose-stepping storm troopers have a chilling effectiveness. Lutze introduces Hitler, beginning with "Mein Führer," and going on to refer to his own loyalty in the past, promises that he will maintain it in the future and follow the orders of "our führer."

Hitler now addresses the men of the SA and SS, speaking of the black shadow that a few months ago had spread over the movement. He is referring to the division within the party and the subsequent murder of Roehm and his supporters. He maintains that "neither the SA, nor any other institution of the party, has anything to do with this shadow," and goes on to claim that there is not even one crack in the structure of the united movement. This remark is followed by huge applause. Continuing, he disclaims any responsibility for the party purges and says: "If anyone sins against the spirit of my SA, this will not break the SA but only those who dare sin against it." Calling lunatics and liars all those who would think that he will ever dissolve what he has built up, Hitler then pledges himself firmly to Germany. He introduces the flag ceremony with the words, "I now give you the new flags," which he intends to "give to the most faithful German hands." Referring to his SA and SS men as having proved their loyalty to him a thousandfold and expecting the same in the future, Hitler ends, as usual, with a threefold "Sieg-Heil!"

The speech is punctuated with bouts of applause in several places, especially whenever the führer referred to the purported loyalty of the SS and SA. During the following consecration of the battle flags Hitler moves along the line of flagbearing troops, clutching his personal banner ("his blood flag"). The confrontation between him and each man is personal and direct. He looks each man directly in the eye, thus seeming to single him out as if he were the only one in the huge stadium. Riefenstahl intercuts the spiritual nature of the flag consecration with shots of cannons being fired in tribute. Wagnerian music, apparently from *Tannhäuser*, accompanies the scene. The flags and standards represent the various regional sections of the SA from all over Germany.

The prominent motif in this sequence is the juxtaposition of the dead with the living, the past with the present, the men with their leader and the spiritual with the material concerns of life, all themes which Riefenstahl combines with consummate artistry.

Scene 11

In this scene the camera is always moving, beginning with the long parade, which shows the variety, strength, and support of German military and labor groups, as well as other service forces from all regions of the country. Superb photography, with a variety of shots, records the troop parade and includes views from the air, from windows and openings in buildings, from bridges, and from moving vehicles. Lively march music emphasizes the spirit of the scene. The film footage is characterized by a rhythmical montage which saves this essentially military review from being tedious. The editing provides for an angle of vision that moves from one vantage point to another, accomplishing what every participant in a parade would like: to be everywhere at once. Occasional close-ups of party leaders, of sidewalk crowds and women are also intercut with Hitler's review of the troops. This provides another feature of Riefenstahl's contrast—a typical one— showing men who do things (i.e., march) and women who just watch. While Riefenstahl builds her montage to give the scene an almost indescribable sense of anticipation and excitement, the rhythm of the parade is not unlike that of other parades.

From the point of view of the history of cinematic technique, *Triumph of the Will* demonstrates the power of the rhythmic montage, providing multilevel impressions of each scene. It is in this manner that the viewer's attention is filled with a sense of excitement which he probably would not have felt to the same degree had he been merely a participant. Riefenstahl thus empathizes with the viewer to a great degree, and her own sense of impatience and boredom infused her with ideas to invent methods which relieve the dull project. This sense of wanting to relieve the tedium is possibly the main quality distinguishing her work. Many viewers of *Triumph of the Will* today may feel a sense of gratitude to Riefenstahl for having taken the side of the spectator. Had she failed to do so, the spectator would have been bored with the endless parades. On the other hand, making a dangerous subject interesting may account in part for her ostracism by the film industry. Following her own instincts, she simply made things interesting, thus in a sense imposing her own will on that of Hitler. This indicates considerable ambition on her part, a desire for recognition of her artistic abilities. This was an ambition, we may add, which was thwarted, because in our time politics and sheer ability cannot be separated. In *Triumph of the Will*, Leni Riefenstahl, undaunted, tries to impose her view on the reality presented, forcing the viewer to see and feel exactly what the director wishes.[32] No single sequence in the film exemplifies this better than scene 11, the longest one, which could easily have become the most tedious. But because the camera is everywhere—from the gutters to the rooftops, giving the viewer an exceptional experience—this sequence becomes exciting. With a continuum of brief shots, with basic motifs and progressive rhythms, Riefenstahl takes the viewer to these various events, but she also makes him a participant in these events. The parade sequence confirms the idea that Germany is a massed, marching column of men. Riefenstahl manipulates and redeems that prosaic space and subject with the omniscience of multiple camera positions and the dynamics of her editing. In fact, just to the left of the reviewing area is a multiple camera position, and the viewer with a quick eye will see Riefenstahl in a black sweater and a long white skirt, standing in front of it while directing the work of her cameramen. In sequence after sequence, the troops march past the führer, while anticipation is built up. Rank after rank, regiment after regiment, band after band—an almost endless parade of military strength develops before our eyes. With arms crossed on his chest, Hitler watches the troops of soldiers, laborers, and motorized forces. He salutes the leaders, and from time to time the people sitting in bleachers behind him rise to their feet in order to salute him. The music begins with themes from *Die Meistersinger von Nürnberg* and continues with the sound of trumpet fanfares, cheering crowds, and military march music. We know that the music master, Herbert Windt, added studio-recorded march music to the actual sound in order to sustain and even enhance the vitality of the varied pictures and the dynamic editing which intercuts shots of the parade with shots of the crowds and of a family looking through a window. Riefenstahl intercuts this action with many shots of medieval buildings. At the end of the sequence, the pace of marching and music become slower. In a long shot the camera pans across the rooftops and gives a view of the city. This is the final event, so it appears, for the majority of men who are passing review before their leader—as they are marching out of the city of Nuremberg.

Hitler, the spiritual leader in other scenes, is here shown as the head of the military forces. Yet Hitler remains somewhat apart from many of the people, surrounded only by party officials and close aides. He views the parade, standing alone in an open car at the curb, and he is separated from the crowd behind him by a great empty space.

## Scene 12

In the closing scene of *Triumph of the Will* Riefenstahl shows the final congress of the 1934 party rally. Crowded Luitpold Hall is dominated by the large illuminated eagle on the platform. The platform itself is decorated with flags, banners, swastikas, and the podium is flanked by large flower displays. At the opposite end there is a sign reading "Alles für Deutschland" ("Everything for Germany"). We see Hitler enter the hall with Hess. The camera position is above and behind the main aisle from which he enters. Hitler is smiling, and he and his aides move quickly to their places on the platform. The crowds welcome them, shouting "Heil." The melody of the Badenweiler March, Hitler's favorite march, is played here as it was at all of his official entries and exits. The band then plays another march to accompany the standard-bearers as they enter the hall up the same main aisle which separates the crowds into two sections. Hess introduces Hitler, saying: "The führer addresses the crowds." Hitler then assumes the word. This is the longest and the most important speech in the film, it has been printed here almost in its entirety.[33]

The Sixth Party Congress of the movement is coming to its close. What millions of Germans outside our party ranks may have considered only a most impressive display of political power has meant immeasurably more for the old fighters; it is the great personal and spiritual meeting of old fighters and comrades-in-arms. And perhaps one or the other among you, in spite of the compelling grandeur of this troop review of our party, was wistfully recalling those days when it was still difficult to be a National Socialist.

At the reference to the old fighters and comrades-in-arms, Riefenstahl shows these very comrades, i.e., Goebbels, Todt, Hess, and others, in close-ups, thus demonstrating whom Hitler presumably meant. By this candid shot Riefenstahl betrays that she knew more about party politics than she was willing to admit in her numerous postwar interviews. The speech continues:

Even when our party had only seven men, it already voiced two principles: first, it wanted to be a true ideologically conditioned movement; and second, it wanted, therefore, to be, without compromise, the sole . . . and only power in Germany. As a party, we had to remain a minority because we had mobilized the most valuable elements of fighting and sacrifice in the nation, which, at all times, have amounted not to a majority, but to a minority. And because these men, the best of the German race, in proud self-confidence, have courageously and boldly claimed the leadership of this Reich and nation, the people in ever greater numbers have joined this leadership and subordinated themselves. [Here great applause sets in].

The German people are happy in the knowledge that the constantly changing leadership has now finally been replaced by a stabilizing force, a man who considers himself representative of the best blood, and knowing this, has elevated himself to the leadership of this nation and is determined to keep this leadership, to use it to the best advantage, and never relinquish it.[34] It will always be only a part of the nation which will consist really of active fighters, and more will be asked of them than of the millions of other fellow countrymen. For the fighters, the mere pledge "I believe" is not enough; instead they will swear to the oath "I will fight!"

The party will for all time to come represent the elite of the political leadership of the German people. It will be unchangeable in its doctrine, hard as steel in its organization, supple and adaptable in its tactics; in its entity, however, it will be like a religious order. But the goal must be that all respectable Germans will become National Socialists. Only the best National Socialists are fellow members of the party.

In the past our adversaries, through suppression and persecution, have cleaned the party from time to time of the rubbish that began to appear. Today, we ourselves must do the mustering out and the discarding of what has proved to be bad and, therefore, inwardly alien to us.[34] It is our wish and will that this state and this Reich shall endure in the millenia to come. We can be happy in the knowledge that this future belongs to us completely. While the older generations could still waver, the young generation has pledged itself to us and is ours, body and soul. Only when we in the party, with the cooperation of everybody, represent the supreme embodiment of National Socialist thought and spirit, will the party be an eternal and indestructible pillar of the German people and of our Reich. Then, eventually, the magnificent, glorious army—those old proud warriors of our nation—will be joined by the political leadership of the party—equally tradition-minded—and then these two institutions together will educate and strengthen the German man, and carry on their shoulders the German state, the German Reich. [During this passage of the speech, Hitler becomes very excited, almost screaming the words, and the audience gets up and shouts "Sieg-Heil!"]

At this hour tens of thousands of party members are already leaving the city. And while some of them are still revelling in reminiscences, others are already beginning to prepare the next meeting—and again people will come and go, will be moved anew, be pleased and inspired, because the idea and the movement are a living expression of our nation, and therefore, a symbol of eternity.

Long live the National Socialist movement! Long live Germany!"

Cinematically, the words of this speech are enhanced by shots referring to themes or images emphasizing Hitler's meaning. When he refers to the party as representing something like a "religious order," Riefenstahl's camera focuses on the eagle with the swastika, one of the insignia, the main one, decorating Luitpold Hall. Hitler's histrionic techniques include waving his arms, pounding his fists, visionary stares into the distance, and enraptured ranting. Riefenstahl takes in all this with close-ups. We see Hitler as an excited politician almost carried away with himself. It seems that he worked with notes, to which he adheres in the beginning. However, he seems to forget them as he becomes more and more excited and propelled by his own dramatic momentum. His voice gets louder, he becomes more excited and exciting. His body moves with the rapidity and heat of his thoughts. He pounds with clenched fists on the podium, jabs his arms in the air, and waves his hands for emphasis. For a person understanding the words he speaks, the entire scene can be exciting, and it is understandable that many Germans were in effect carried away by Hitler's demagoguery. However, for an outsider, not immediately familiar with the German language and hence just perceiving the gesticulations and some wild sounds, the scene might appear humorous. It is not surprising that Charlie Chaplin found so

much to make fun of in his *The Great Dictator*, although his
method of ridicule underrated the real dangers of Hitler's powers.

It has been pointed out by critics that this speech allows Hitler to
appear more ridiculous and hence more human than the previous
speeches. It is difficult to assess whether or not Riefenstahl
intended things that way, but it is decidedly anti-climactic.

The party convention is now officially closed after Hess says that
"The party is Hitler, but Hitler is Germany: just as Germany is
Hitler," finishing up with a three-fold "Sieg-Heil!" Before Hess can
speak these words, he has to wait a few minutes in order to allow
the applause following Hitler's speech to die down. A brief,
fleeting smile of self-satisfaction appears on Hess's face, as he
waits. After this short remark, he turns around, seems to face Hitler
directly, and he raises his arm in the well-known Nazi gesture of
greeting. The melody of the "Horst-Wessel Lied" is heard, and
everyone gets up to sing it.[36] In the final scene it is played first by
a band and then by a pipe organ carrying the melody alone to the
end. And the sequence closes with a long shot of the entire Luitpold
Hall, followed by a medium shot of the swastika which ends in a
dissolve into the final shot. The camera shoots from below and
slightly to the right, and we see a column of men marching toward
us from the left-middle background of the frame, slightly upward
and toward the right foreground, almost diagonally crossing the
frame. They cover only one half of the frame and are silhouetted
against the sky, moving slowly upward, with faces that are not
recognizable. The men begin to walk right into the audience. The
film ends with the very infectious singing of the "Horst-Wessel
Lied," which is actually sung by the marching men (rather than
merely played by a chorus offscreen), and it would be easy to
imagine that the spectators, after leaving the movie house, will
continue humming the melody for some time, thus carrying with
them, if not all the images shown them, at least the songs. The
unifying power of these well-known songs, and in fact, the effect
of the music in the film generally, cannot be overemphasized. It
does a lot to carry the spirit of unity and solidarity into the
audience, perhaps even more than the images themselves, which to
an audience relatively untrained in appreciating mass media and its
language, might not have the force that is usually attributed to them
by critics.

While it has sometimes been maintained that the film was actually not used for propaganda purposes and while it is not known how many Germans saw it, the film ran for at least four weeks in all major German cities. Probably every German who was in his teens or older saw it. The postwar generation is not familiar with it, since the film is almost never shown to the general public now.

There is little doubt, however, that no director or producer could have made a film such as *Triumph of the Will* without having an avid interest in the subject: Hitler and the Nazi party.[37] Moreover, *Triumph of the Will* could not have been turned into the outstanding film that it is, if the director had not also been an artist. Riefenstahl's skill as a filmmaker is as evident in the production as in her homage to Hitler.[38] As a matter of fact, the well-known German actress, Hildegard Knef, recalls having heard Riefenstahl say that she had a vision when she first listened to Hitler speak. "I saw the surface of the earth as a semiglobe," Riefenstahl reportedly said. "It opened up, and a huge fountain gushed forth into the sky and fell right back to earth. It was as if the entire surface of the earth was being whipped by a storm."[39]

Although this particular vision did not find expression in *Triumph of the Will,* Riefenstahl's talent enabled her to transform the tedious spectacle of Nuremberg into an exciting event. She treated the rally at Nuremberg as a pageant of new leaders who intended to improve the world through their own daring, discipline, and ability, with Hitler established as the official savior. Riefenstahl never denied her fascination with Hitler, which she admitted even as late as 1977 and which left its impact on the film. To many filmmakers who left Germany while she herself remained behind, she answered: "A commission was proposed to me. Good. I accepted. Good. I agreed, like so many others, to make a film. . . . It is history. A pure historical film. . . . It reflects the truth as it was then."[40]

In retrospect, we realize that Leni Riefenstahl meant to show the truth as she saw it. That her "truth" happened to coincide with that of Hitler is ultimately the reason for the ostracism and criticism she has experienced throughout her life. It is not possible to forget to what catastrophic consequences this truth led. In view of our pres-

ent knowledge of it, Riefenstahl must be considered guilty by association, although she herself did not raise a finger to kill a single
person in connection with the Nazi crimes.

## Reception

Riefenstahl paid heavily for making *Triumph of the Will*. She
was ostracized by the film world and denied the opportunity to
continue her career. She was held in prison for three years or longer
and subjected to interrogations by the allied powers. She was
accused of participating in Nazi crimes by a British newspaper, a
charge of which she was cleared by the courts. In the opinion of
one commentator "it was the common citizens of the world who
passed sentence on her."[41]

In Berlin, where *Triumph of the Will* was first screened, it was
well received and acclaimed for its artistry. Goebbels awarded her
the National Film Prize on May 1, 1935, with these words:

This film represents an exceptional achievement in the film production of
the past year. It is closely relevant to us because it reflects the present: it
describes in unprecedented scenes the gripping events of our political
existence. It is a filmed grand vision of our Führer, who is shown here for
the first time on the screen in the most impressive manner. The film has
successfully overcome the danger of becoming a mere propaganda
feature. It has lifted up the harsh rhythm of our great epoch to eminent
heights of artistic achievement. It is a monumental film, thundering with
the tempo of marching columns, based on iron principles redhot with
creative passion.[42]

However, audiences across Germany appreciated the film less
than one would have expected.

In general, moreover, film critics have held negative opinions.
These opinions indicate, however, that it might have been possible
to admire Riefenstahl's artistic talent alone, if she had not made this
a film in collaboration with the Nazi party. However, *Triumph of
the Will* cuts across too many controversies, offends too many
sensibilities to be regarded dispassionately and viewed solely as a
work of art. It shows the inextricable combination of form and
content in art. Lotte Eisner recognizes this most clearly. Leaving
aside all party politics and history in her discussions, she points to
the problematics of the film in purely aesthetic terms when she

writes that "the human body becomes an ornament like the warriors in Lang's *Siegfried*. Riefenstahl's frequent use of the close-ups confers gigantic proportions on the meanest objects: the policeman's hands linking [*sic*] against their cartridge belts take on the appearance of some giant-stopping palisade. Here man becomes statue." Eisner calls attention to the faces in close-ups which seem like granite, with their vast strongly modeled surfaces and inhumanly sculptured chins. "They evince the same impression of emptiness and boredom as the colossal hulking statues erected by Arnold Brecker, the Third Reich's most conspicuous sculptor...ponderous pomposity is inevitable and official art will always commission it in mistake for the heroic."[43]

Susan Sontag also discusses the questionable nature of the film by analyzing its "fascist aesthetics," in her provocative article "Fascinating Fascism." She demonstrates in connection with *Triumph of the Will* what she means by "fascist aesthetics," maintaining that Fascist art is preoccupied with "situations of control, submissive behavior and extravagant effort." In her opinion, it exalts two seemingly opposite states, egomania and servitude. The relation of domination and enslavement takes the form of a characteristic pageantry: the massing of groups of people, the turning of people into things, the multiplication of things and groupings of people/things around an all-powerful hypnotic leader figure or force. Fascist art centers on the orgiastic transactions between mighty forces and their puppets and "glorifies surrender."[44]

Other critics have been less concerned with aesthetics than with politics, thus failing to appreciate the film as a work of art. Kracauer assumes that the party rally was staged for the film, which is inaccurate. His central argument deals with the way that the conflict between reality and art may illuminate one's understanding of the film: "Though a very impressive composition of mere newsreel shots, this film represents the complete transformation of reality, its complete absorption into the artificial structure of the Party convention."[45] Richard Griffith writes that Riefenstahl, with camera and shears, created an "evil psychic world which cannot be destroyed by the ideological artillery of America."[46] David Hull maintains that "objectively Leni Riefenstahl's films helped the Nazi cause. This does not mean that she was a personal monster, nor that every 'moral' aspect of her film is deplorable. For her achievements on this level, she has been widely and justly condemned—if not always for the reasons stated by her critics—and it seems unlikely that history will reverse the verdict. But it is also necessary to assess her as an artist accountable only to another kind of history, and it seems possible that on this level, film history will preserve the honors which have been given to her."[47]

In another example of critical opinion the film was described as "an example of what genius in this medium can accomplish without the restraint of conscience and humanity," as a "Machiavellian masterpiece," and "a diabolic combination of reality and stylization, Wagnerian mysticism and present-day immediacy."[48]

Germans either avoid writing about Riefenstahl altogether or tend to be extremely critical of all her work and especially her involvement with the Third Reich. Left-wing German critics would probably agree with Ulrich Gregor, a well-know film historian, who described *Triumph of the Will* as outspokenly Fascist.[49] A lone voice in the desert of adverse criticism is that of Richard Barsam who, very cautiously, writes that "the paradox of *Triumph des Willens* is that it can repel us and attract us at the same time."[50] Riefenstahl herself claims that there is a Mafià-like international conspiracy working against her.[51]

The controversy over Riefenstahl shows that *Triumph of the Will* (and it is essentially over this film that the controversy rages) poses a profound problem to all those who love art and abhor fascism. This work has frequently been praised as one of the greatest propaganda films in history. Another propaganda film is Eisenstein's *Battleship Potemkin* (1925) which has never been accused of glorifying repressive totalitarianism. While there are many differences, as well as similarities, between these two films, perhaps the most important difference is that *Triumph of the Will*, in essence, appeals to and arouses fear in the viewer. *Battleship Potemkin*, on the other hand, appeals to the viewer's sense of brotherhood and solidarity. In *Battleship Potemkin*, Eisenstein, like Riefenstahl, shows crowds of people, gives close-ups of human faces, shows us the great variety of expression and types of the Russian faces, yet he never allows us to see a beautiful or not-so-beautiful face of any of the hated pro-czarist leaders. Eisenstein's sympathies are clearly with the small, the humble, the different, the ordinary Russian citizens. He shows them as brave, passionate, united in brotherhood, suffering, and good-natured. He never shows them as puppets of the powers that be; on the contrary, they are presented as resisters. The propaganda value in this is that Eisenstein's resisters appear to be the majority; in reality, resisters are always in the minority. However, something in the human heart (at least that of viewers of extraordinary films) feels strongly compelled towards empathy for the underdog. The underdog is king in Eisenstein's *Battleship Potemkin*. In Riefenstahl's *Triumph of the Will* the swastika is king, that is to say, an abstract, though beautiful form. It goes beyond the scope of this work to show how Eisenstein technically supports his inclinations, his emotions and predilections. A few examples may suffice. Eisenstein shows maggots, wounded babies, sleeping sailors, weeping women. He builds up a montage in which these basic elements are juxtaposed with critical images of the Russian czarist regime (i.e., the crumbling gates of the building in which the reactionary forces are located, guns, cannon balls). As Eisenstein himself said, a work of art was for him primarily a "structure of pathos." Riefenstahl's *Triumph of the Will* essentially demonstrates the structure of power, however beautiful this structure may be. The largely negative reaction to Riefenstahl's film is based upon the fact that perhaps without wanting to, she appeals to the spectator's fear.

### Tag der Freiheit (1935)

When Hitler saw *Triumph of the Will* at the Ufa-Palast-am Zoo in Berlin, he was delighted. But not all of his associates shared his enthusiasm. Especially members of the army were disappointed, because they felt they were underrepresented in the film. General Blomberg was furious when he saw that his forces were seen for less than a minute and a half. He went to Hitler and demanded that additional footage be shot and included in the completed version of *Triumph of the Will*. He wanted the German Army publicized equally with the Nazi party and the SS and SA. This presented a delicate problem for Hitler, since he needed the full support of the German Army at this time, yet he had promised Leni Riefenstahl that he would not interfere with her film. Hence he suggested to Riefenstahl that Blomberg and other officers of high rank should get together and be filmed as background for the title of the film. Riefenstahl refused, explaining: "I told him no. I can't do it. And for the first time he looked shocked. He told me that if I acted like an ass I would have enemies."[52]

Riefenstahl changed her mind, however, apparently out of fear for Hitler who had looked at her and said that she had forgotten to whom she was speaking. "That was the first time I was really scared of him."[53] Thus Riefenstahl decided to shoot a separate film. Using a montage technique both pictorially and aurally, she shot it with cameramen in a single day, thus making Blomberg very happy. The film lasts approximately fifteen minutes and is available at the Museum of Modern Art in New York.

The film begins with a dark screen, while on the sound track we hear a bugle call. Flags now appear and are filmed as shadows against the sky. The title *Tag der Freiheit (Day of Freedom)* is flashed onto the screen. Soldiers, silhouetted against a white background, with shouldered guns and wearing helmets, are shown. They move the guns to the floor and back to their left shoulders. The title "Nürnberg 1934" now appears on the screen. A command is given and the soldiers march forward while the camera photographs them from behind. "Direction: Leni Riefenstahl" is the next title flashed on the screen. Then: "Music: Peter Krieder. Team: Hans Ertle, Walter Frentz, Albert Kling, Guzzi Lantschner, Kurt Neubert, Willy Zielke." A high shot now follows, showing the soldiers marching toward the viewer.

Flags are shown as shadows against the sky, and the camera focuses on a pair of polished boots outside a tent. From here the camera pans over a city of tents, in front of which we see a guard walking back and forth. It is a quiet morning but human activity begins immediately. One man fills a small vessel with water, another strokes a horse; we see people waking up, coming out of their straw-filled tents. The camera focuses on a group of men who are naked to the waist. They are doing their morning toilette, washing, brushing teeth. The mood is one of joviality and freshness. The men sing well-known German folksongs, including "Dornröschen war ein schönes Kind" and others. We get a glimpse of the various units of the army, including the navy and other sections. The camera now takes a shot of the kitchen, where we see the men eating out of their simple brass dishes. After another tracking shot of the tent city, the camera focuses on a group of horses, lined up in a single file and restlessly moving their legs. A shot showing us the horses' legs indicates that they are of high quality, with narrow calves. A group of horsemen emerges from a foggy background. The camera moves to a column of soldiers, lined up exactly like the horses, suggesting the same discipline, quality, and readiness for action implied by the shot of the horses.

Throughout the film the sky is overcast and gray. Riefenstahl tells us that the weather was very bad during that one day when she shot the film. While this film presents an army review, usually a rather tedious affair, Riefenstahl again manages to break the boredom with her editing and montage. The band now plays a happy tune, and we see soldiers marching across the frame from the background at the right to the front on the left. A shot follows, focusing on a column of horses crossing a wooden bridge, riders on their backs. The horses break into a gallop, and then are seen entering a lake. This scene dissolves into a shot of a close-up of a bugle, which allows the spectator to look directly into its opening, while it is sounded. In the background there now appears Speer's architectural eagle, which was featured many times in *Triumph of the Will*, surrounded by flags with the swastika, all enveloped in thick fog.

The camera now pans over a crowd watching the army exercise. The infantry is viewed first, and we see the men marching in columns, then breaking up, running across the field as if in mock battle. Machine guns are fired, men run in groups. The following shot shows us soldiers on motorcycles practicing getting on and off the machine as fast as possible. Occasionally these mock battle scenes are intercut with shots of horsemen and the watching crowd in the background. The camera focuses on the platform occupied by Hitler and other party officials, all of whom are watching the mock battles through binoculars. This shot is followed by a sequence presenting tanks and antitank guns, with close-ups of several mechanical details, indicating the precision with which the vehicles and arms are forged. A cut to Nazi party officials follows, with close-ups of their faces, which are grim, without the trace of a smile. Now a plane appears in the sky, shot as a shadowy bird. The camera then takes a shot from above the plane, displaying the precision welding and other mechanical details that would be of interest to a military expert. This shot constitutes an indirect praise of the superb workmanship that has gone into the making of this warplane. The bugle appears on the screen and is sounded, preceded briefly by another close-up of the eagle and the swastika in its claws. This and the following sequence seems to consist of footage from *Triumph of the Will*.

The camera travels to the military planes and then intercuts to cannons on the ground, as if to show how the planes might be shot down. In the following sequence, artillery men are preparing their antiaircraft guns, opening the barrels, moving the cannons, getting ready for action. Discipline and smooth military operation is the theme of this sequence.

Another close-up of Hitler follows, showing him watching the military proceedings from his platform, surrounded by party officials, including Lutze and Himmler.

In the final sequence of this film the camera follows a group of planes engaged in flying practice and presents rather intricate patterns and configurations of several planes against the sky. The German national anthem ("Deutschland, Deutschland über alles") is heard on the soundtrack and, with a last shot of the eagle and swastika, the film ends.

The title of this brief film comes from a stanza in the "Horst-Wessel-Lied." Like *Triumph of the Will*, it is characterized by a kind of editing which allows the viewer to follow the otherwise tedious proceedings with great interest. Thus, frequently brief but beautiful nature scenes, showing fog rising from the ground, alternate with the more mechanical shots presenting the details of a machine gun or a military plane. It is possible to believe that Blomberg was happy with this film, since it presents the army in all its efficiency and discipline, including its up-to-date weapons.

This film has generated little critical comment, since it was lost for many years. Even today, few film critics know that it is available.

Miss Riefenstahl recalls that one day a representative of the German Propaganda Ministry came to her house and demanded her prints and negatives, which were to be stored near Bolzano. She gave him, among other things, all three negatives of *Tag der Freiheit*, and they were not seen again until one of them turned up many years later at the Museum of Modern Art. For a long time it was assumed that Riefenstahl had actually destroyed the film herself.

# 5

## Beauty is not Names:
## *Olympia*

THE OLYMPIC GAMES held in Berlin in August 1936, afforded the Nazis an opportunity to impress the world with the achievements of the Third Reich. Hitler decided to make the Olympics a great national spectacle that would show off Germany to best advantage. Such promotion was necessary because in 1936 there was already acute international awareness and criticism of the treatment of the Jews in German sports. So the signs "Jews not welcome" were taken down from shops, hotels, beer gardens, and places of public entertainment, and the persecution of the Jews was temporarily halted.

Hitler appointed Dr. Carl Diem, who for twenty years had been the secretary of the German government's commission for sports and recreation, to handle the details of the festivities for the Eleventh Olympic Games. Dr. Diem had plans to make the German games even more lavish than the Tenth Games, which he had attended in Los Angeles. He succeeded brilliantly. As the party convention of 1934 had demonstrated, the Germans were masters at mass pageantry—something which they really loved—and the Olympic Games afforded a new opportunity to show this mastery.

A few months before the Olympic Games, German troops had marched into the demilitarized Rhineland. This action was an open breach of the Treaty of Locarno, and Hitler as well as all of his aides feared that there would be military countermeasures on the part of the Allies. The tension caused by the entire event has been described by Albert Speer who, in his *Inside the Third Reich,* wrote that Hitler waited with great trepidation for the first reactions from the Allies and remembers that "the special train in which we rode to Munich on the evening of that day . . . was charged with the tense atmosphere that emanated from the Führer's section...Hitler sighed with relief: At last! The King of England

137

will not intervene...."[1] The remilitarization of the Rhineland remained uncontested. The Olympic Games were thus used to create a harmonious atmosphere, exhibiting a peace-loving Germany which made the other powers forget that this very same Germany had just broken the Treaty of Locarno.

Hitler expected more than 100,000 visitors in Berlin and asked Dr. Diem to make arrangements so that these crowds would be easily accommodated. A new stadium was built, but at first there were difficulties regarding the plans. Otto March, the architect, had designed a concrete structure with glass partitions similar to the Vienna stadium. Hitler went to inspect the site and came back in a state of anger which prompted him to curtly inform State Secretary Pfund to cancel the Olympic Games. "They could not take place without his presence, he said, since the Chief of State must open them. But he would never set foot inside a modern glass box like that."[2]

Thus Speer was asked to make a sketch overnight, showing how the steel skeleton already built could be clad in natural stone and have more massive cornices added. The glass partitions were eliminated, and Hitler finally was content. As a result of these changes, the cost of the building increased, but money appeared to be no problem.

Hitler was quick to recognize the opportunities the Olympic Games would offer his megalomania. When Albert Speer pointed out to him that the athletic field in Berlin did not have the prescribed Olympic proportions, Hitler said: "No matter. In 1940 the Olympic Games will take place in Tokyo. But thereafter they will take place in Germany for all time to come. And then we will determine the measurements of athletic fields."

A number of technical devices had to be developed for the games. Thus a strong loudspeaker that would not echo was needed. It was devised from the speakers that had been used at the Nuremberg party rally two years earlier. Moreover, new scoring devices had to be developed as well as equipment to provide improved pictures of close finishes in the athletic events. Other new devices installed at Berlin included an electrical torch device to determine winners of the fencing contests and a computer to show the judges' decisions in the diving contests. These were produced by Diem's staff on time for the opening of the games. Artists designed the medals and award certificates. Invitations were issued, and the Olympic Games of 1936 were promoted on a large scale.

Great thought and care was bestowed upon the treatment of the Olympic participants. The Olympic village, located in a forest near a number of ponds and lakes west of Berlin, consisted of 160 houses and meeting halls, built of brick, stone, and concrete. The participants of the various nations were allowed to enjoy their customary comforts. The Japanese had the opportunity to sleep on their mats on the floor if they so desired; the Americans got their American mattresses; and the Swiss had their feather comforters. The North German Lloyd shipping line catered and served food for the approximately four thousand athletes expected.

The specific problems that Dr. Diem encountered during the preparations were outlined in one of the monthly newsletters published by his office. Thus he had to worry about "how many telephones should be furnished for the Reich Sports Field; which should be local and which should be connected to the central exchange; how many lights; where should the microphones and loudspeakers be installed; how high should the flagpoles be; how many steps; with what should the seats be covered; should there be flooring on the galleries; how should the temperature of the water in the swimming pools be regulated. . . ," and other organizational questions.[4]

The Reich minister for People's Enlightenment and Propaganda, Joseph Goebbels, did everything he could to promote the Olympic Games. Filming the games, as he knew, would be additional advertisement, and the film about the games was announced long before it was completed. A filmed Olympia would reach more people than could attend the games themselves. Hitler wanted the festival to be seen by as many people as possible so that through the games he could present spectacular views of the new Germany. It is with this thought in mind that Goebbels granted Riefenstahl permission to organize a film company that would have exclusive rights to film the Olympic (summer) Games in Berlin.

Why Riefenstahl? According to Glen Infield, Luis Trenker was first offered the project of filming the Olympic Games. This offer was allegedly made to him by the president of the Reich Film Association, but Trenker declined in order to edit his movie, *Der*

*Kaiser von Kalifornien* (*The Emperor of California*). Riefenstahl then "hurried" to Hitler, who gave her the production rights to the events with all necessary authority.[5] Riefenstahl then founded a company especially for the purpose of filming *Olympia,* a fact which Goebbels announced on May 17, 1936: "Dr. Goebbels has given total filming rights of the Olympic Games of summer, 1936, to the Olympic Film GmbH under the management of Leni Riefenstahl. The Olympic Film GmbH will work in cooperation with the German newsreels. Pictures of the Olympic Games on normal film from other sources are not permitted."[6] The production rights for special shots of the competition on the regatta course in Grünau were granted to Ottomar Krupski. These shots were to be recorded on 8mm film and later copies by Riefenstahl's team to be included in the final version of the Olympic film.

The agreement between Riefenstahl and the Reich Ministry for People's Enlightenment spelled out the details in seven clauses.[7] The total production cost was estimated to be 1.5 million marks and was scheduled to be disbursed to Riefenstahl in four installments, beginning with the first one of 300,000 marks on November 15, 1935, nine months before the shooting of the film, and ending with a similar sum on January 1, 1937, half a year after the film was supposed to be shot, with two installments in between. Riefenstahl herself was to receive the amount of 250,000 marks as a personal compensation, which would allow her to travel and cover other personal expenses connected with directing the film. This was a handsome sum, and there are no indications that Riefenstahl used the money for any purposes other than making a first-rate film. She was requested to submit vouchers for her expenses to account for the total utilization of the 1.5 million marks, something which she thoroughly disliked. The agreement further stated that Riefenstahl alone would be responsible for the artistic form and the organizational management of the Olympic film. Moreover, the German newsreels, Ufa, Tobis-Melo, and Fox were placed under the authority of Leni Riefenstahl as had been done when *Triumph of the Will* was produced.[8] The conditions appeared to be reasonable, and Riefenstahl accepted them. Despite these fairly decent conditions, it seems that Goebbels opposed her filming of the Olympic Games from behind the scene. This is something which Riefenstahl has complained about again and again, and at least one crew member confirms that this was true.[9] In retrospect, however, this is the most controversial issue surrounding the making of the film. It appears difficult to reconcile the contradiction between the existence of the agreement on the one hand and the largely undisputed fact of Goebbel's attempt to sabotage the making of the film, on the other. One explanation is that Hitler, who really wanted *Olympia* to be made by a first-rate filmmaker, was willing to give Riefenstahl what she wanted. Goebbels, on the other hand, for whatever personal motives he may have had, tried to undermine Hitler's orders whenever he had a chance. This sort of activity is not unusual in politics. Moreover, it confirms Riefenstahl's arguments, voiced repeatedly during and after the war, that in her opinion Hitler was not bad but that he was surrounded by small, mean, and vicious people who were ultimately responsible for the atrocities committed by the Third Reich. This argument is familiar to anyone who lived during the years of the Third Reich or had an opportunity to question those who believed in the führer. We know now that, as President Roosevelt so graphically expressed it, "The fish stinks at the head," i.e., when something is wrong with an organization, the leadership is responsible for it. It is possible that Hitler gave different instructions to Riefenstahl and Goebbels. This was a well-worn administrative ploy, which Riefenstahl either failed to see or simply ignored. According to herself and her supporters, she was an idealist and believed that people were good rather than bad. She primarily remembered the results of an event, but failed to recall the political details. All this might help to explain why she was fascinated by Hitler and believed him to be a decent person.

Concerning the role of the National Socialist government in the making of *Olympia*, Riefenstahl claims that she had gone to Ufa Film Company a year before she wanted to make *Olympia*, asking them to make an agreement with her. But they were not interested. Thereupon she went to Tobis and the director, Friedrich Mainz, agreed immediately. She told him that she would make two films. "He knows that the government is against [*sic*].... Yet he guarantees 1.5 million Reichsmark. After he makes this agreement with me, he got a lot of trouble with Goebbels and the Ministerium."[10] This would mean that both the price established to make the film of the Olympic Games and the director designated to produce it were determined by an agency separate from the National Socialist government. According to Riefenstahl: "On higher orders [she means Goebbels] the German newsreel cameramen who were very important to my film were removed from the control of Leni Riefenstahl." In another context she stated that the best cameramen available in Germany were not allowed to work for her, because big companies already had a monopoly on them.[11]

Riefenstahl's claims are contradicted in the sixth clause of the agreement between the Reich Ministry for People's Enlightenment and Propaganda where we read that the Reich Ministry for People's Enlightenment and Propaganda undertakes to place the German newsreels Ufa, Tobis-Melo, and Fox under the authority of Riefenstahl. Still, it is possible that the Nazi government made an agreement which it did not really wish to keep. That the government actually commissioned the making of *Olympia*, however, can hardly be denied. The important officials were careful to hide the involvement of the National Socialists in the financing of the film. Thus one of the documents indicates that the Olympic Film Company was established solely for the purpose of making the film *Olympia*: "All the resources required by the company to reproduce the film are also being supplied exclusively by the government. The company had to be established, because the government does not wish to appear publicly as the producer of the film. It is planned to liquidate the company when the production of the film is concluded."[12] From this document we can conclude that Hitler intended to use Leni Riefenstahl as a front for the Nazi party and give the International Olympic Commitee and the world the impression that the famous actress and director was filming the Olympic Games as a private project using private funds and her own film company.

It is possible that Riefenstahl was not aware of being used by the Nazis for political purposes. She was interested in making a film with as much public support as possible because this would give her the best opportunity to make a good film. What would be a "good film" was a matter left entirely to her own intuition, as a clause in the agreement between her and the Reich Ministry for People's Enlightenment made clear. In this clause it is stated that she would have complete artistic control over the project. For an artist the temptation to create under the best possible circumstances is impossible to resist.

The announcement in the German film journal *Illustrierter Film Kurier* advertising *Olympia* contains expressions which are typical of the language of the National Socialists, especially that used by Goebbels. The descriptions are vague; the writer appeals to the "spirit," refers to "strength and beauty," advertises the film in a way which transcends mere factual information. There are references to the human "yearning for ideas" and "a yearning for beauty and perfection" from which "a flame will be born." Other key words are "antiquity," "modern times," and "endurance." The film was obviously seen as an attempt to integrate the 1936 summer Olympics into the time span that had elapsed since the first Olympic Games in ancient Greece. By implication, the 1936 Olympic Games make a claim for becoming immortal like those of ancient Greece.

The film did prove to be a good investment. Within six months of its premiere, *Olympia* earned 4,210,290 marks, more than double the amount that Tobis had advanced, and the money continued to come in. Long after the contracts had been signed to establish the Olympic Film Company and to finance the project, Olympic Film contracted with Tobis to distribute the film itself. Tobis, represented by Friedrich Mainz, agreed to guarantee the sum of one million marks for the distribution rights. Moreover, Tobis Film Company periodically sent one copy of an accounting report to Olympic Film and two copies to the Reich Ministry for People's Enlightenment and Propaganda. This was done, perhaps, as a device to keep the public from knowing that the Nazi government had financed the film company. The records can be viewed at the Bundesarchiv, Koblenz.

The question that continues to haunt commentators and film viewers alike is why Riefenstahl accepted the assignment to make the film, especially since she had told Hitler in 1934, when she was asked to do *Triumph of the Will*, that she would never again make a film for the National Socialist government. She had agreed then to make *Triumph of the Will* under three conditions, i.e., (1) that funds be arranged by her rather than the party; (2) that no one, including Hitler but especially Goebbels, be allowed to see the film until it was finished; and (3) that Hitler never ask her to do a third film.[13] In essence, all three conditions were kept, yet Riefenstahl made *Olympia*. Possibly Riefenstahl's vanity, uncontested even by her, overpowered all other considerations, and she thus created a work which has been hailed as the greatest of its kind by nearly all who saw it. In retrospect, it may be easier to see why Riefenstahl failed to reject this opportunity to increase her fame. She was not one of the truly great filmmakers in 1938 (like Fritz Lang, for example). She wished to enter what Andrew Sarris calls the pantheon of recognized film directors which has always been closed to women. At any time it would have been easier for a man to let a chance pass by than for a woman, precisely because for a woman in a man's world the chance either comes once or not at all. Neither men nor women commentators seem to have forgiven Riefenstahl for taking advantage of her comparatively comfortable relationship with the leading figures of the Third Reich when she made *Olympia*, but all lovers of film art kow that *Olympia* would never have been created if Riefenstahl had said "no."

## Production

Regarding the actual production of the film, Riefenstahl said that it took her a long time before she knew whether or not she was going to make this film. "My first interest in it was sports," she says. She wanted to create a liaison between sports and cinema. Sports had always been her love, and ceremonial cinema she had learned to create in *Triumph of the Will*. Evidence indicates, however, that originally Riefenstahl had planned to make one feature film out of *Olympia*. She decided only under the pressure of practical circumstances to turn the film, once intended to be one normal-length feature film, into two normal-length feature films.[14]

She faced a number of problems that no film director had ever faced before. Film at that time did not have a high range of sensitivity. This meant that the depth of field was severely limited, an important consideration in a film dealing with sporting events. In a film of this kind, the participants, moreover, were moving most of the time, either running, perhaps disappearing under water, leaping high into the air, or throwing a discus or javelin that would be nearly impossible for a camera to follow. Moreover, the Amateur Athletic Federation restricted Riefenstahl's activities to insure that she and her cameramen remained at certain prescribed distances from the field.

She maintains she did not have much money, or at least not enough to really do a good job on a sports film, which in her opinion was not considered good business by film industries. So she claims that 1.5 million marks was less opulent than might have been believed. As a result of this, she and her crew had to be more inventive. She developed several new camera techniques. For the most part, the effects obtained by her crew were improvised coups. People did not know or it was not pointed out to them how many things she and her crew actually discovered. The noiseless camera, for example, was made so because it was not supposed to bother the athletes. It was invented by one of Riefenstahl's cameramen. The camera for underwater shots was invented by another one of her cameramen. During this time she was looking for other tricks, and even the most modest tricks were used. Thus they had the idea of digging trenches (it was very hard to obtain permission for this) from which they might film the jumpers, in order to give a better rendering of this effort.

There were other problems. When studying the requirements for filming the hundred yard dash she decided that she wanted a camera with a variable speed on a catapult that would ride on the rails alongside the track. She also wanted the catapult to have a variable speed so that the camera could always be kept just a few steps ahead of the runner. The noise of the camera and the wheels of the catapult on the rails had to be muffled so that they would not distract the runners. Thus the engineers devised a camera whose whirring could scarcely be heard. This was of some importance, because in 1936 there were no zoom lenses. Without a zoom lens, a close-up, always a Riefenstahl specialty, would be difficult to make under these conditions, because the camera had to be close to the subject, something that was not feasible most of the time. Riefenstahl, however, recognized that there "was no principle at all that demanded that the camera always be far away from the object or even on the object." She gradually discovered that the constraints imposed at times by the Olympic Committee even could serve her as a guide, but it was important to know when and how to respect or violate these constraints.

At the time of a race, for example, we had installed a hundred meter track, and the camera ran along it very well, but it seemed to me that the mileage of the race should be completed with extreme proximity and following the movement at a constant distance. As there was no question of getting close to the runner, it called for the use of the telescopic lens. I withdrew to find a vantage point. It was at this moment that we began to employ the gigantic telescopic lenses that were to serve us from then on. It was the fusion of static shots, rhythmic shots and shots animated by technical movement that were to give the film its life, its rhythm.

Thus, in the face of each problem, it was necessary to feel her way, to make tests, and each test resulted in a new idea. The team also had cranes and ladders, but rapidly eliminated the first because they had an inconvenient way of oscillating. Zchail, one of Riefenstahl's cameramen, who specialized in this type of work, often had a depth of field of no more than thirty centimeters (i.e., twelve inches). Under these conditions the pictures would have been ruined with the slightest oscillation. Steel towers were built in the middle of the stadium to take in the total panorama.[15]

In the riding sequences, for instance, the movements of the horses caused a great deal of vibration. Vibration was a difficult interference for the cameras at that time. In order to reduce the vibration caused by the horses' movements, the camera was placed on a rubber bag filled with feathers. This method made it possible to take shots from high overhead. As a result of it, the cameramen could reproduce the motion of horse and rider in a competition. Another innovation by Riefenstahl was the use of automatic cameras which she placed in baskets. The baskets were attached to balloons and the latter released to drift over the stadium. The balloons were furnished with automatic cameras which led to the necessity of running ads in the paper everyday so that when the balloons came down in Berlin, people would know that they had cameras inside. With this system, out of thousands of meters of exposed film, ten were good. "But they were very good," Riefenstahl says.[16] Thus, they had one balloon-borne camera just above the finish line of the sculls (which was equally assured by a 120 meter traveling shot). Unfortunately, at the last minute, the Olympic Games Committee vetoed the balloons and that was the end of that experiment. Riefenstahl says she cried when she heard that.

In other contexts, for instance, while the marathon was in progress, Riefenstahl and her crew had a little basket in which was a miniature camera that was set off automatically by movement. All this was done so that the runner would not notice anything.

Special camera techniques were also required to film the diving events after the divers had reached the water and had to be photographed underwater. Riefenstahl's cameramen would climb to a high diving board, focus their lens, dive with the Olympic diver into the water, and film him as he and they dipped in. Thus the cameramen would continue shooting as they hit the water and many times they would have to change a lens at the bottom of the pool. This method required a good deal of practice and rehearsal. According to Riefenstahl herself, it was necessary to train her cameramen for six months with special cameras to fulfill assignments of this kind.[17] This method called for first-rate cameramen who would also be willing to submit to the ordeal of training beforehand and to the diving procedure while the film was in progress.

To try to take good shots of the competition swimmers, Riefenstahl had to invent yet another technique. She attached a camera to a frame on the side of a small rubber raft for shots above one hundred meters. The difficulty with this technique was that she did not have permission to propel the boat, in which she or her cameramen might be sitting, by oars, because this would cause waves in the pool and disturb the event. She solved this problem by having the raft pushed along with a pole. "In this way we were able, during a shot, to start with a face, seen from close, and move off from it. There were also underwater shots, sometimes followed by emergence, shots made at water level as well as shots made with the lens half-submerged.[18]

Solving these technical problems was not always easy. "I knew that the film could be interesting only on one condition," she confessed. "I knew that the restraints imposed by the events, while serving as a guide, had to be violated at times. Otherwise I would have just a newsreel film." It had become evident to her that the film could only be interesting if she could capture the form (*Gestaltung*) of the events, by which she means the collective image, not names and statistics, not records and figures. "Remember: Beauty is not names," she told an interviewer.[19] For that reason she began to think about ways of placing the cameras in different spots.

The topic of the film attracted her for a number of reasons in addition to her natural interest in sports. The title of her book, *Schönheit im Olympischen Kampf* (*Beauty in the Olympic Struggle,* 1937), written in connection with making the film, implies two things: the complete domination of the body by the will, and the great atmosphere of tolerance, introduced by the feeling of camaraderie and loyalty, which is at the very heart of the contest. "In a confrontation like the Olympic games, all men and all races must, for themselves and others, give the best that they have." From this results an extraordinary atmosphere that is lifted well above ordinary life and "this is what I sought to render." "I seek harmony. When harmony is produced, I am happy."[20]

In general, Olympic athletes tend to be people whose accomplishments stand above those of ordinary citizens, primarily because Olympic athletes are ambitious, self-disciplined, and dominated by a strong will. Showing men and women with such qualities is perhaps an undemocratic activity. Most people do not participate in the Olympic Games. Hence, the very idea of extraordinary physiques and accomplishments which were frequently attained as a result of very hard work, extreme willpower, and a good deal of extraordinary talent, was held reprehensible by many people, especially because the film was produced in Nazi Germany. Filming Olympic Games in any other country might have been forgivable. However, Riefenstahl showed beautiful bodies, successful male and female athletes of all races, nations, and colors, and she did this in a Germany which was then singularly undemocratic. Thus she exhibited a contradiction between her film and the reality which was the background to this film: she filmed members of many races and nations, implying that they were equal, yet she made the film in a country which had officially denied that all nations and races were equal. Does this mean that she, through her art, wanted to contradict official policy? Most likely she was politically naive. Her film does not celebrate the masses, except in occasional shots of the bleachers with cheering crowds, which serve to relax the tension created by the competitions. Riefenstahl shows individuals who decided to distinguish themselves from the masses and leave behind a new world record associated with their names. It is possible that the Olympic Games held in Germany in 1936 were so successfully filmed because the inherent spirit in them is somewhat undemocratic. According to eyewitnesses, Riefenstahl was absolutely fascinated by the faces and bodies of the male Olympic athletes of other races, and she repeatedly asked her cameramen to shoot the faces of the Japanese participants and especially the face of Jesse Owens. Riefenstahl has always admired physical superiority, a fact which is reflected in *Olympia* as well as in her later work about the Nuba. It is well known that Goebbels

Photo right: Hans Ertl built himself a special camera for underwater shots during the filming of *Olympia*
Courtesy of Gordon Hitchens, New York City

objected to the emphasis Riefenstahl gave to the athletes of races other than Caucasian. According to one collaborator, this is the reason why Riefenstahl deliberately delayed the completion of the editing of the film, hoping thus to avoid having to make changes for propaganda purposes.[21]

Film connoisseurs today generally agree that since 1936 there has not been a film about the Olympic Games which attained the high artistic level of *Olympia*.

During the production of the film and even before the Olympic Games took place in Berlin, there were a number of serious political problems. As a principle, Jews were not to be excluded because there had been protests from the United States. Several groups, including the United States National Council of Methodist Churches, the American Federation of Labor, as well as former Governor Al Smith of New York and most American newspapers had expressed strong objections against United States participation in the 1936 Olympic Games. However, the Amateur Athletic Union voted by a narrow margin to send the American Olympic teams to Berlin after Rudi Ball, ice hockey player, and Helene Mayer, champion fencer, both Jewish, had been assured consideration for places on the German Olympic teams. However, several American Jewish athletes ultimately refused to participate in the games and protests in the United States continued.[22]

It has often been maintained that Riefenstahl's work was the first feature film ever made of the Olympic Games. This is not true: Arnold Fanck filmed the winter sports section of the 1928 Olympic Games in Garmisch-Partenkirchen. His work was not successful. There have been attempts to imitate Riefenstahl's film on a scale as large as that provided under the auspices of the Nazi regime. The most noteworthy of these was the film of the 1968 Olympic Games in Japan. This film was not very successful. About her own film Riefenstahl said that it was very difficult to make it because most sport films are dull, and she did not want hers to be dull. To this day her statement has remained accurate and been contradicted only by her own *Olympia*.

Riefenstahl maintains that from the start she had intended to show that the form must "excite" the content and give it shape.[23] She also said that she had the whole thing in her head and that she treated it like a vision. She felt like an architect building a house. "The law of film is architecture, balance." If the image is weak, so

Photo left: The Olympic torch is lit in "Festival of Peoples," Part I of *Olympia*
Courtesy of Deutsches Institut für Filmkunde

Riefenstahl argues, the director would have to strengthen the sound, and vice versa. Riefenstahl also wanted the total impact on the viewer to be one hundred percent, "never more or you tire them."

This argument indicates that Riefenstahl perceives the film as an art form which should not allow the viewer to think for himself or assume a detached position. Riefenstahl wants the film to be a totalitarian experience. She also claims that for a film like *Olympia* it was important to alternate both sound and picture: "When one is up, then the other must be down . . .," and "you move at times from reality to more and more poetry and more unusual camera work."

There were other definite formalistic principles which Riefenstahl insisted had to be observed in a film like *Olympia*. Thus she argues that the beginning had to be quiet. She told interviewers that it was important to interest nonsports people in sports. She also wanted to separate the different human races and insisted that each race should be identified by its own particular sport. "Each was to do a different thing."[24]

The principles given by Riefenstahl in reference to *Olympia* represent good structural aesthetics, although Riefenstahl maintains she based these principles upon her own intuition. She expressed her aesthetic principles faithfully in *Olympia*. In her view, the secret to *Olympia* is the sound, which took her three months of mixing. "No general crowd noises, but like music," she commented. She planned the sound so that it would be "coming in waves. . . . No synchronized sound, but all made by us in the studio." Even horses breathing and runners panting had to be made audible on film, because "people cry too much," she told an interviewer.[25]

Regarding the quality of her crew members, Riefenstahl maintains that she only had thirty cameramen instead of the one hundred everyone maintained she had. Moreover, of these, only six were first-rate, because they had feature and newsreel background (Hans Ertl, Walter Frentz, Guzzi Lantschner, Kurt Neubert, Hans Scheib, and Willy Zielke). In retrospect, she was proud of having inspired the excellent teamwork among her crew. In view of her success in the *The Blue Light* and *Triumph of the Will*, it would not be an exaggeration to say that Riefenstahl seems to have been unique in inspiring precisely this kind of teamwork. It is not clear now whether the inspiration came as a result of her personality, her beauty, her own devotion to the cause, or all three. "I must say we formed an extraordinary crew. For entertainment, as well as while working, we always stayed together, even on Saturday and Sunday. When we stayed together in the tents, we talked, always letting the ideas come, and they always came. That's good practice. There were also nocturnal conversations."[26] Riefenstahl also claims that she only had one camera for each shot, with the exception of the first day of the games when Hitler gave the opening speech. In that case she needed more than one camera, because a retake would have been impossible if technical difficulties had arisen during the speech; thus, auxiliary cameras were used for that event.

Riefenstahl's crew was composed of six cameramen who formed the principal section. Sixteen other cameramen and assistants took care of the trials at other locations. Only members of her main crew were permitted to enter the stadium. In addition, she employed nonprofessionals whom she asked to carry small cameras and mingle with the crowd in order to get reaction shots.[27] The cameramen were placed so that the skill of each was put to best use. Thus Hans Ertl was in charge of diving and field and track events. Walter Frentz had to photograph the sailing regatta, the marathon, and the balloon cameras which later had to be eliminated. Guzzi Lantschner supervised the shooting of swimming events, riding, gymnastics, and rowing. Willi Zielke was responsible for filming certain sections of the prologue. Although she was the only woman among highly skilled cameramen, her work was respected as that of a professional. One of her assistants tells us that "she would assign you to a position. . . . she would tell you what lens to use, what focal lens, how many frames to run, what filter to use. She knew exactly what she was talking about."[28]

At some distance from the Reich Sport Field (athletic facilities in addition to the Olympic stadium) the Geyer works were located, which upon Riefenstahl's request supplied her with a building for technical and administrative purposes. Here was her center of activity where she worked constantly when she was not in the Olympic stadium or on other filming locations. "If I start a work, I forget food, I forget that I am a woman, I forget my dress. I only see my work," she explained, continuing, "I forget because I am fascinated by my work."[29] The teams with whom she worked confirmed her fanatical devotion to her work. In her attempt to have her cameras show the power of the human spirit over all physical obstacles, she was constantly on the move, searching, experimenting, or encouraging her crew. However, she was not really inclined to forget her appearance. In fact, she was always dressed in fashionable, yet practical, clothes, and her hair always looked as if she had just stepped out of the beauty parlor. While making *Olympia* may have been difficult and frustrating at times, records indicate that it provided her with a well-paying job which involved power, a great variety of experiences, creative activities, and a certain measure of fame.

## Analysis

Part 1 of *Olympia, Festival of Nations* is tense and emphasizes the spirit of competition. Part 2, *Festival of Beauty* is lyrical and stresses the beauty of the human body, individually and collectively. In both parts of the film Riefenstahl makes use of her self-proclaimed artistic principles. Before a new and exciting sporting event, she generally intercuts a tranquil scene. Sometimes such a scene is no more than a dark screen. At other times she shows clouds in the sky, a bell in a steeple, or flags blowing in the wind. Frequently she intercuts the sporting events with scenes from nature, showing trees reflected in the water, a rising or setting sun. The result is that the viewer is appreciably excited by the film but he is never exhausted. He is present at all the exciting competitions, but he does not have to elbow his way through the crowds. While he cannot shake the hand of a gold-medal winner, he can see the past stress and present bliss on his face.

The prologue, consisting of approximately 950 feet of 35mm film, most of which was shot on location, combines features of parts 1 and 2, though it tends to be on the lyrical side. It functions as a kind of spiritual godfather to both parts. Beginning with a double-exposure picture of the crumbling ruins of Greece, indicating the passage of time between the ancient Olympic Games and the 1936 version in Berlin, it is intended to show the link between ancient Greece and modern times. In addition to classical ruins, friezes, pillars—all photographed against a beautiful, clear sky—it shows dissolves and fade-ins of Greek stone sculptures featuring Apollo, Alexander the Great, and includes especially

Myron's famous statue of the discus thrower. There are also shots of the Acropolis, the Temple of Zeus at Olympia, and men and women in the nude, all photographed with a hazy background intended to represent the Greek spirit of health. A solitary runner, cheered on by crowds along the streets as he passes through the Greek villages on his way, finally arrives in Berlin. This sequence is intercut with shots of other runners carrying the torch in a relay, which begins at a temple and proceeds through what appear to be Greek woods. From time to time this sequence is intercut with shots of the sun reflected in the water. At one point a runner makes his lonely way along the beach, with sunlit Greek villages in the background. The last man in the relay, who lights the fire in the Olympic stadium in Berlin, is the German athlete Schilgen; he is blonde and clearly distinguished from the other runners in the relay. In several versions of the prologue to *Olympia* appear female nudes dancing in forests and doing gymnastic exercises.

A total of 400,000 meters (1,200,000) feet of film were exposed when *Olympia* was shot, but the edited version consisted of only 6,150 meters. The original German copy of the film was synchronized simultaneously in four languages and later distributed in sixteen languages. After World War II, the German voluntary self-control agency (FSK) released a de-Nazified edition of the film. Most of the scenes showing Hitler and other Nazi officials had been cut out. Parts of the musical score of the "Horst Wessel Lied" had been eliminated. In many versions of *Olympia* distributed in the United States the scenes showing the female nudes were expurgated. Although the nudes are handsome to look at and obviously do not serve pornographic purposes, they tended to offend the sensibilities of certain viewers, especially since it is conjectured that one of the nudes was Riefenstahl herself.[30] The shots of the nudes in the prologue were made on the Baltic sea, although in the film the impression was created that the nudes were photographed in Greece. It appears that the nudes in the prologue were an afterthought. Riefenstahl was of the opinion that the footage shot on location in Greece lacked interest and suspense, and so she later added the sequences with the nudes. The nude scenes together with the Greek sculptures were intended to establish a connection between ancient Greece, where the nude body found expression in Greek art, and the modern Olympic Games, celebrated in Germany. In the prologue the female nudes are very graceful, doing gymnastic exercises which imitate the undulating motion of the grass surrounding them, thus placing them in unison with nature.

Most of the prologue was shot in Greece before the Olympic Games began. Riefenstahl flew to Athens, meeting her two camera-men there. They subsequently drove through Czechoslovakia Austria, Hungary, and other countries by way of a goodwill gesture and also to promote the Games. Riefenstahl herself selected the runners carrying the torch from Olympia to Berlin. One of these was a former Olympic medal winner, sixty years old in 1936. Riefen-stahl and her cameraman Jaworsky followed in a Mercedes con-vertible, photographing the runners and torch bearers as they moved along. Another runner was an unusually handsome young man, who appeared among the first twenty runners. Riefenstahl asked Jaworsky to shoot every move he made, because she was fascinated by his physical beauty. Actually, Anatole, as he was called, was not Greek by birth, although he looked like a Greek statue, but was the child of Russian and Yugoslav parents, who happened to be stranded in Greece.

His physique exhibited the celebrated perfect harmony of a typical Greek sculpture, but he was alive, made of flesh, not of stone, and thus represented a well-chosen type for incorporating the spirit of the Olympic Games, as Riefenstahl wanted it. After the shooting of the prologue, Riefenstahl took Anatole with her, providing him with a passport and handsome new clothes. She got him a job in the film industry in Berlin. Her crew members found her choice of Anatole perfectly sound. "As usual, she had a perfect instinct for what was good for the film," Jaworsky remembered. Naturally, Riefenstahl's fascination with the beauty of this young man gave rise to rumors that she had a love affair with him. According to an eyewitness, Anatole thought of Riefenstahl as "that crazy woman," who for some reason, had decided to choose him. However, attuned to Greek ways of life, he refused to jump or run at siesta time, even though Riefenstahl and her crew, pressed for time, ignored siesta. Instead of running around the ruins of Delphi, as Riefenstahl requested, Anatole chose to sit down and eat his lunch until siesta was over.[31]

In *Festival of Nations*, the various national Olympic teams are shown marching into the stadium. The German team extends the right arm in the familiar Nazi greeting. A chorus in the background sings "Olympia" and a speaker says that "we pledge to be honorable competitors during the Olympic games." The events shown in part 1 are (1) discus throw, male (won by U.S.A.); (2) discus throw, female (won by Germany); (3) 100-meter dash, male (won by Jesse Owens, U.S.A.); (4) shot-put, male (won by Germany); (5) 800-meter dash, male (won by U.S.A.); (6) broad jump, male (won by Jesse Owens, U.S.A.); (7) high jump, female (won by Hungary); (8) 400-meter race, male (won by U.S.A.); (9) hammer throw, male (won by Germany); (10) high jump, male (won by U.S.A.); (11) hurdle race, female (won by Italy); (12) hurdle race, male (won by U.S.A.); (13) javelin throw, male (won by Germany); (14) 10,000-meter race, male (won by Finland); (15) 400-meter relay, female (won by Great Britain); (16) 400-meter relay, male (won by U.S.A.); (17) pole vault, male (won by U.S.A.).

*Festival of Beauty* is less organized than *Festival of People*. It also tends to emphasize team sports like hockey and soccer. It gives scenes of various disciplines without indicating the winners and without creating the suspense characterizing part 1.

In *Festival of Nations*, after a candid shot of the Olympic village, where the various athletes are shown in training among lakes and ponds, we see men jumping, intercut with a picture of kangaroos jumping, which is intended to provide comic relief. Next are men practicing boxing; then follows a brief sequence showing sections of a soccer game in which members of all races and nationalities seem to be interested. A brief shot of a basketball team at work follows next, after which the film shows a discus practice session. Weight lifters and javelin throwers come next—and thus the whole first sequence is established as a review of part 1 of *Olympia*.

The next sequence focuses on male athletes of various nationalities resting in their lounge chairs in the Olympic village. In the following we see young women practicing gymnastics. They are shown moving on their knees, in the grass, wearing gymnastics suits. The group of female gymnasts becomes larger and larger and the final shot in this sequence shows a huge athletic field with gymnasts in perfect geometrical order, working in unison. This scene is one of the favorite stills from *Olympia*, and it has frequently been used to indicate the Fascist intent in the film. After several "quiet" scenes and others showing the background of the Olympic film, there follows a sequence, in slow motion, of gymnastics, including work on the balancing beam, parallel bars, and the horse.

We see both men and women doing exercises; the winner and the points achieved are seldom announced in Part 2 of the film. There are Japanese gymnasts on rings, doing exercises photographed against the sky, other male gymnasts on parallel bars, shot from below. We see a man swinging on horizontal bars, again photographed—this time in slow motion—against the sky. This gives the cameramen a chance to show a flying human body against the sky, rotating around the horizontal bar. The lyricism of this sequence is followed by the famous diving sequence. Again, the announcers do not mention the number of points awarded by judges to an athlete; instead, they concentrate on the names of the winners in the diving sequence. It is difficult, in this section of the film, to pay attention to the names, for only the anonymous bodies flying into the sky and then diving into the water matter here. Riefenstahl has transcended all sense of competition and created simply beautiful forms.[32] The viewer feels a sense of exhilaration which is not tied to nationhood or race, but is perhaps an expression of the joy in the beauty of the movement of these flying bodies. The individual diver does not matter—and the commentator, who has vociferously accompanied the first part of *Olympia*, frequently keeps a long silence in this sequence. Interesting, though not new for modern viewers, are the sequences showing the divers as they dip into the water. The camera captures the bodies flying through the sky and entering another medium, the water.

The men's final breast-stroke swimming events (won by Japan) follow next, and are followed by other swimming competitions, including free-style. The sailing competitions, held in Kiel on the Baltic sea, are shown next. Twenty-five nations participated. While this, for many viewers, is the least interesting event to observe, since most spectators would not be able to distinguish between the various types of sailboats and appreciate the different achievements, Riefenstahl makes this sequence lively by intercutting it with shots of the sky, of a lone man up a high mast, and the billowing sails in the wind, providing the viewer with a feel of the fresh breeze, the sunshine and spraying waters that accompany this sport. After this sequence, hockey follows. The film shows various aspects of team cooperation, and brings out the dramatic highlights.

A high point in part 2 of *Olympia* is the riding sequence. It provides the most suspenseful material. It was very difficult to shoot but it provides the spectator with a sense of adventure and fear, a sense of admiration for the horsemen, which Olympic Games have rarely been able to transmit, with or without film. The beauty of the terrain, the liveliness of the horses—all contribute to the high drama of this sequence. The Germans, traditionally winners at this event, fared well in this discipline, although they had severe competition. The next sequence shows the pentathlon, a feat including riding, fencing, pistol shooting, swimming, and jumping. It is an event for aristocratically born men involving enormous physical strength and considerable skill.

Bicycle racing—with a mass start—is the next event in *Festival of Beauty,* followed by the famed marathon race. Riefenstahl spent a lot of time and thought on the marathon. She mentions in her interviews that she tried to build up a montage of music and image, showing the increasing fatigue of the marathon runner. In this sequence the camera finally concentrates on the legs of the runners and the music becomes slower and slower, thus indicating the general fatigue and—more important—the exertion necessary to overcome this fatigue. The marathon is one of the highlights in the entire film in cinematic, in athletic, and in human terms. In order to make this race interesting, Riefenstahl resorted to all kinds of cinematic devices. She photographed the runners from above, she concentrated her cameras on their legs, and she shot shadows of their bodies, silently running along the endless roads. In many ways, she made the ordeal of the marathon so difficult-looking on film that many a spectator would be discouraged to attempt it. She showed the haggard faces, the many runners who collapsed, and others who gave up because of fatigue. Finally, she showed the exhausted winner, the slender, fragile-looking Japanese Kitei Son. A runner from Great Britain was second, and the third was again a Japanese. In this case, beauty and strength, a Riefenstahl principle in *Olympia,* exhibited forms which have nothing to do with fascism.

The decathlon, another tiring event, provides the next sequence in part 2. As the name implies, it involves ten events which took two days to accomplish. The American Glen Morris was the winner of this event. This sequence constitutes the climax of *Olympia,* part 2.

It combines ten feats of endurance and will, and the rendering of it on film shows great beauty.

Part 2 of *Olympia* closes, in most prints, with flags billowing in the wind and with a shot exhibiting the Olympic bowl of fire and featuring a chorus singing the song "Olympia."

The film *Olympia,* in addition to the sporting events, includes many scenes which highlight the events shown. The greatest accomplishment in this film is that its director put the sporting events into the general web of life. This principle makes *Olympia* interesting to viewers, no matter if they like sports or not. This "web of life" included Hitler, the SS, flags featuring the swastika, blue skies, clouds, water reflecting sun or moon, pigeons, and masses of cheering crowds on bleachers, dressed in saris, dressed in Abyssinian hats, in kimonos, and fashionable European clothes. The film highlights the most dramatic sporting events. In part 1 the pole-vaulting probably provides the most breathtaking experience. The viewer appreciates the efforts of the athletes and is regally entertained at the same time.

It is another achievement of *Olympia* that it shows women to be beautiful and strong at the same time. Good examples of this were the German athlete Gisela Mauermeyer, winner of the women's discus, and a Hungarian beauty, winner of the women's high jump. Jesse Owens, with his beautiful childlike face and handsome sinewy legs, is also a hero—I would say *the* hero in the film. Other heroes, less obvious, were the letter pigeons, the reporters, and, above all, the cheering crowds, shouting in Italian, Japanese, English, French, or German. Black athletes were frequently the winners in these games, and the announcer always gave them their due. Occasionally the film features Nazi insignia. There were flags with swastikas, there were SS boots, and there was Hitler as well as the "Horst Wessel Lied." But there were also the beautiful sky, music, and the award ceremonies.

Riefenstahl was infatuated with flags, both in *Olympia* and in *Triumph of the Will.* Her infatuation with flags has been noted by well-known film critics. She lingers over night views of torch light, slashing the darkness, and flags transparent next to the flames. In sunlight she sought to catch figures against the light, the shadows cast by a marching column, or men enveloped in the phosphorescense. "A set of flags and poles undulates like a field of ripe corn. The human body becomes an ornament, and the

Photo right: The human body seems to transcend the law of gravity in the famous diving sequence from "Festival of Beauty" Part II of *Olympia*
Courtesy of Gordon Hitchens, New York City

columns filmed from above . . . are suddenly transformed into a blurred, hazy vision."[33]

*Olympia* shows a world of beauty beginning with the flight into antiquity, as fire and torches are lit, and ending with the realistic concreteness of the competitions recorded in a way which only a film is capable of doing. The "sixteen days" provided a permanent record to the sporting world that beauty is not names.

The Winter Games of the 1936 Olympiad were held in Garmisch-Partenkirchen, Bavaria. Goebbels had asked a member of his staff to film the Winter Games: and, according to Henry Jaworsky, there was a lot of competition between Riefenstahl and the director of the Winter Olympics film, Hans Weidemann. The film did run in the movie theaters in Germany but does not appear to have been a great success. In general, the Winter Games were less spectacular than the Summer Olympics, due in part to the extremely cold weather.

## Reception

Internationally, *Olympia* was well-received. It won the Grand Prix at the 1938 International Film Festival in Venice, where it was cited as the "world's best film of 1938." Henry McLemore, United Press correspondent, who had personally covered the Berlin Games, wrote in 1938 that "last night I saw the finest motion picture that I have ever seen. . . . This is not propaganda but the most glorious filming of the greatest meeting of the athletes in the history of the world."[34] The *Los Angeles Times* of December 17, 1938, featured a review which was also largely favorable. In the opinion of its writer, the film turned out to be much more than a "chronicle of the world-famous competitions," and it was described as a triumph of the camera and an epos of the screen. In a Finnish newspaper, *Olympia* was characterized as a first-class work of art—beautifully executed, grandiose, impressive, and fascinating.[35] The Swedes, who awarded Riefenstahl the Polar Prize for this film, wrote that *Olympia* was a factual documentary which was "almost poetry."[36] The Swiss decided that the film surpassed all expectations.[37] In France, critics thought that "a film of this magnitude and such a glorification of human effort" left even the most recalcitrant viewers deeply moved.[38] In Hungary, a newspaper article described *Olympia* as "perfect," and Dutch

Photo left: Kitei Son, Japanese winner of the marathon in *Olympia*, Part II
Courtesy of Gordon Hitchens, New York City

critics thought that it was "glorious" that something like *Olympia* could actually be seen.[39] Italian critics wrote that this "woman of extreme grace, beautiful bearing, and secure elegance knew how to produce and organize the two greatest works known to the history of film."[40] A Danish paper found that Leni Riefenstahl had created a unique epos of beauty, of strength, and of a joy of life.[41] A Belgian critic described *Olympia* as a triumph of poetry and of sensuous and pure lyricism.[42]

For whatever reason, the world press found that *Olympia* was a great work of art. Not surprisingly, German reviews were also favorable. The German censorship board found the film "politically valuable, artistically valuable, culturally valuable, suitable for the education of the common people, and an educational film," thus awarding it the highest rating possible in the German film industry under the control of Goebbel's Ministry for Propaganda and People's Enlightenment.[43] German journalist Erwin Goelz, writing in *Der deutsche Film* under the pseudonym of Frank Maraun, wrote that *Olympia* was a "triumph of a documentary that succeeded where the film the Americans tried to make at Los Angeles during the previous Olympic Games failed." He also explained why he thought that *Olympia* was so successful. Clearly imbued with Nazi ideology, Goelz maintained that the film was good because in it Germany had created for the Olympic Games of 1936 a wonderfully perceived and symbolic framework which, from the very beginning, had elevated the Games above a mere sports reportage. In his view, *Olympia* was also the result of National Socialism which was penetrating the total life of the nation and made the viewer see reality and idea together. He concluded his review by insisting that only in the ideological structure of National Socialism was it possible to create this great documentary as an artistic achievement.[44]

More recent German reviews are infinitely more critical of the film. Ulrich Gregor, a leftist contemporary German film critic, believes that *Olympia* is "Fascist in spirit," because the film treats sports as an heroic, superhuman achievement, a kind of ritual." Gregor draws his inferences especially from the narration where words like "fight" and "conquest" are frequently heard. The fact is, however, that even in non-German narration, such words had to be used in order to describe the competition.[45] We may add that all competition consists of fight and conquest to some extent, to which the combatants in general submit voluntarily. Critics writing from the point of view of Ulrich Gregor evidently find all forms of competition, including sporting events, reprehensible, not to say Fascist. Such a judgment implies an oversimplified, indeed, facile definition of "fascism" and obscures its real dangers.

The difficulty with *Olympia* is that it was made in Hitler's Germany. As long as the memory of that Germany is still alive in the viewer, the film cannot be judged with absolute objectivity. The ambiguous nature of the reaction to *Olympia* was pointed out by Riefenstahl, who quotes two contradictory opinions regarding the propagandistic effects of the film. The German Voluntary Self-Control Agency found that "Leni Riefenstahl has consciously and in a sophisticated fashion presented Jesse Owens and other colored athletes so magnanimously as to give the world the impression that there was then no racial prejudice in Germany." On the other hand, a French magazine wrote: "During the entire film of the 1936 Olympic Games, Leni Riefenstahl does nothing but glorify Nazi athletes. So little does she concern herself with the other competitors that all countries must energetically protest the spirit in which these scenes were made."[46] Although there are many contemporary film critics who would describe *Olympia* as one of the great documentary films of the century, the film still remains controversial.

# 6

## Of Men and Wolves: *Tiefland*

### Production

RIEFENSTAHL had made plans to shoot *Tiefland* (*Lowlands*, 1954) immediately after completing *The Blue Light*. In the summer of 1934 she traveled to Spain. She was not in good health at that time, and the strain of shooting this film made her condition even worse. Moreover, she had chosen an amateur, Franz Eichberger, to play the leading male part, a fact which contributed to the difficulty of getting the production underway, although Riefenstahl later always maintained that Eichberger was an excellent actor. However, he never got another part in the German movie industry.

Originally, she had planned to produce the film with her own production company, but her health broke down completely in the summer of 1934; and, after having had to direct several scenes from a stretcher, she decided to shelve the project and return to Berlin, where Hitler pressured her into making *Triumph of the Will* (see chapter 4). She did not resume work on *Tiefland* until 1942.

Again, many complications developed. Since Goebbels was in charge of all films produced in Germany, Riefenstahl, as well as other film directors had to get his authorization before she could produce any films; hence she occasionally had to report to Goebbels her progress on *Tiefland*. Goebbels' diaries show that by 1942 the film had already cost five million marks and that it was not expected that the film would be completed before another year was out. Goebbels described the circumstances surrounding this film as "unfortunate." He referred to innumerable complications regarding *Tiefland*, mentioned Riefenstahl's ill health "from overwork and worry," and urged her earnestly to go on leave before taking up further work. He also congratulated himself on

163

not having had anything to do "with this unfortunate case," so that he bore no responsibility.[1] Tobis film company was going to receive the rights to this film in return for 40,000 marks, a sum which evidently was to be advanced by the German government.

Although much of *Tiefland* was shot on location in Spain and in the German and Austrian Alps, studio space had to be rented in Prague for a number of scenes. Since studio space was difficult to obtain during World War II, Riefenstahl asked for help from Dr. Max Winkler, the economic advisor in the German ministry, which he provided. Other difficulties involved securing the talents of her favorite cameraman, Albert Benitz. Benitz was especially necessary for the concluding scenes of the film, namely the duel between Pedro and Don Sebastian.

While Riefenstahl worked on *Tiefland*, taking shots in Spain and elsewhere, war raged throughout Europe. The summer of 1944 in particular was not a happy one for Riefenstahl, both for political and for personal reasons. The personal problems were primarily related to her health. Moreover, in August 1944, Riefenstahl's father and brother died. In Riefenstahl's own words, her brother "died a hero's death" in the firm belief in his führer and in Germany's victory. In the fall of 1944 she was on her feet, again trying to complete *Tiefland*, but another staffing problem developed. She now needed Hermann Storr, the chief sound technician who had previously worked on the film. Storr was on the crew of a film directed by Veit Harlan, who worked closely with the Nazi Ministry of Propaganda and People's Enlightenment. Since Veit Harlan's films were more in tune with the political interests of the Nazi government, he could choose his favorite professionals. Riefenstahl appealed to Veit Harlan's sense of appreciation for her films and to his human dignity and, with all the additional support of a prominent Nazi leader, she managed to secure the services of Storr.[2]

In 1944 Germany's military fortunes were turning: studios were bombed out, actors and other professionals were being drafted into the army, and no money was available for films which were not of immediate political interest to the Nazis. Riefenstahl could not complete *Tiefland* until after the end of World War II, although she had secured the expert assistance of both Veit Harlan and G. W. Pabst. The two directors were in charge of what she termed "secondary" scenes. Pabst, for instance, directed primarily the scenes in which Riefenstahl's opponent in the film, Donna Amelia, acted. Neither Harlan nor Pabst received official credit for participation in *Tiefland*. Possibly they did not want to be mentioned.

Certain records in the Archives of the Federal Republic of Germany in Koblenz indicate that in 1943 Riefenstahl's production company, which was to produce *Tiefland*, was practically bankrupt, for Riefenstahl asked that the Nazi government bail her company out and give it special status within the war economy. Her request was granted.[3] Apparently, the cost of the film did not cause her to compromise her artistic intentions. An anecdote exists suggestive of her working methods even at a time of diminishing funds and wartime difficulties. When Riefenstahl's crew was working on this film in the studio, her designer was asked to recreate a forest, tree-by-tree, on the set, similarly to the forest created for Fritz Lang's film *Die Nibelungen*. When the forest was completed, she praised it highly, but on the next day she asked to be raised on a crane in order to select shooting angles. While sitting high above this artificial forest, she called down that it was just marvelous but also requested that a tree be moved several feet. This was a difficult thing to do, since the trees were enormous and very heavy. At the end of the day, Riefenstahl had almost every tree shifted by several feet. She herself denies the truth of this story.

A weakness in *Tiefland* is related to the fact that by the early 1940s, Riefenstahl no longer had the same relationship to the topic which had compelled her to take it up in 1934. She had outgrown the emotional bonds attaching her to the theme. *Tiefland* thus was little more than an escape for her, albeit a costly one for the German film industry. It provided Riefenstahl with an opportunity to flee into the mountains. While Spain had been her chosen terrain for shooting, the war finally made travel into foreign countries impossible, and several scenes had to be shot in Germany and Austria.

In retrospect, it is still difficult to see why Riefenstahl continued with a film in the success of which she no longer believed. According to one interview, she was primarily interested in photographic aspects. "I fled into photography."[4] She wanted to make sure that black-and-white photography would remain subtle enough to survive as a competitor against the new color films which were becoming more and more popular in the movies.

Riefenstahl has frequently maintained that she found the dual activity of acting and directing very strenuous, yet she assumed both roles in *Tiefland*. She claims that this was due to the fact that she could not find a leading actress whom she liked. Moreover, German director Pabst, who could have directed her acting, in her view was no longer the same director he had been before he had gone to Hollywood. His Hollywood experience had changed his style. Thus the scenes which he directed in *Tiefland* are characterized by extreme overacting, something which he may have come to appreciate in Hollywood.

The frequent interruptions during the production of *Tiefland*, quite aside from the long time span which had elapsed between its first conception and its final shape, disturbed the quality of the film also. Either the studio, the actors, or both were unavailable when Riefenstahl needed them. Once she even had to destroy all the sets developed for a sequence of shots, because she could not get the actor she wanted. He was working for the well-known director Gustav Gründgens. In other instances, Riefenstahl had been promised a studio several times but later was denied access to scarce studio space because Goebbels supported the production of films that would tend to raise the morale of the hungry, bombed-out, and demoralized German citizens, something which *Tiefland* could not claim to do at all. As a result of all these mishaps, the inner suspense, according to Riefenstahl, petered out of the film. She admits that this fact is especially noticeable in her own acting which she described as "dead," claiming in her interview with Herman Weigel that she did not have the guidance she needed.[5] As a matter of fact, Riefenstahl never was a first-rate actress, but she might have developed into one, if she had worked under the guidance of Pabst who, unlike Fanck, was a very good director of actors. Riefenstahl evidently was aware of her deficiencies as an actress, and this may have been one of the reasons for her wanting to become a film director.

In addition to all these difficulties, much of the exposed film featuring *Tiefland* was confiscated by the French after the war. The lost material was of particular importance in relation to the milieu surrounding the Marquez of Roccabruna; it contained footage made in Spain, and pictures of the bulls as well as the drought. Some of this material was never returned to Riefenstahl and this, according to her, was the reason why the film has no real ending.

## Analysis

The plot of *Tiefland* is based upon an opera composed by the Czech, Eugene d'Albert, which Riefenstahl saw in her youth in Berlin and never forgot. The libretto was composed by Rudolph Lothar, adapted from *Terra Baixa*, a late nineteenth-century Spanish play by Angel Guimera. D'Albert composed the music and the work was premiered in Prague on November 15, 1903. It was performed at the Metropolitan Opera in New York five years later, scoring a success, though in an abbreviated version. When performed in Oslo in 1913, *Tiefland* provided Kirsten Flagstad with an opportunity to make her opera debut and get launched on her phenomenal career. The original opera is characterized by a highly melodious musical score, which still enjoys great popularity among singers, although opera directors generally dislike the work because of its allegedly sentimental story. However, *Tiefland* still appears on the programs of European and American opera houses.

Riefenstahl in her film adapted both the libretto and the music. Herbert Windt, her favorite composer, added several musical phrases of his own, and other segments of the original composition were retained. The essential difference between the original plot and Riefenstahl's film is that Riefenstahl converted sections of the plot, which in the opera were merely narrated, into cinematic images. The most dramatic section is the struggle between the shepherd Pedro and the wolf, which in the opera is merely narrated by Pedro, providing the singer with a marvelous aria. In Riefenstahl's film, it is acted out, photographed against the craggy mountains, and given dramatic intensity. In addition, the wolf scene assumes symbolic significance, because the wolf, strangled by Pedro with his bare hands, symbolizes the slave driver, Don Sebastian, Marquez of Roccabruna, who lives in the lowlands. The peasants also call him "the wolf."

In Riefenstahl's film the action takes place at the foot of the Pyrenees in the lowlands and mountains of Catalonia. The plot opens with the revelation that Don Sebastian, Marquez of Roccabruna, is in debt. The harvests have been bad, because this has been a year of drought. In order to keep enough food for his bulls—the best fighters in the kingdom—Don Sebastian has the water of the vital stream, needed by his peasants for his fields, diverted so that it irrigates his private pasture lands, as a result of which the land worked by the peasants dries up. The peasants, moreover, lack water even for their households. It is, therefore, highly unreasonable for Don Sebastian to keep the water to himself. When he is asked to return the water to the peasants who are in fact tilling his own land, he rejects their request, thus showing himself to be cruel and despotic, as well as stupid, though the stupidity is not emphasized in Riefenstahl's film.

One evening, while driving through the village of Roccabruna, he sees Martha, a beggar girl and excellent dancer, in an inn. He falls in love and makes her his mistress. When it becomes clear that he has to marry the mayor's daughter in order to pay his debts, he insists on an expedient: he marries the mayor's daughter, Donna Amelia, marries off Martha to Pedro, the naive shepherd from the high mountains, but insists that Pedro will not be Martha's husband, and that, instead, he himself will come to visit Martha on their wedding night. When Don Sebastian arrives, Martha has come to love Pedro, and the film ends with a duel between Pedro and the Marquez of Roccabruna, at the end of which the latter lies dead, strangled by Pedro's bare hands in the same way in which during the opening sequence of the film the wolf was found dead after a struggle with Pedro. The final scene shows Martha and Pedro in the mountains walking toward the sun.

As always, Riefenstahl works with strong contrasts. The main theme in this film, as indicated vaguely in the title, is the conflict between the life of the pure and simple people in the mountains, symbolized by Pedro, and the life of the corrupt people, represented by Don Sebastian, inhabiting the plains. The theme is corroborated throughout the film in the dialogue, in the cinematographic development, and by the plot itself. The dramatic energy of *Tiefland* derives from the constant cinematic juxtaposition between the craggy mountains, shown against waterfalls, flowers, and other beautiful forms of nature, and the plains, usually shown as arid flatlands, with withered vegetation and unhappy or bored people.

The opening scene shows a mountain terrain during the night, with the moon visible only enough to cause the huge shadows to be cast by the mountains, reminiscent of those in *The Blue Light*. Gentle, operatic soft music accompanies this idyllic scene. The music imitates flutes and horns, music that is usually played in the mountains. We see a herd of bleating sheep, accompanied by the sound of bells. The camera now travels to a simple hut, enters it, and focuses on a young man sleeping on a cot; he is the shepherd responsible for the herd of sheep grazing on the mountains. The camera travels back to the herd and suddenly focuses on a wolf, standing on top of a mountain crag, yawning.

The music changes to more violent rhythms, announcing the imminent danger that is threatening this mountain idyll. Suddenly, movement comes into the sheep; they run in all directions, aware of the dangerous wolf. This symbolism in the context of the film is obvious. Innocence versus viciousness is shown in the confrontation between the sheep and the wolf. (One wonders how the director and the Nazi authorities reconciled such action with Germany's own attacks on largely defenseless neighbors). The wolf comes prowling down the mountain, ready to attack his prey, but it is somewhat hindered by the barking of the small dog. The shepherd Pedro is awakened by his dog and goes out to fight the wolf, who has just killed one of his sheep. The two fight each other, Pedro starting the fight by throwing a slingshot which hits the wolf on the nose. This is a battle of two equals. It is a fair battle. It is almost an aristocratic battle, because Pedro's slingshot has the same function as the proverbial glove. It provides a challenge for battle, which is accepted by the wolf. The scene ends when the wolf is dead, strangled by Pedro's bare hands. Pedro washes his wounds in the mountain lake. The most dramatic section of this scene is the part in which Pedro and the wolf roll down the hill, forming a veritable beast with two backs. The difficulty of overcoming the wolf is indicated in Pedro's distorted face, frequently featured on stills from this film. It indicates the extreme exertion necessary to kill the enemy of his flock.

After the wolf-fighting scene, we see magnificent photography of the mountain range, focusing on the water generated by this terrain and then traveling on to the plains. We see the sun rising in the mountains, and the water coming down in great torrents. The fog disappears from the summits, and we enter the plains, observing the river flowing through fields which are dried up. A shot of the peasants follows next. They are hammering away at the dam, so that the water will be diverted in a different direction. The camera now shifts to Pedro, descending from the mountains, carrying a wolf's pelt on his shoulder. Organ music accompanies his descent. Again the camera shifts—this time to the black-clad rural workers with their hoes in their hands, walking off the scene and apparently into the spectators with a threatening gesture. The shifting between the mountains and the plains is disconcerting. In the next sequence the peasants of the valley bow to the approaching master of Roccabruna, but they are rejected. The black-clad peasants against the white plains and the blue skies provide an interesting contrast to the moist, flourishing mountain terrain shown whenever the mountains are in the picture.

Pedro comes down from his mountain, and the camera focuses on him. The peasants had requested that the "Master let the water run freely again." In reply they are told, "No, the dam remains. The Marquez needs the water for his bulls." Pedro, symbolizing the beauty of the mountains, enters the village with several sheep and the wolf's pelt slung over his shoulder. Here follows a shot of the covered wagon in which rides Martha, played by Leni Riefenstahl herself, who plans to dance for the villagers. She symbolizes a mediation between the corruption of the plains and the innocence of the mountains; she prepares for her dance in village inns, attracting children of the village square. Flamenco music accompanies this scene.

The camera suddenly shifts to an elegant lady, Donna Amelia, daughter of the mayor of Roccabruna, dressing in magnificent chambers, worrying about obtaining the Marquez of Roccobruna for her husband. The magnificent beauty of the interiors is effectively contrasted with the natural simplicity of both the mountains from which Pedro recently descended and Martha's beggar wagon. It is clear, despite the beauty of the surroundings, that Donna Amelia represents evil. Conversations between her and others confirm this impression. She is willing to pay a lot of money to become the wife of the Marquez of Roccabruna.

The scene shifts to a Spanish chamber, where sits Don Sebastian, a little tyrant, bored, obviously the master of all this. He is concerned about using additional pressure against his peasants so that they will pay their rent and enable him to pay his own debts. The scene then shifts to the cellar of the castle where Pedro eats a supper with the servant girls. The humor, gaiety, simple beauty of this "downstairs" milieu is contrasted with the boredom, emptiness, and vicious plotting characterizing the "upstairs rooms" where the *haute volée* of Roccabruna, presided over by arrogant Don Sebastian and the sleepy mayor of the town, has assembled.

Pedro, the shepherd, struggling with the wolf in *Tiefland*
Courtesy of Deutsches Institut für Filmkunde

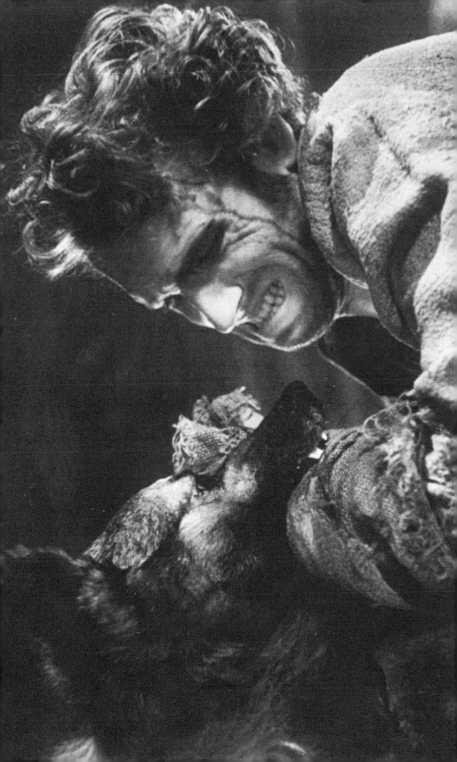

The following sequence takes place in a simple village inn visited only by men, most of whom are obviously rural workers. They are sloppy, but enjoy watching the dancing of Martha. Her dancing is rather chaste, though it arouses the simple workers. Pedro watches the scene through the window and is immediately charmed by Martha. The arrival of Don Sebastian indicates that he was indeed bored by members of his own social class whom he has left in order to be entertained in this inn. This scene has certain Fascist overtones: the master, Don Sebastian, peremptorily stomps into the inn, is immediately greeted by the peasants with bowed heads and other forms of self-humiliation, and as the master, is welcomed by a woman who can entertain him. He has the power to take her, and she submits without question. The rest of the film bears out this theme: although Don Sebastian is a cruel task master, he loves the beautiful, humble, and talented Martha, whom he decks out with clothes fit for a Spanish princess. He is nasty to everyone but her. The entire sequence involving Don Sebastian and Martha gives credit to Riefenstahl's method of expressing vital matters through indirection. However, in doing so, she also upholds traditional values: Martha is submissive to Don Sebastian and, in fact, seems to be attracted by his viciousness. Requested to love him, she simply obeys. While this may be a hangover from the European film tradition of the 1920s, when women often flopped to the ground before a strong man who simply "took them," in the context of Riefenstahl's work it also has become a well-worn cliché. Another cliché is the erotic dream of a woman wishing to be the object of desire of two or more men. This was an underlying topic in *The Blue Light* and it surfaces again in *Tiefland*. Riefenstahl liked to be viewed as an innocent yet highly erotic female. She dealt with the problem of being innocent and powerless, on the one hand, and of being independent and powerful, on the other, by dividing her life into fact and fantasy. In her fantasy she dreamed of the innocent, lovely, desirable Yunta or Martha. In real life, she chose to be a director, in charge of an organization with many employees which made it possible for her to indulge her dreams.

The remainder of *Tiefland* shows scenes reminiscent of *The Blue Light*. As a matter of fact, in her interview on Camera Three, Riefenstahl maintained that many of the actors for *Tiefland* had participated in *The Blue Light*. The black-clad and somber peasants, the serfs of Don Sebastian, in one of the most powerful

Photos left: *Tiefland*, the contenders for the water—(top) Don Sebastian's bulls, "the best in the kingdom"; (bottom) the peasants lined up for water in a scene reminiscent of *The Blue Light*      Courtesy of Deutsches Institut für Filmkunde scenes, confront their master with their troubles. These scenes are shot against the plains and feature the picturesque hats of the villagers, their black robes and worn faces, and provide a contrast with the elegant robes and lighthearted laughter of the moneyed aristocracy surrounding Don Sebastian in the rooms of the castle. Martha in a sense partakes of both worlds. As his mistress, she is handsomely dressed but good-natured and innocent, and she travels back and forth between the world of simplicity and innocence and the world of corruption without losing her identity.

At one point in the film she runs away from her master into the mountains, is found by Pedro, and is forever converted to the life of innocence that reigns high in the mountains. She wants to leave Don Sebastian; however, he insists that he would rather kill her than part with her. His agents catch her and bring her back, and he is still as passionately in love with her as ever. Martha, as seen and acted by Riefenstahl, is the innocent, untouched beauty with a golden heart, who knows no evil and is actually afraid of violent sexuality. She is ultimately useless in the castle. She does not work, nor does she think or otherwise transcend her physical beauty. Her only achievements are her innocence, her beauty, and her goodness of heart, born of naiveté. That Martha, a beggar woman, should be so noble of heart is a beautiful aspect of the film but hardly credible in reality and thus makes for a good deal of melodrama.

The melodrama continues in the scenes involving the serfs of the Marquez who, when the water in their wells dries up because the Marquez has diverted the river, distribute whatever water is left in a fair and democratic way among all the households of the village. Martha's goodness becomes evident in the scenes where she tries to mitigate the sad life of the serfs, once by offering the miller a piece of jewelry given her by Don Sebastian, so that the miller can pay his rent, and once by holding back Sebastian's horse whip at a moment when he was about to hit an old peasant woman who had called him a slave driver. At this point in the film, Martha finds out that the peasants in the village call Don Sebastian "the wolf" and that he is cruel to everyone but her. She also learns that Sebastian has had many mistresses, of whom he gradually got tired and whom he eventually sent away. Martha's own preciousness is thus enhanced because Sebastian loves her and, she claims, will never beat her, but he does hit her when he discovers that she gave away the jewelry he had given her. She runs away, looking strangely out of place among the mountains in her white robe. For an unknown and dramatically unmotivated reason she runs into the mountains as a place of refuge, wanting to find, though this is clear only in retrospect, a place of purity—which she does, for here she meets Pedro who saves her and nurses her back to health.

It is this Pedro whom she finally marries, and who knows nothing about the schemes surrounding their marriage. As a result he is called "fool" and given the sign of the cuckold by the other villagers. When Martha finds out that Pedro came down from the pure mountains not because he was mercenary, but because he loved her, she no longer despises him.

Riefenstahl omitted a melodramtic high point of the original opera, *Tiefland*, where Martha asks Pedro to kill her because she had been another man's mistress first. Riefenstahl omitted this bit of business to show that two pure and innocent people are automatically attracted to each other, though Martha had also loved her arrogant and cruel Don Sebastian.

A real weakness in the film is the overemphasis on Martha's goodness, which seems somewhat incredible in view of the fact that she is a simple beggar girl, who was accompanied by a rather primitive rascally "manager." When offered water in Pedro's cabin, for instance, she rejects it claiming while swooning, that the "peasants" need it more, evidently still dreaming about the hard lot of the peasants in the lowlands.

Don Sebastian's love for Martha is a form of possessiveness which Martha obviously relishes. His threat to kill her rather than part with her scares her and excites her at the same time. She thus submits to the shoddy marriage scheme devised by Don Sebastian, although she does so with tears in her eyes, and it is not clear from the film whether these tears well up because Martha feels sad about losing her position as first mistress with Don Sebastian, or because she feels sorry for the unwitting Pedro, or both.

The end of the film seems dramatically unresolved. Martha, by now a sophisticated lady, accustomed to being served, well-dressed and handsome at all times, and Pedro, the naive shepherd, walk up the mountain together. This unlikely pair is presumably hoping to find purity and happiness among the eternal summits. Pedro had never "known" a woman, in the biblical sense, until he saw Martha at the inn. She thus became the one and only woman for him. For Sebastian, she was the last, and most cherished, in a long series of women, and thus Martha's value as an object of desire of two entirely different men is high. In the last dramatic sequence, Pedro, the shepherd, wins over and destroys Don Sebastian, the wolf, because of his physical strength and his familiarity with wolves. One of the touches of irony is that Don Sebastian has consistently paid a certain reward to anyone who killed a wolf in his territory. There will be no one to reward Pedro after he kills the human wolf, Don Sebastian. The duel between the two men, fought with knives, takes place during a heavy thunderstorm (shot in a studio) accompanied by flashes of lightning and heavy rain. Here Pedro reestablishes his honor by killing the wolf with his bare hands.

*Tiefland* is not a very good film. It suffers from too much cutting. A technique which was very useful in creating suspense and interest in both *Triumph of the Will* and *Olympia* failed in this film with its melodramatic plot. The symbolism of innocence (lambs, mountains, etc.) versus corruption is oversimplified and predictable. While there are a number of excellent shots reminiscent of the higher photographic quality in *The Blue Light*, they are comparatively few in number. Moreover, many scenes were obviously shot in a studio. The character of the beggar girl Martha as the pinnacle of innocence and beauty is not convincing as a reality. It is only a dream. Riefenstahl herself felt that *Tiefland* failed to provide a good example of her excellent work. Shortly after the film was released in 1954, she withdrew it for twenty-five years. Beginning in January 1979, distribution resumed in the United States. The naiveté, of which she has frequently been accused, is demonstrated here by the fact that she builds up the theme that love conquers all without paying any attention to the social and economic circumstances which serve as determinants to the attraction between men and women. Thus Riefenstahl again shows herself to be an idealist. In *Tiefland* the idealistic principles—duty, goodness, simplicity, and honesty—win the day.

## Reception

*Tiefland* was not well-received by the German public. It was hardly noticed by the non-German public. This may have had something to do with the eclipse of Riefenstahl's reputation in 1954; but it is also attributable to the inherent weakness of the film itself. Artistic ambitions and the accuracy of her shots were praised by the German newspaper, the *Frankfurter Allgemeine;*[6] but other critics found a connection between the "undulating fogs" and the "undulating bosoms" in the film, describing it as sentimental and without class.[7] It was also judged to be a film possessing artistic and technical quality, though lacking epic interest.[8] Since the film had been withdrawn from circulation for twenty-five years and was only recently made available to American movie audiences, its reception in the United States cannot be assessed at this point.

# 7

# Unrealized Projects

IN COMPARISON with other well-known filmmakers, Riefenstahl has completed few films. In part this is due to her association with the Third Reich. After 1945 her life was characterized by a good deal of bad luck regarding her film projects. However, even films she had intended to do before 1945 were left incomplete.

In 1929 she began making plans for a film to be called *Die Schwarze Katze* (*The Black Cat*). The script was written by Dr. Fanck and, according to Riefenstahl, it was the best scenario he ever produced.[1] This was to be a mountain film, shot in the Dolomites, recording the experiences of cameraman Hans Schneeberger. The main theme was the dynamiting of Casteletto during World War I. At that time Schneeberger had been a lieutenant who maintained a strategic position with sixty men until the very last minute before the building was blown up. Every single man was buried in the rubble. Of the sixty soldiers only eight survived, and with these eight the lieutenant succeeded in maintaining the military position until relief arrived. It seems to have been a story of heroism and survival under difficult circumstances.

The title of the film referred to a woman, the daughter of a mountain guide, whose uncanny climbing abilities brought her the name "the black cat." Riefenstahl was supposed to play the part of the black cat, a part which she would have found just wonderful and which would also have proved artistically satisfying. We now see that she turned to *The Blue Light* because, in a sense, it compensated her for the fact that *Die schwarze Katze* had not been realized. Fanck failed to get financing for his script. He offered the scenario to Ufa, which rejected it, and it was subsequently rejected by other major film companies, because at that time war films were not considered desirable in Germany.

177

*Photo left: Leni Riefenstahl in her editing room in 1977*
Courtesy of Leni Riefenstahl-Produktion

There is an interesting historical footnote involving *Die schwarze Katze*. Luis Trenker, who was on several film crews with Riefenstahl and Hans Schneeberger, heard of the idea for the film. Since he had been in the same army unit in World War I as Schneeberger and also had participated in the events surrounding Casteletto, he stole the idea and wrote his own script, to be called "Berge in Flammen" ("Mountains on Fire") and converted it into a successful film before Fanck and Riefenstahl could even begin the realization of *Die schwarze Katze*. This led to a law suit which Trenker won and Harry Sokal, who owned the rights to *Die schwarze Katze* lost. *Berge in Flammen* became a very popular film in Germany.

According to Riefenstahl, all those who saw the manuscript liked the story, but nobody was interested in a war film in 1929. It was then that Fanck sat down to write a new script and within a single night produced the scenario for the film *Die weisse Hölle vom Piz Palü*, which he filmed instead and for which he found it easier to get financial backing.

In 1933 Riefenstahl became involved in a project called "Mademoiselle Docteur." This was a spy story, based upon real events and on the experiences of a real spy by that name who worked during World War I. Riefenstahl was interested in playing the part of the female spy, an idea that was again suggested to her by Fanck. She had always wanted interesting and challenging roles in films, and "Mademoiselle Docteur" surely would have been a fascinating acting experience. The project was to start immediately upon the return of Fanck and his crew from Greenland. Ufa had already agreed to support the film production; the scenario had been completed by Gerhard Menze; and G. W. Pabst or Franck Wysbar were to direct it. Hans Schneeberger was to be cameraman again. However, in the summer of 1933 the German War Ministry prohibited the production of this film on the grounds that a film on espionage would "reveal too much about the subject." In view of later events, this prohibition is ominous, because it suggests that the Third Reich had military plans as early as 1933, a suggestion which has been confirmed since. Ufa had already signed the agreement with Riefenstahl when she was informed that the film could not be made. Riefenstahl was told that the ban was not directed against her, but that it was a ban against all films dealing with espionage. In 1936 a film based upon the story of Mademoiselle Docteur was made in

France, under the direction of G. W. Pabst, with Dita Parlo playing the female lead.

After completing *Olympia,* Riefenstahl made plans to film *Penthesilea,* a project that surely was the most expensive failure for her. She had thought of filming *Penthesilea* for many years, in fact, ever since Max Reinhard had called her "his Penthesilea" in 1926, and she read all there was to read about the queen of the Amazons. She wrote three sets of production notes, dated August 7, 9, and 11, 1939. These extensive notes indicate what she had in mind with the project. *Penthesilea* was a favorite idea of hers, but she found that this material (based on Kleist's play), which presented the battle between the sexes in picture form, was not suitable as a stage play. In her opinion, Kleist's language was too antique to be believed, though she found it very beautiful. Riefenstahl also thought that Kleist's language was the reason why the play was so rarely performed. Undoubtedly, however, a major reason why *Penthesilea* is so rarely performed on the German stage is the enormous difficulty involved in staging a play with numerous battle scenes, long poetic speeches, and an untraditional subject matter. Riefenstahl wanted to turn it into a great film opera.

The plot of Kleist's play, summarized, is as follows. The Amazons attack the Trojans who are fighting the Greeks, and the latter thus find an unexpected ally. Wishing to make the Amazons their formal ally, the Greeks, represented by Ulysses and Achilles, meet Penthesilea, who rejects their proposal to become allies, and instead leads the Amazons against both the Greeks and the Trojans. She has a chance to kill Achilles in battle, but spares his life, because she has come to love him. When Achilles' chariot crashes in battle against the Amazons, Penthesilea pursues him, but he gets away as a result of a trick which forces Penthesilea and her Amazons to fall violently from a cliff. The battle between Achilles and Penthesilea now becomes passionate, and friends of both try to persuade them to discontinue the fight. Penthesilea continues to attack the Greeks, but at the same time directs her priestess to prepare the rose festival, during which the Amazons allow their captives to love them and beget children on them in order thus to assure the continuation of the Amazon tribe. Penthesilea has fallen in love with Achilles and has to defeat him in combat in order to lead him to the rose festival as her lover. However, Achilles wins in combat, and Penthesilea is in a suicidal mood. She has a chance to flee from her captivity but does not want to, since she loves Achilles. Her love for the man she has to defeat brings about an insoluble emotional conflict. The Greeks have routed the Amazons and Achilles gives orders to pursue and annihilate them. Penthesilea is unaware of this, since she has fainted. When she comes to and recognizes Achilles, she confesses her love for him and he does likewise. The Amazons have collected their forces and are attacking the Greeks in order to free their queen, but Penthesilea does not really want to leave; the Amazons then throw themselves between Achilles and Penthesilea, separate them and threaten the life of Achilles who is forcibly carried away by Ulysses. Penthesilea berates her Amazons for having freed her and separated her from Achilles. The latter, through a herald, challenges Penthesilea to a duel, knowing that she can love him only after she has defeated him in battle. Penthesilea misunderstands this voluntary submission, thinking it is a challenge, and she gets ready to kill him. In fact, she goes mad. Both Greeks and Amazons try to prevent this combat, the Amazons throwing themselves before Penthesilea to stop her. She has them driven away by dogs. Penthesilea meets the disarmed Achilles, who willingly has submitted himself to her so that she can lead him to the rose festival as her lover, something he desires because he loves her also. She fails to see Achilles' self-imposed weakness and murders him, literally dismembering his body with the dogs and drinking his blood. When she recovers from her madness and returns to reality, she dies out of sheer sorrow and a broken heart.

Riefenstahl thought that this story would make a good radio play or a great film, and she wanted to produce that great film. By the time World War II broke out (September 1, 1939)—at which time the project had to be shelved indefinitely—she had already engaged most of the actors, written the script, and laid out the plans in detail. Before she wrote the script, she read many books on the Amazons and repeatedly studied Kleist's play. She wanted the film to have historical authenticity. In addition, she intended to turn into images whatever was expressed in words, exactly as she was later to do in *Tiefland*. Referring to the well-known German film based upon Kleist's play *Der zerbrochene Krug* (*The Broken Pitcher*), starring Emil Jannings in the male lead, she decided that she did not want to produce filmed theater, which she found unartistic.

She had intended to shorten Kleist's play but wished to retain the beauty of the language and present the Amazons on the stage in a stylized manner, similar to the way she had seen them represented in Greek reliefs and other forms of sculpture. The acting was to be stylized especially in the scenes where the Amazons appear on the stage. She also intended to shoot the film in color, but very sparingly used, "graphically, like cave drawings."[2]

She wanted to stylize nature as well, showing a sun that would be ten times its normal size and oversized trees with extraordinary forms. All this was an attempt to bring form and content together. Riefenstahl maintains that Kleist's language is stylized and, hence, the cinematic form had to be stylized also. She had in mind the type of stylized sculpture that appeared in the prologue of *Olympia*, like the heads of Apollo or Alexander, with the difference that the sculptures in Penthesilea would suddenly come to life. The actors would have to speak while in darkness; the light would be switched off while the words are heard and turned on again when merely the stylized heads would be seen. She planned to have no language at all in the beginning of the film and to bring in only choruses of the female priests. The verses of Kleist were to be heard for the first time in her film only when Penthesilea and Achilles meet. All this indicates that she was well-prepared for shooting the film and, in fact, had already selected the place, Libya, where several scenes were photographed. Since she was to play Penthesilea herself, she received training in the sports that were required for the film. She learned to become a superb horsewoman who would be able to ride a horse without a saddle, sitting on it backward. The battle scenes were to be shot in Libya, and other scenes were to be photographed on the German island of Sylt in the Northern Sea.

By 1939, one hundred young women had already been trained to play the Amazons. Riefenstahl did not want girls to play the Amazons. Instead, she wanted real women who would be perceived by the spectator as real women. Apparently she had in mind women who were erotically attractive and in control of their own destinies, who could be as strong as men, who were dedicated to their profession, who could sustain hardship, feel love, assume responsibility, and live or die for a cause, in other words, complete human beings. Penthesilea would undoubtedly have been one of the most magnificent female characters in movie history. Compared to Riefenstahl's vision as it emerges from her program notes for the film, all attempts in modern cinema to create a superwoman or a wonderwoman appear pale and bloodless. Riefenstahl's Penthesilea was intended to be a goddess and a human superindividual, and characterized by royal dignity; she was to be unrestrained and possess a wild, feline nature. Riefenstahl visualized her as wavering from one extreme to the other: "The almost stylized element in her character that infuses her with something divine must again and again be relaxed and interrupted by an impulsive and wild temperament."[3]

Penthesilea would have fitted well into Riefenstahl's aesthetic universe, for she would have embodied beauty as well as strength, just as the athletes in *Olympia* or, later, the Nuba of Kau. Achilles—tall and handsome, according to the *Iliad* — was conceived as being blonde, with curly hair, a bit cruel and wild—and a true match for Penthesilea, who finally murders him in a fit of madness. Of special interest is Riefenstahl's idea of the scene in which the Amazons return from flight to attack the Greeks in order to free their queen, who is the prisoner of Achilles, whom she loves. This is the turning point in the play by Kleist, anticipating the fatal misunderstanding between Penthesilea and Achilles, both high-minded, strong, and beautiful, as well as proud individuals, willing to submit themselves to each other out of love, but prevented from doing so by their misunderstanding and the other members of their society. In this part of the film, the Dionysian element was to reach its climax. There would be an ominous silence first, according to Riefenstahl, and then there would follow a trembling of the universe, of the wind, the leaves, the grasses, the animals, the rippling of the water, of the dust on the ground—all in preparation of a violent storm. She had grand ideas about showing this storm as leaping flames, overflowing rivers, and splitting rocks. Penthesilea was to be shown as at one with these unleashed forces of nature; she was to appear like a mad maenad, her hair shooting out like snakes around her head, the incarnate daughter of Dionysos. Thus Penthesilea was seen to be related to, perhaps even the cause of, the upheaval of nature, which, by implication, would have shown her as a goddess, more powerful than any man she could love or defeat.

In planning this film, Riefenstahl wanted to emphasize the expressiveness of the gestures of the Greeks and the Amazons in order to show the atmosphere of a different age, the age of antiquity; for antiquity has always been closer to her than any other age. Riefenstahl even confessed that she felt as if there had been a transmigration of souls and that she had lived the life of Penthesilea at some previous time; in this sense, Kleist's Penthesilea spoke every word as if it had been from the depths of Riefenstahl's own soul. It is not hard to see how Riefenstahl—a self-assured woman, talented, fairly wealthy, famous, beautiful, healthy, athletic, a favorite with the authorities of her own country—would identify with a fictional character like Penthesilea.

The acting in *Penthesilea* was to be stylized, but there were also to be scenes in which "a woman really has to fall from a horse when a warrior grabs her," i.e., the actresses were not to be spared from difficult stunts. The stylization, in other words, would be produced as a result of photographic means, of the distribution of light and shadow, as well as the acting.

In 1943 she also had plans to make a film about Van Gogh. But nothing is known about that project. After completing *Tiefland*, she wanted to do a project called *Die roten Teufel* (*The Red Devils*). She had engaged Brigitte Bardot and Vittorio de Sica as actors. She herself was going to be the producer and the scenarist. Joachim Bartsch and Harald Reinl were to assist her with the script. The basic theme, according to Riefenstahl, was that of *Penthesilea*. However, she wanted the topic to be demonstrated on skis and in the form of a comedy, but essentially demonstrating a struggle between the sexes, as in *Penthesilea*. She had plans to shoot the film in color and introduce contrasting effects, showing the immobility of the snow-covered spaces and the movement provided by the skiers. The rivalry between a team of male and female skiers would provide the essential theme and permit her to develop images in three colors, the "reds" and the "blues" mixing on the immaculate whiteness of the snow, thus creating seductive, three-colored motifs. The script was completed by 1954 and preparations had been made for the shooting.

The completed script can be found in Leni Riefenstahl's personal archives. On the basis of her plans for this film, we can see that she was still under the influence of her early mountain films with Arnold Fanck. The main theme in *Die roten Teufel* was a competition between a team of Tyrolean Reds, a team of male skiers dressed in red (hence the name of the film), and a team of

Norwegian women skiers, dressed in blue, both groups having chosen to live in training huts high up on the mountain slopes, far away from the tourist accommodations of St. Paradiso, a winter resort, where this ski comedy was to be acted out. The principal characters were to be an Amazon-like woman, called Christa, captain of the women's team, and Michael, a skiing champion on the opposite team, with whom Christa, despite vigorous resistance, eventually falls in love. It seems that this film was to have provided Riefenstahl with an outlet for her nostalgia for the hard but good times she enjoyed as a skier and actress in the mountain films of the 1920's, before the advent of the Third Reich. Moreover, certain aspects of *Die roten Teufel* were reminiscent of the international flavor suffusing *Olympia*. According to Riefenstahl's own notes, the film would show the audience not only Americans, Germans, Austrians, Norwegians, Swiss, French, and Italians, but also Japanese, Indians, and other Orientals.

However, the project failed. In part this was the result of newspaper articles containing critical material about her. Announcements in newspapers read: "Taxpayers, watch out, here is money being spent for Leni Riefenstahl."[4] In reality, according to Riefenstahl, the financing of this feature film had been offered by distribution contracts with the Herzog Film Company. Bardot, at that time still unknown, had been recommended to her by Jean Cocteau. She had won Vittorio de Sica for this part because Caesare Zavatini, who had read the script in an Italian translation, convinced his friend and associate, Vittorio de Sica, to assume one of the principal parts.

Riefenstahl then pursued plans to make another mountain film, a mountain film in color. To be called *Ewige Gipfel* (*Eternal Summits*), it was to be a documentary about the first ascent of several famous mountain peaks by well-known climbers. In it Riefenstahl wanted to demonstrate that high mountan peaks will always have a great attraction for man.

In 1955 Jean Cocteau considered making a film about the German monarch Frederick the Great (1740-1786) and Voltaire, the French philosopher, who for many years was a close advisor and even friend of Frederick. This was to be called *Frederick and Voltaire*, and Jean Cocteau had planned to play both roles. The underlying theme was the love-hate relationship between the

Germans and the French which for centuries has characterized their political history.

Cocteau was planning to present the theme in his own way, wishing nevertheless to work under the direction of Leni Riefenstahl. Both he and Riefenstahl researched the subject, collected stories, and worked out several scenes at his villa on the French Riviera. Together they developed the form, but Riefenstahl could not find a distributor for such a film, and hence it was never made.

Another unrealized project, a somewhat new and unusual theme for Riefenstahl, was a film titled *Drei Sterne am Mantel der Madonna* (*Three Stars on the Cloak of the Madonna*). Anna Magnani was to play the Madonna, a mother of three sons, whose lives the film was to narrate. In the course of the film, she was to lose her sons, one by one, and the death of each one would be commemorated by a star sewn on her cloak. Magnani, however, feeling that she was too young for the role, declined to play the part and hence this project failed also.

In addition to these projects, Riefenstahl wrote scripts for a film, *Sol y Sombra* (*Sun and Shade*), a Spanish expression based upon the seating arrangements in a typical Spanish bullfighting arena. It was intended to be a documentary film about Spain. Finally, she had plans to make a film tentatively titled *Tanz mit dem Tod* (*Dance with Death*), the plot of which was to be located in Florence. The story was drawn from Riefenstahl's own experiences as a dancer and was to be based upon the life of Harald Kreuzberg, a famous dancer with whom Riefenstahl had performed in Berlin. It is not clear why these last projects were not realized.

One of the most interesting and mysterious unrealized projects is the film *Schwarze Fracht* (*Black Cargo*, 1956). It was to be co-directed by Riefenstahl, Africans, and Arabs. The script had been written by Riefenstahl herself, Kurt Heuser, and Helge Pawlinin, and it was based upon the book by Hans-Otto Meissner. Several shots of animals were made and a few scenes on a river were photographed before the project had to be shelved. The plot is concerned with a woman who, like Riefenstahl, found herself in an adventurous situation. Wishing to continue the work of her husband, who had mysteriously died while researching a primitive tribe in Africa, a woman anthropologist locates the tribe after a long and exciting search. She discovers that its members are being forced into slavery by Arab slave traders. With the help of a British undercover agent, she frees the enslaved tribe, while its members are being secretly transported to Arabia. She discovers that her husband had been murdered by the slave traders, and she learns from the natives that nearby is a cave with strange and mysterious letters scratched on the wall. These writing had precisely been the object of her husband's search, because they provided a key to the history of the peoples and culture of central Africa.

The *Black Cargo* project bore great significance for Riefenstahl, since she intended to shoot not merely a film, but put her talents in the service of a human cause. In her notes for this film, she pointed out that "men are hunted down and sold into slavery" in the darkest corner of the earth. She mentioned the fact that the Belgian missionary La Gravière had called this matter to the attention of the United Nations, as a result of which the slave problem of our age had become known to the public. "Each month up to 5000 blacks from equatorial Africa are abducted from their homes and sold primarily to the newly-rich oil sheiks in Arabia. A strong, young man or beautiful girl costs between $1,600 and $4,000."[5] The United Nations and the Anti-Slavery Society failed to stop the hunting and trading of slaves, whose cries for help went unheard in the vast impenetrable spaces of the central African bush. Riefenstahl ostensibly wanted to make her film *Black Cargo* in order to turn the attention of the civilized world to the problem of the slave trade. This seemed a worthy cause for Riefenstahl's film talents, and it is a pity that numerous misfortunes and financial difficulties ultimately forced her to abandon the whole project. The wary reader will wonder why Riefenstahl did not turn her attentions to the many people who were abducted into another kind of slavery by the Nazis, a kind of slavery which, as we now know, was at least as horrible and worthy of our protests as the slavery imposed by Arabian oil sheiks upon the men and women of equatorial Africa. If Riefenstahl really did not know the existence of concentration camps until after World War II, as she has frequently claimed, she seems to have wanted to make amends for that ignorance by calling our attention to the iniquities prevailing in central Africa.

In 1960, Riefenstahl received an offer from the British firm of Production Adventure, which wanted to produce a remake of *The*

*Blue Light.* In collaboration with Ron Hubbard and Philip Hud-
smith, she wrote an entirely new script, quite different from the
original. The film was to be made in the style of a ballet film. It was
intended to be a fairy tale in dance and color, reminiscent of *The
Red Shoes*; but again the project failed to materialize.

By 1973, Riefenstahl was working on a film about the Mesakin
Nuba in Central Africa. To this day the film has not been
completed, one reason being that the exposed material was ruined
as a result of a technical error in a film processing laboratory. The
footage, shot in the late 1960s, had been submerged in the wrong
kind of chemicals by the film processing laboratory which
developed it, turning much of the material green. Riefenstahl had
shot at least twelve hours worth of material, of which, in her
opinion, 18,000 feet are still worth turning into a film, that is to say,
she had enough footage for a nine hour movie. For sound she
wanted to use much music, singing, and speaking, and she herself
has already synchronized whatever has been completed as film.
Riefenstahl herself had learned the language of the Mesakin Nuba.
Since a large part of the material in this film is of a scientific nature,
it needed a good deal of elaborate explanation. Yet Riefenstahl
dislikes superimposed narration in a film, and this is another reason
why she has so far failed to complete her film on the Nuba. The
footage was shot on 16mm, for financial reasons, and she hopes to
be able to blow it up to 35mm. Those who have viewed sections of
it are enthusiastic. However, only excerpts have been shown so far.
The B.B.C. has telecast sections of the Nuba film in connection
with a documentary on Leni Riefenstahl. It is not clear if the film,
once completed and distributed, will only deal with the Mesakin
Nuba or include also footage taken of the Nuba in Kau who live
southeast of the Mesakin Nuba territory, and whom Riefenstahl
celebrates in her second book on the African tribe, *The People of
Kau*. In the absence of the completed Nuba film, we have to rely on
the two books about the tribe containing rare and beautiful stills, in
order to determine what Riefenstahl had in mind when she
exposed herself to considerable hardships and dangers while
searching for and ultimately photographing the Nuba. While the
Mesakin Nuba were friendly and approachable from the
beginning, the Nuba of Kau made it extremely difficult for
Riefenstahl and her assistant, Horst Kettner, to take pictures of
them. As a matter of fact, only after her assistant eased the pain

Photo top: Leni Riefenstahl among the Masakin Nuba in 1968 or 1969
Courtesy of Leni Riefenstahl-Produktion

caused by the severe wounds of one Nuba fighter, was it possible
for Riefenstahl to become acquainted with the Nuba of Kau. The
two tribes speak entirely different languages and are, in fact, two
different peoples, distinguished by their way of life which
civilization, as Riefenstahl knows it, does not cherish. The Nuba of
Kordofan (Mesakin) who, as a result of encroaching civilization,
had completely lost their ancient way of life by 1974, knew no
theft, discord, and major illnesses when Riefenstahl first began to
live with them. They lived in complete harmony, according to
Riefenstahl, something which she has implicitly and explicitly
admired as an ideal and tried to express in her cinematic work. The
Nuba of Kau also live according to principles cherished by
Riefenstahl. Among these is the celebration of the human body
which Riefenstahl repeatedly emphasizes in her book on the Nuba
of Kau. "Their use of form and colour sprang from the very fount of
art. Girls and men alike, they made a genuine cult of their bodies,"
Riefenstahl writes, referring, among other things, to the highly
developed art of body painting among the Nuba. She also admired

their courage, even heroism, most noticeable whenever they had to endure pain. This was especially true of the women, who had to undergo a tatooing procedure three times in their lives. The men, many of whom spent about ten years of their lives as fierce fighters, frequently subjected themselves to the most savage stabbings and knife blows, not to wage war and conquer territory, but simply to win applause for their strength and physical prowess. In fact, both books on the Nuba constitute a celebration of the beauty and glory of the healthy and young human body. Implicit in Riefenstahl's work of the distant and more recent past is a certain disapproval of modern civilization which allows the human body to become weak and flabby. The clearest expression of her appreciation of the beauty of the healthy body is in *Olympia*. While there may be those who claim that making a cult of the body is an activity with Fascist tendencies, such a claim would surely be spurious with respect to the Nuba, whose uninterrupted isolation from Western civilization made it difficult, not to say impossible, to hear of a Hitler or Mussolini.

Riefenstahl's recent activities, including her unrealized projects, indicate that she essentially adhered to the same principles and themes which characterized her early work. She always admired physical beauty, disliked civilization, and sought a life away from civilization; she praised suffering and hardship as a form of strengthening body and soul, thus holding on to the belief that the human body is essentially subject to the power of the human will.

# Notes and References

## Chapter One

1. Andrew Sarris, *Interviews with Film Directors* (Indianapolis, 1968), p. 394.

2. Glenn Infield, *Leni Riefenstahl* (New York, 1976), p. 14.

3. Sarris, p. 400.

4. Ibid.

5. *Kampf in Schnee und Eis* (Leipzig, 1933), p. 32, hereafter cited in the text as *K*.

6. Arnold Fank, *Er führte Regie mit Gletschern, Stürmen, Lawinen* (Munich, 1973), pp. 157-58.

7. Sarris, p. 388

8. Ibid.

9. *From Caligari to Hitler* (Princeton, 1947), p. 257.

10. Ulrich Gregor and Enno Patalas, *Geschichte des Films* (Reinbek bei Hamburg, 1976), I, 61.

11. Sarris, p. 389.

12. Ibid.

13. Infield, p. 229.

14. Ernst Hanfstaengl, *Unheard Witness* (Philadelphia, 1957), p. 203.

15. Communicated to the author in a personal interview on July 28, 1979.

16. Gordon Hitchens, "Interview with a Legend," *Film Comment*, Winter, 1965, p. 8.

17. B.B.C. interview, 1972.

18. Infield, p. 66.

19. Sarris, p. 392.

20. David Hull, *Film in the Third Reich* (New York, 1973), p. 23.

21. Ibid.

22. Ibid., p. 53.

23. Karl Loewenstein, Hitler's Germany: *The Nazi Background to War* (New York, 1939), p. 75.

24. Infield, p. 78.

25. Loewenstein, p. 5.

26. Abba Eban, *My People: The Story of the Jews* (New York, 1968), p. 393.

27. Communicated to the author in a personal interview on July 28, 1979, in New York.

28. Sarris, p. 394.

29. From the interview described in note 27.

30. Documents in the Archives of the Federal Republic of Germany in Koblenz indicate that a Mr. Ott, a subordinate of Goebbels, had many complaints about Riefenstahl's spendthrift ways. Goebbels simply shrugged them off, insisting that one should not be "petty." See R 55/503.

31. Interview with the author on July 28, 1979 (see note 26).

32. *Film Comment*, Winter, 1965, p. 25.

33. Infield, p. 187.

34. Infield, p. 188. According to David Hinton, *The Films of Leni Riefenstahl* (Metuchen, N.J., 1978), p. 151, it appears that Riefenstahl's telegram to Hitler, congratulating him on his march into Paris in 1940, was not considered an authentic document by postwar German authorities, because Riefenstahl's message was not printed on official telegram stationery. The telegram is on file at the Berlin Document Center.

35. According to Glenn Infield, this comment appears in File R 109 III/Vork. 16 of the Bundesarchiv, Koblenz. However, when I went to check the records, this file had been removed.

36. Interrogation Report PWB/SAIC 13, National Archives, Washington, D.C.

37. Herman Weigel, "Interview mit Leni Riefenstahl," *Filmkritik*, no. 188 (August 1972), 410.

38. "Blut und Hoden," *Der Spiegel*, no. 44 (1976), 228-32.

39. Charles Ford, *Leni Riefenstahl* (Paris, 1978), pp. 152-53.

## Chapter Two

1. Oskar Kalbus, *Vom Werden deutscher Filmkunst* (Altona-Bahrenfeld, Germany, 1935), I, 91.

2. Fanck, p. 136 and passim.

3. 21, no. 6 (1924).

4. Kalbus, I, 92.

5. Fanck, p. 161.

6. Hinton, p. 8.

7. Communicated to the author by Henry Jaworsky in a personal interview on July 28, 1979, in New York.

8. Mark Sorki, "Six Talks with G. W. Pabst," *Cinemages*, 3 (1955), 12.

9. In a rather hostile letter addressed to the German magazine *Der Spiegel*, Sokal accused Riefenstahl of having become an anti-Semite

overnight, after reading Hitler's *Mein Kampf.* Riefenstahl denies the charge. See *Der Spiegel,* no. 46 (1976), 14, and no. 47 (1976), 18.

10. Kracauer, p. 258.
11. Sarris, p. 456.
12. 15, no. 2003 (1933).
13. Kalbus, II, 37.
14. Ibid.
15. Ulrich Gregor and Enno Patalas, *Geschichte des Films* (Reinbek bei Hamburg, 1976), I, 61.

## Chapter Three

1. Sarris, p. 338.
2. Herman Weigel, "Interview mit Leni Riefenstahl," *Filmkritik,* August 1972, p. 437.
3. Gordon Hitchens, "Henry Jaworsky Interviewed," *Film Culture,* Spring, 1973, p. 129.
4. Weigel, p. 437.
5. Communicated to the author by Henry Jaworsky during an interview on July 28, 1979, in New York.
6. L. Andrew Mannheim, "Leni," *Modern Photography,* February 1972, p. 117.
7. Interview on B.B.C., June 1972.
8. *Newsweek,* September 16, 1974, p. 91.
9. *Filmkritik,* August 1972, p. 398.
10. Kracauer, p. 259.
11. (Berkeley, 1969), p. 11.
12. Ibid., p. 17.
13. (New York, 1970), p. 56.
14. Ibid., p. 58.
15. Ibid., p. 33.
16. Eisner, p. 313.
17. Gregor and Patalas, II, 144.

## Chapter Four

1. Interview reported in Kevin Brownlow, *Film: The Magazine of the Federation of Film Societies* (London), no. 47 (1966). Riefenstahl later on denied having exactly said this about Ruttman's work. See *Filmkritik,* August, 1972, p. 433, n.
2. Herman Weigel, "Randbemerkungen zum Thema," *Filmkritik,* August, 1972, p. 428.

3. *New York Times,* April 16, 1933, sec. 4, p. 2.

4. "We National Socialists do not place any particular value on seeing our SA march across the stage or the screen. Their area is the street. But anybody approaching the solution of National Socialist problems in the field of art, has to realize that...in this case art does not derive from the will but from ability. A National Socialist attitude ostentatiously exhibited does not by any means serve as a substitute for a lack of true art. The National Socialist government has never required the production of specifically SA films. On the contrary, it even sees a danger in an excess of them. But if a film wants to present the experiences of our SA or the National Socialist idea, this film has to be of the foremost artistic quality. Therefore, it is not easy but, on the contrary, extremely difficult, because it is an obligation to the entire nation to make an SA film. The task posed to the maker requires the use of the best talents, and only truly great artists can solve it. National Socialists do not condone artistic failure under any circumstances. On the contrary, the greater the idea which is represented in artistic form, the higher are the artistic demands made upon it." (Joseph Goebbels in a speech made on the birthday of Horst Wessel in 1933, quoted in Oskar Kalbus, *Vom Werden deutscher Filmkunst,* II, p. 119.)

5. Sarris, pp. 391ff. In this interview, Riefenstahl commented on her flagpost elevators: "In this way one day I had a little elevator installed on one of the great masts that carried oriflammes that would rise to the top and thanks to which my camera was able to effect, at any given moment, a movement that I considered rather successful."

6. See *Hinter den Kulissen,* p. 16, where Riefenstahl claims, in contradiction to allegations elsewhere, that "preparations were being made already in May."

7. On ibid., p. v, we read: "District Leader of Franken [Frankenführer] Streicher helped us over many difficulties. Through the cooperation of the city of Nuremberg it was possible to aid the totally novel exploitation of all technical means for the film. All the resources we needed, down to the street cars and fire ladders, were placed at our disposal by Oberbürgermeister [mayor] Liebel." According to Riefenstahl and others, the brochure was ghostwritten by Ernst Jaeger. In fact, a check for 1000 marks, made out to Ernst Jaeger, presumably for this service, is on view at the Federal Archives in Koblenz. No matter who actually wrote the brochure, Riefenstahl took the credit, and the work probably provides the best information on the composition of the crew and methods of shooting the film.

8. Ibid., p. 28. See also Leni Riefenstahl, "Wie wir *Triumph des Willens* drehten," *Die Woche,* no. 41 (October 13, 1934), 1130-32.

9. The observant viewer of *Triumph of the Will* will notice that the cameramen are quite visible throughout the film. We detected at least twelve sequences where they are obviously going about doing their work. If the party congress had been staged solely for the benefit of the cameras, more care would have been taken to camouflage all or many of the cameramen who are especially visible in scene 11. At one point we can even see Leni Riefenstahl herself, wearing a black sweater and white skirt.

10. Infield, p. 103.

11. *Hinter den Kulissen*, p. 13.

12. Riefenstahl indirectly admits this when she says that *Triumph of the Will* can be used as propaganda. See *Filmkritik*, August, 1972.

13. Folke Isaksson and Leif Fuhrhammar, *Politik und Film* (Ravensburg, 1974), p. 185.

14. See Richard Barsam, *Film Guide to Triumph of the Will* (Bloomington, 1975).

15. Ibid., p. 62.

16. The text of the "Horst Wessel Lied," a song about a young Nazi student and storm trooper, killed in 1930, who left a marching song based on familiar party melodies, is as follows:

Die Fahne hoch! Die Reihen dicht geschlossen
SA marschiert mit ruhig festem Schritt.
Kameraden, die Rot-Front und Reaktion erschossen
Marschier'n im Geiste in unser'n Reihen mit.

Die Strasse frei den braunen Bataillonen
Die Strasse frei dem Sturmabteilungsmann.
Es schau'n auf's Hakenkreuz voll Hoffnung schon Millionen
Der Tag für Freiheit und für Brot bricht an.

Zum letzten Mal wird jetzt Alarm geblasen
Zum Kampfe steh'n wir alle schon bereit.
Bald wehn Hitlerfahnen über alle Strassen
Die Knechtschaft dauert nur noch kurze Zeit.

Die Fahne hoch! Die Reihen dicht geschlossen,
SA marschiert mit ruhig festem Schritt.
Kameraden, die Rot-Front und Reaktion erschossen,
Marschier'n im Geiste in unseren Reihen mit.

*The Banner High!* (English translation by the author. No attempt has been made to imitate the rhyme and rhythm in the English version.)

> The Banner High! Tightly closed are our ranks
> SA is marching with its solid tread
> Comrades shot by the Red-Front and the Reaction
> Are, in spirit, marching with us.
>
> Clear the street for the brown battalions
> Clear the street for the man from the SA
> Millions look upon the swastika full of hope
> The day of freedom and for bread begins to dawn.
>
> The alarm is sounded for the last time
> We are all ready for the battle.
> Soon the Hitler flags will hang above all streets
> Servitude will last only a little longer.
>
> The banner high! Tightly closed are our ranks
> SA is marching with its solid tread.
> Comrades which were shot by the Red-Front and the Reaction
> Are, in spirit, marching with us.

17. In German the text reads: "Am 5. September, 1934, 20 Jahre nach Ausbruch des Weltkrieges, sechzehn Jahre nach Deutschland's Niederlage, neunzehn Monate nach dem Beginn der Deutschen Renaissance, flog Adolf Hitler wieder nach Nürnberg um die Reihen seiner treuen Anhänger zu besichtigen."

18. The plane shown in the sky was not Hitler's, but as a result of skillful editing, Riefenstahl gives the impression that the plane had carried Hitler himself.

19. See Barsam, p. 33, who writes that Hitler here is shown as "a man above men as well as a leader whose powers are vested both in his personal popularity and in the combined strength of his faithful troops."

20. Among other songs, we hear the well-known "Drunten im Unterland" and "Rosenstock, holder blüh."

21. For the English version of the entire speech, see Barsam, pp. 39-40.

22. The phrase "Red Front and reaction killed" is from a line from the "Horst Wessel Lied."

23. The German title is "Wir sind Arbeitssoldaten."

24. Barsam, p. 46.

25. In *Hinter den Kulissen*, (p. 23) Riefenstahl admitted that only the most beautiful faces of the Hitler youth were sought out by her and her cameramen.

26. Most commentators, including Siegfried Kracauer, insist that they only see blonde Germans in the film. But—as a somewhat accurate reflection of the physical attributes of the Germans themselves—the film shows a mixture of many brown-haired and blond young, middle-aged, and old people. Blonde is by no means the predominant hair color in the film.

27. It is strange that Riefenstahl, a woman, paid no attention to women at all in this film. There were many women's organizations in Nazi Germany, such as the B.D.M. (Bund deutscher Mädchen), and others, but the fact is that throughout the two hours of the film women are shown at most for two minutes, and even then they appear only as spectators, watching the proceedings from windows or participating as costumed peasants from one of the German regions.

28. In seventeenth- and eighteenth-century Europe, the monarch was considered to be God's representative on earth. Hitler is obviously alluding to that idea.

29. In the film *Star Wars*, the last scene is quite reminiscent of this particular scene in *Triumph of the Will*: the aisle, where the heroes march down, flanked by faithful partisans on both sides, seems to be an imitation of Riefenstahl's famous shot.

30. For the background of this entire affair see Alan Bullock, *Hitler: A Study in Tyranny* (New York, 1971), pp. 242-43.

31. Riefenstahl's original intention in this sequence had called for a scene in which Hitler, Himmler, and Lutze would be followed by the camera mounted on a small car. But the SA cleared the roadway (although she had permission to take the shot this way), and inadvertently also sent her camera car away. While she was not able to take the shot as planned, she nevertheless managed to capture one of the most memorable scenes in the entire film with her own camera mounted in an elevator which moved in one of the flag masts holding the battle standards behind the speakers' platform. In several instances the spectator can see this elevator moving up and down the mast.

32. The wish to impose her own will upon that of Hitler was, however indirectly, expressed by her in an interview with a German magazine in which she complains that "everybody only thinks of Hitler when they think of me. How about my work? Does it count for nothing?" See *Der Stern*, no. 35 (August 18, 1977), 41.

33. See Barsam, pp. 62-63.

34. The reference to "blood," while ominous in view of later implementations of Nazi racial politics, is somewhat disingenuous, since Hitler him-

self was probably half-Jewish or, at any rate, not pure German blood.

35. The comment about the mustering out and the discarding of what is alien to the Nazi party indicates that Hitler was planning to tighten the rules regarding admission to his party.

36. During the candid close-ups in this sequence, we see that Hermann Goering, for one, had not memorized the words of the "Horst Wessel Lied."

37. In an interview printed in *Der Stern*, Riefenstahl is reported as "admitting bravely that she was enthusiastic about Hitler" (*Der Stern*, no. 35 [August 18, 1977], 41.)

38. In *Hinter den Kulissen* (p. 28), Riefenstahl writes, "Thus there arises above the basic motif of this victorious title a film from the German present . . . a triumphal march of recognition, of courage, of power for our German people to fight and win," although she fails to specify against whom the German people fight and over whom or what they win.

39. *Die Zeit*, no. 48 (November 24, 1978).

40. Sarris, p. 392.

41. Infield, p. 227.

42. Barsam, p. 67.

43. Eisner, p. 337.

44. *New York Review of Books*, February 6, 1975, pp. 23-30.

45. Kracauer, p. 300.

46. "The Film Till Then," in *The Film Till Now*, ed. Paul Rotha (London, 1949), pp. 590-91.

47. Hull, pp. 139-40. Judging by the recent interest in Riefenstahl's work, it seems that Hull's prediction has come true.

48. Robert Vas, *Sight and Sound*, no. 32 (Autumn, 1963), 201.

49. Gregor, pp. 24-25.

50. Barsam, p. 72. New books on Riefenstahl, notably by Charles Ford and David Hinton, are more favorable to Riefenstahl and her work.

51. See *Newsweek*, November 29, 1976, p. 72.

52. Interview, B.B.C., June 1972.

53. Infield, p. 105.

## Chapter Five

1. Speer, p. 72.

2. Ibid., p. 80.

3. Ibid., p. 70.

4. Infield, p. 114.

5. Ibid., p. 115.

6. Bundesarchiv, Koblenz, File Number R 4311/731, p. 102.

7. Ibid., File Number R2/4788, pp. 433, 435.

8. For the complete agreement see Infield, pp. 116-17.

9. Communicated by Henry Jaworsky to the author in an interview on July 28, 1979, in New York.

10. Gordon Hitchens, "Interview with Leni Riefenstahl," *Film Culture.* Spring, 1973, p. 104.

11. Sarris, p. 465. Many other details about the techniques that Riefenstahl's crew devised for the film are discussed in this interview.

12. Infield, pp. 118-19 and note.

13. Hull, p. 74.

14. Bundesarchiv, Koblenz, File Number R 55/503, p. 52.

15. Sarris, p. 397.

16. Ibid.

17. Hull, p. 133.

18. Sarris, p. 396.

19. Gordon Hitchens, "An Interview with a Legend," *Film Comment,* Winter, 1965, p. 9.

20. Sarris, pp. 394-95.

21. Henry Jaworsky in an interview with the author on July 28, 1979, in New York.

22. Infield, p. 126.

23. Aesthetically, Riefenstahl is a formalist. What she means here is that the beauty of the form should generate interest in the content of an action. Instead of showing the record of a sprinter in terms of figures, for instance, Riefenstahl photographs the slender, sinewy legs, as she did in the case of Jesse Owens. It is these legs, in other words, which are responsible for bringing about the sprinter's world record (Hitchens, *Film Culture,* Winter, 1965, p. 9).

24. Hull, p. 132.

25. Hitchens, *Film Culture,* Winter, 1965, p. 9.

26. Sarris, p. 395.

27. Infield, p. 134.

28. Henry Jaworsky, as quoted in *Film Culture,* Spring, 1973, p. 173.

29. Hitchens, *Film Culture,* Spring, 1973, p. 181.

30. Infield, p. 131.

31. Communicated to the author by Henry Jaworsky during an interview on July 28, 1979, in New York.

32. While most of the time the faces of the divers are not directly visible, the photography, almost always in shots against the light, makes it clear that the bodies of Caucasians and occasionally Japanese dominate the scene.

33. Eisner, p. 336.

34. *Hollywood Citizen News,* December 12, 1938.

35. *Helsingin Sanomat,* August 8, 1938.

36. *Svenska Dagbladet* (Stockholm), July 17, 1938.

37. *Berner Tageblatt,* May 14, 1938.

38. *Liberté* (Paris), July 5, 1938.

39. *Esti Ujsas* (Budapest), September 9, 1938; *Het Nationale Dagblad* (Leiden), August 8, 1938.

40. *La Stampa* (Turin), August 28, 1938.

41. *Vestkysten*, August 3, 1938.

42. *Le Vingtième* (Brussels), June 24, 1938.

43. Infield, p. 147.

44. No. 11, May 1938.

45. I refer the reader to the most popular version of *Olympia* distributed in the United States, including the print available at the Museum of Modern Art, New York. The commentator, the well-known British announcer Marshall from B.B.C., frequently used the words "fight," "a dangerous rival," "victory," and other expressions relating to struggle and competition.

46. Leni Riefenstahl, "Statement on Sarris/Gessner Quarrel about *Olympia*," *Film Comment*, Fall, 1967, p. 126.

## Chapter Six

1. Hull, p. 138.

2. Infield, pp. 191-93.

3. See Bundesarchiv, Koblenz, File Number R55/69, p. 31.

4. Herman Weigel, "Interview mit Leni Riefenstahl," *Filmkritik*, August 1972, p. 407.

5. Ibid., p. 408.

6. April 28, 1954.

7. *Deutsche Zeitung*, February 17, 1954.

8. *Filmwoche*, February 6, 1954.

## Chapter Seven

1. Herbert Linder, "Riefenstahl Filmographie," *Filmkritik*, August 1972, p. 435.

2. Herman Weigel, "Interview mit Leni Riefenstahl," *Filmkritik*, August 1972, p. 406.

3. Leni Riefenstahl, "Notizen zu *Penthesilea*," *Filmkritik*, August 1972, p. 416. A translation of Riefenstahl's notes to *Penthesilea* can be found in *Film Culture*, Spring 1973, pp. 194-215.

4. *Filmkritik*, August 1972, p. 440.

5. Hinton, p. 129.

# Selected Bibliography

## Primary Sources

1. Books

*Hinter den Kulissen des Reichsparteitagsfilms.* Munich: Zentralverlag der
NSDAP, 1935. Though Riefenstahl claimed credit for this publication
by having her name printed as the author of it, this brochure, describing in detail the making of *Triumph of the Will,* was ghostwritten by
Ernst Jaeger, editor of the *Illustrierter Film Kurier,* who was paid 1000
marks for his services.

*Kampf in Schnee und Eis.* Leipzig: Hesse und Becker, 1933. Herein are
contained Riefenstahl's memoirs concerning her role and experiences
during her early years as a film actress and director up to 1933. It
describes in some detail the joys and tribulations suffered by her and
her film crews in the mountains in order to obtain beautiful pictures.

*Schönheit im Olympischen Kampf.* Berlin: Deutsch Verlag, 1937. Consisting primarily of stills from the film *Olympia,* this book contains
a preface in which Riefenstahl emphasizes that not victories but beauty,
grace, and strength were the principles which inspired her to make
this film. She also mentions the difficulties she had in getting close to
the athletes with her cameras. This book also seems to have been ghostwritten by Ernst Jaeger.

*The Last of the Nuba.* New York: Harper & Row, 1974. Originally published in German in 1968, this was Riefenstahl's first book-length publication on her life and work among the Nuba tribe in Africa. It consists primarily of fantastic and candid shots of the tribesmen and
women with a text explaining the life and customs of the Nuba.

*The People of Kau.* New York: Harper & Row, 1976. Riefenstahl's second
book on the Nuba, containing more stills and texts regarding her work
among the tribe in Africa, was originally published in Germany in 1976.

2. Periodical Articles

"Nie Antisemitin gewesen." *Der Spiegel,* no. 47 (1976), 18. A letter to the
   German newsmagazine in which she denies having ever being anti-
   Semitic. She claims that she told Hitler that she abhorred his race
   theories and denies having read *Mein Kampf* before April, 1932.
"Statement on Sarris/Gessner Quarrel about Olympia." *Film Comment,*
   Fall, 1967, p. 126. This is Riefenstahl's response to articles in *Variety*
   and *Village Voice* commenting on the first showing of *Olympia* at the
   Museum of Modern Art, New York. Riefenstahl quotes two completely
   contradictory critiques of *Olympia.*

3. Interviews

LENI RIEFENSTAHL Part I and Part II (One half-hour each; 16mmcolor/
   sound films).
   Produced by CAMERA THREE at WCBS-TV (New York City) for
   broadcast by the CBS Television Network.
   (Produced and directed by John Musilli. Written by Stephan Cho-
   dorov.) Original broadcast dates: April 1, April 8, 1973.
   Subsequently rebroadcast on the series CAMERA THREE over the
   PBS Network: 2/7/80, 2/14/80. The interview covers her entire
   career and is essentially presented as a monologue by Leni Riefenstahl,
   intercut with stills from her various films.

### Secondary Sources

1. Filmography

LINDER, H. "Filmography of Leni Riefenstahl." *Filmkritik,* August 1972,
   pp. 435-441. Though in German, it is the most recent and most accurate filmography of all of Riefenstahl's films, including those in which
   she acted and which she directed.

2. Books

BALÁZS, BÉLA. *Theory of Film.* New York: Dover Publications, 1970.
   One of the first works dealing with the theory of film, bridging the
   eras of silent and sound film. Sections of the original version were
   written in 1924 before Balázs collaborated with Riefenstahl on *The
   Blue Light.* These provide special insight into the use of close-ups in
   Riefenstahl's films.
BARSAM, RICHARD M. *Filmguide to Triumph of the Will.* Bloomington:
   Indiana University Press, 1975. Providing a shot-by-shot analysis of

*Triumph of the Will*, this first book-length description of Riefenstahl's most controversial film provides a fair assessment of its director's artistic accomplishment.

BENTLEY, ERIC, ed. *The Classical Theater.* Vol. 2. *Five German Plays.* New York: Doubleday Anchor Books, 1959. Contains an English translation of Kleist's *Penthesilea*, the play which so long fascinated Leni Riefenstahl.

BUCHER, FELIX. *Screen Series: Germany.* New York: A. S. Barnes, 1970. Although by no means complete, this book provides useful data about the German film and is one of the most accessible reference works on the subject.

EISNER, LOTTE. *The Haunted Screen.* Berkeley: University of California Press, 1969. By far the best book on the German expressionist film. Eisner is extremely critical of Riefenstahl, always questioning the originality of her cinematic accomplishments.

FANCK, ARNOLD. *Er führte Regie mit Gletschern, Stürmen, Lawinen.* Munich: Nymphenburger Verlagshandlung, 1973. These memoirs provide many anecdotes and interesting details regarding Fanck's role in the German film industry. On occasion, Fanck's statements contradict those of Riefenstahl, and in general, Fanck is bitter about his comparative eclipse in the German film industry.

FORD, CHARLES. *Leni Riefenstahl.* Paris: La Table Ronde, 1978. Ford's discussion of Riefenstahl's life and work is brief and contains very little new material. The author argues that Riefenstahl's talent as a filmmaker has been ignored because of her involvement with the powers of the Third Reich.

GREGOR, ULRICH, AND PATALAS, ENNO. *Geschichte des Films.* 2 vols. Reinbek bei Hamburg: Rowohlt, 1976. The authors, both well-known German film historians, here provide a conspectus of the history of film. Tending toward the political left, the authors are highly critical of Riefenstahl's work.

HANFSTAENGL, ERNST. *Unheard Witness.* Philadelphia: J. B. Lippincott Company, 1957. Hanfstaengl's memoirs, in addition to throwing much light upon Hitler's character during his rise to power (1920-34), contain an often-quoted passage describing the allegedly first meeting between Hitler and Riefenstahl in 1932.

HARDENBERG, FRIEDRICH FREIHERR VON. *Henry von Ofterdingen.* Translated by Palmer Hilty. New York: Frederick Ungar, 1964. A novel by Novalis (pseud.), this is a fairly recent translation of a famous work, originally published in 1802, which features the myth of the blue flower. It merits reading, if only for an understanding of German cultural history.

HINTON, DAVID. *The Films of Leni Riefenstahl.* Metuchen, N.J.: Scarecrow Press, 1978. The most recent English-language book-length discussion of Riefenstahl's work. Its author is concerned with a rehabilitation of Riefenstahl's reputation as a great film director.

HULL, DAVID STEWART. *Film in the Third Reich.* New York: Simon and Schuster, 1973. The best general analysis of films produced during the Third Reich. While there are occasional errors, the work serves as a good introduction and reference work on Nazi film.

INFIELD, GLENN. *Leni Riefenstahl: the Fallen Film Goddess.* New York: Thomas Y. Crowell, 1976. Written by an American ex-pilot, the work constitutes the first book-length biography of Leni Riefenstahl. Unfortunately, it contains many errors and is definitely intended to denounce Riefenstahl once and for all. Riefenstahl has tried to prevent its translation into German.

ISAKSSON, FOLKE, AND FUHRHAMMAR, LEIF. *Politik und Film.* Ravenburg: Otto Maier, 1976. A fine book. Originally published in Swedish, it deals with the relationship between politics and film on an international level. The book merits translation into English.

KALBUS, OSKAR. *Vom Werden deutscher Filmkunst.* 2 vols. Berlin: Ross Verlag, 1935. One of the most important books on the early years of the German film. It discusses the most important films made between 1919 and 1934, providing the reader with analysis of plot, background, acting, and directing. Unfortunately, it is not easily available in the U.S. It merits translation into English.

KRACAUER, SIEGFRIED. *From Caligari to Hitler.* Princeton: Princeton University Press, 1947. This famous psychological study of German films up to 1933 contains several errors regarding Riefenstahl's films and is open to attack because of its author's thesis regarding the relationship between German mountain films and their function as the harbingers of the Third Reich. Nevertheless, it is a seminal study.

MANDELL, RICHARD. *The Nazi Olympics.* New York: Macmillan, 1971. The most complete description and analysis in English of the 1936 Olympic Games in Germany, including the Winter Olympics in Garmisch-Partenkirchen. Although there are several errors of fact, especially with respect to Leni Riefenstahl, the book provides a useful guide to the background and details surrounding the eleventh Olympiad.

SARRIS, ANDREW, ed. *Interviews with Film Directors.* Indianapolis: Bobbs Merrill, 1968. Sarris edits a series of interviews with film directors. The interview with Riefenstahl printed here was originally conducted by the French critic Michael Delahaye and published in *Cahiers du Cinéma* [September, 1965] as "Leni et le loup." It was reprinted in *Cahiers du Cinéma* (no. 5) [1966]) with an English translation by Rose Kaplin.

SPEER, ALBERT. *Inside the Third Reich*. New York: Macmillan, 1970. Since Speer was the principal architect for Hitler and participated actively in many films made during the Third Reich, his memoirs are important for any study of any aspect of the Nazi era. Before meeting Speer for the first time, Riefenstahl had collected newspaper clippings about him, which she showed him in 1934.

3. Periodical Articles and Other Sources

BARKHAUSEN, HANS. "Footnote to the History of Riefenstahl's *Olympia*." *Film Quarterly*, Fall 1974, pp. 8-12. Deals with the financial backing of the Olympia Film Co. which was established by the NSDAP in order to produce the filmed Olympiad.

BISHOP, CHRISTOPHER. Speech given to the Toronto Film Society at its Sixth Exhibition Meeting, February 3, 1957, Capitol Theater, Toronto. This is the best brief discussion of the historical background to *Triumph of the Will* ever written. Available only as notes for the film screening.

ESTES, JIM. "Nazi Film—A Triumph of Evil Genius." *San Francisco Chronicle*, July 28, 1959, p. 35. As the title implies, this is one of the many articles claiming that Riefenstahl lent her artistic talents to an evil cause.

GARDNER, ROBERT. "Can the Will Triumph?" *Film Comment*, Vol. 3, No. 1, Winter 1965, pp. 28-31. A well-known filmmaker and film critic here pioneers as almost the first sympathetic critic of Riefenstahl's life and work.

GREGOR, ULRICH. "A Comeback for Leni Riefenstahl." *Film Comment*, Vol. 3, No. 1, Winter 1965, pp. 24-25. The author claims that he is speaking for himself and his generation in condemning the work of Leni Riefenstahl as inherently Fascist.

GUNSTON, DAVID. "Leni Riefenstahl." *Film Quarterly*, Fall 1960, pp. 4-18. Although this article contains a number of factual errors—not surprising considering its date of publication—it is one of the best pieces on Riefenstahl ever written: critical but fair. It is also distinguished by an excellent style, rarely seen in scholarly works on film history.

HEBERLE, HELGE. "Notizen zur Riefenstahl-Rezeption." *Frauen und Film*, no. 14 (December, 1977), 29-34. A recent, left-wing German critique of Riefenstahl and her work.

HITCHENS, GORDON. "An Interview With a Legend." *Film Comment*, Winter 1965, pp. 6-11. One of the first interviews Riefenstahl ever published; much later research is based upon it.

―――― "Leni Riefenstahl Interviewed," October 11, 1971, in Munich. *Film Culture*, Spring, 1973, pp. 94-121. One of the most recent interviews Riefenstahl gave to an American, it contains a good deal of information on her work on the Nuba.

MANNHEIM, L. ANDREW. "Leni." *Modern Photography,* February 1974, pp. 88-119. Describes a few photographic innovations that are credited to Riefenstahl.

SCHILLE, PETER. "Lenis blühende Träume." *Der Stern,* no. 35 (August 18, 1977), pp. 28-43. One of the first articles on Riefenstahl's underwater photography.

SCHULBERG, BUDD B. "Nazi Pin-Up Girl: Hitler's Nr. 1 Movie Actress." *Saturday Evening Post,* March 30, 1946, pp. 11-41. This often-quoted article deserves being described as a "hatchet-job." Its author was obviously carried away by his anti-Nazi sentiments at the time of writing it.

SOKAL, HARRY R. "Über Nacht antisemitin geworden?" *Der Spiegel,* no. 46 (1976), p. 14. A letter in which Sokal, once Riefenstahl's fiancé, claims that Riefenstahl became a racist and anti-Semite overnight after reading Hitler's *Mein Kampf.* Harry Sokal was a producer of three films in which Riefenstahl was involved, including *The Blue Light.*

SONTAG, SUSAN. "Fascinating Fascism." *New York Review of Books,* February 6, 1975, pp. 23-30. While this is the most insightful recent piece of writing on the aesthetics of Riefenstahl's Nazi films, it also suffers from a striking though forgivable ignorance of the particulars of German cultural and political history. It is probably the most influential article read by U.S. film critics on Riefenstahl at this time.

DER SPIEGEL. "Blut und Hoden." *Der Spiegel,* no. 44 (1976), 228-32. The author(s) of the article, discussing Riefenstahl's books on the Nuba, suggest that there is a relationship between Riefenstahl's love for the black uniforms of the SS and the black bodies of the Nuba tribesmen.

WEIGEL, HERMAN. "Interview mit Leni Riefenstahl." *Filmkritik* (August 1972), pp. 426-33. This is the only serious interview conducted by a German film writer with Riefenstahl, and it provides a good deal of information, especially on Riefenstahl's more recent activities.

# Filmography

1. Films in which Leni Riefenstahl Appeared

## DER HEILIGE BERG (THE HOLY MOUNTAIN); (UFA, 1926)

| | |
|---|---|
| Director: | Dr. Arnold Fanck |
| Screenplay: | Dr. Arnold Fanck |
| Photography: | Sepp Allgeier, Albert Benitz, Helmar Lerski, Kurt Neubert, Hans Schneeberger |
| Set Decoration: | Leopold Blonder, Karl Böhm |
| Music: | Edmund Meisel |
| Cast: | Leni Riefenstahl, Luis Trenker, Frieda Richard, Friedrich Schneider, Hannes Schneider, Ernst Petersen |
| Running Time: | about 78 minutes; 3,100 meters |
| Premiere: | December 17, 1926, Berlin UFA-Palast am Zoo |

Note: One copy is in the Riefenstahl Archives, and one in the Federal Archives, Koblenz, Germany.

## DER GROSSE SPRUNG (THE GREAT LEAP); (UFA, 1927)

| | |
|---|---|
| Director: | Dr. Arnold Fanck |
| Photography: | Sepp Allgeier, Richard Angst, Albert Benitz, Charles Metain, Kurt Neubert, Hans Schneeberger |
| Set Decoration: | Erich Czerwonski |
| Music: | Werner R. Heymann |
| Cast: | Leni Riefenstahl, Luis Trenker, Hans Schneeberger, Paul Graetz |
| Running Time: | about 73 minutes; 2,931 meters |
| Premiere: | December 22, 1927, UFA-Palast am Zoo, Berlin |

Note: The film is available for rental from Parufamet/Germany. In England it is known as *Gita, the Goat Girl*. A copy is also available in the Riefenstahl Archives, as well as in the Federal Archives, Koblenz, Germany.

## DAS SCHICKSAL DERER VON HABSBURG (THE FATE OF THE HAPSBURGS); (Leofilm and Essemfilm, 1929)

Director:            Rudolf Raffé
Screenplay:          Max Ferner
Photography:         Marius Holdt
Cast:                Leni Riefenstahl, Erna Morena, Fritz Spira, Maly
                     Debschaft, Alfons Fryland, Franz Kammauf
Running Time:        about 60 minutes; 2,400 meters
Premiere:            Early 1929

Note:   The film is probably lost.

## DIE WEISSE HÖLLE VOM PIZ PALÜ (THE WHITE HELL OF PIZ PALÜ); H. R. Sokal Film, Berlin, 1929)

Director:            Dr. Arnold Fanck
Assistant Director:  G.W. Pabst
Screenplay:          Dr. Arnold Fanck, Ladislaus Vajda
Photography:         Sepp Allgeier, Richard Angst, Hans Schneeberger
Set Decoration:      Ernö Metzner
Music:               Willy Schmidt-Gentner
Cast:                Leni Riefenstahl, Gustav Diessl, Ernst Petersen, Ernst
                     Udet, Mizzi Götzel, Otto Spring
Running Time:        84 minutes; 3,330 meters
Premiere:            November 15, 1929, UFA-Palast am Zoo, Berlin
16mm Rental:         Museum of Modern Art, New York; Aafa Special
                     Distribution (in Germany); Beta-Film, Munich

Note:   The original silent film was reedited with a sound track in 1935.

## STÜRME ÜBER DEM MONTBLANC (STORMS OVER MONT BLANC); (Aafa-Film, Berlin, 1930)

Producer:            Harry Sokal
Director:            Dr. Arnold Fanck
Assistant Director:  Karl Mayer
Screenplay:          Dr. Arnold Fanck
Photography:         Sepp Allgeier, Richard Angst, Hans Schneeberger
Set Decoration:      Leopold Blonder
Music:               Dr. Guiseppe Becce (several filmographies list Paul
                     Dessau)
Cast:                Leni Riefenstahl, Sepp Rist, Ernst Udet, Mathias
                     Wieman, Friedrich Kayssler, Alfred Beyerle, Ernst

Petersen, David Zogg. Beni Führer, Rähmi (mountain guide), the Lantschner brothers, the Leubner brothers, Harald Reindl, Lucki Föger, Claus von Suchotzky

Running Time: about 74 minutes; 2,964 meters
Premiere: December 25, 1930, Princess Theater, Dresden

Note: The original title was "Über den Wolken" ("Above the Clouds"). The film is also known as *Avalanche*. The film is still available for rental in Germany.

**DER WEISSE RAUSCH (THE WHITE FRENZY)**; (H. R. Sokal Films, Berlin, 1931)

Director: Dr. Arnold Fanck
Screenplay: Dr. Arnold Fanck
Photography: Richard Angst, Kurt Neubert, Hans Gottschalk
Set Decoration: Leopold Bittner
Music: Paul Dessau, Fritz Goldschmidt
Sound: Leopold Bittmann, E. Specht
Cast: Leni Riefenstahl, Hannes Schneider, Guzzi Lantschner, Walter Riml, Rudi Matt, Lothar Ebersberg, and fifty international skiing champions
Running Time: 60 minutes; 2,565 meters
Premiere: December 10, 1931, Ufa-Palast am Zoo, Berlin

Note: In 1963-1965 a new version (65 minutes) was issued by Dr. Fanck. The film was originally titled *Sonne über dem Arlberg* (*Sunshine Over the Arlberg*). In 1956, it won an award at the Sports Films Biennial in Italy. The film is still available for rental in Germany.

**S.O.S. EISBERG (S.O.S. ICEBERG)**; (Deutsche Universal; Universal Corp., N.Y., 1933)

Director: Dr. Arnold Fanck
Assistant Director Tay Garnett (for the English version, Werner Klinge)
Screenplay: Dr. Arnold Fanck, Fritze Loewe, Ernst Sorge, Hans Heinrich, E. Knopf, F. Wolf, Tom Reed
Photography: Richard Angst, Hans Schneeberger
Pilots: Ernst Udet, Franz Schrieck
Scientific Advisors: Dr. Fritz Loewe, Dr. Ernst Sorge
Set Direction: Fritz Maurischat, Dr. Ernst Petersen, Arno Richter
Music: Paul Dessau
Cast: Leni Riefenstahl, Ernst Udet, Gustav Diessl, Sepp

|                    | Rist, Gibson Gowland, Walter Riml, Max Holzboer |
| Running Time:      | 71 minutes; 2,827 meters; American release, 76 minutes |
| Premiere:          | August 30, 1933, UFA-Palast am Zoo, Berlin |
| 16mm or 35mm Rental: | Universal Films, New York |

2. Films Directed by Leni Riefenstahl

**DAS BLAUE LICHT (THE BLUE LIGHT)**; (Leni Riefenstahl Studio Films, 1932)

| Producer:          | H. R. Sokal |
| Assistant Director: | Béla Balázs |
| Screenplay:        | Leni Riefenstahl in collaboration with Béla Balázs |
| Photography:       | Hans Schneeberger, Henry Jaworsky |
| Music:             | Guiseppe Becce |
| Editor:            | Leni Riefenstahl |
| Cast:              | Leni Riefenstahl, Mathias Wieman, Max Holzboer, Beni Führer, Martha Maire, Franz Maldacea |
| Running Time:      | 70 minutes; 2,344 meters |
| Premiere:          | March 24, 1932, Berlin |
| 16mm Rental:       | Janus Films, New York; Museum of Modern Art, New York (1952 version) |

Note: The film was reedited in 1952 with a new sound track, which, in Riefenstahl's opinion, was better than the original sound track.

**SIEG DES GLAUBENS (VICTORY OF FAITH)**; (Ministry of Propaganda, Germany, 1933)

| Photography:       | Sepp Allgeier, Franz Weimayr, Walter Frentz, R. Quaas, P. Tesch |
| Music:             | Herbert Windt |
| Cast:              | Members of the NSDAP at the 1933 Nuremberg rally |
| Running Time:      | Approximately 45 minutes; 1,700 meters |
| Premiere:          | December 1, 1933 |

Note: The film has been lost.

**TRIUMPH DES WILLENS (TRIUMPH OF THE WILL)**; (Leni Riefenstahl Studio Films, 1935)

| | |
|---|---|
| Producer: | NSDAP and Leni Riefenstahl |
| Business Managers: | Walter Traut, Walter Grosskopf |
| Photography: | Sepp Allgeier (overall direction) |
| Cameramen: | Karl Altenberger, Werner Bohne, Walter Frentz, Hans Gottschalk, Werner Hundhausen, Herbert Kebelmann, Albert Kling, Franz Kock, Herbert Kutschbach, Paul Lieberenz, Richard Nickel, Walter Riml, Arthur von Schwertführer, Karl Vass, Franz Weihmayr, Siegfried Weinmann, Karl Wellert |
| Assistant Cameramen: | Sepp Ketterer, Wolfe Hart, Peter Haller, Kurt Schulz, Eugen O. Bernhard, Richard Kandler, Hans Bühring, Richard Böhm, Erich Stoll, Josef Koch, Otto Jäger, August Beis, Hans Wittman, Wolfgang Müller, Heinz Linke, Erich Küchler, Wilhelm Schmidt, Ernst Kunstmann, Erich Grohmann, Unit of Svend Noldan, Hans Noack, Fritz Brunsch |
| Aerial Photographs: | Albert Kling |
| Art Director: | Albert Speer (architectural planning) |
| Set Decoration: | City Councilor Brugmann, Architect Seegy |
| Music: | Herbert Windt |
| Sound: | Siegfried Schulz, Ernst Schütz |
| Sound Effects: | (March music dubbing): Band of the SS Bodyguard of Adolf Hitler directed by Bandmaster Müller-John —and sometimes by Leni Riefenstahl |
| Cast: | Members of the NSDAP, participants in the 1934 Nuremberg party rally, and inhabitants of the city of Nuremberg |
| Running Time: | 110 minutes in most versions; 3,109 meters; original version, 140 minutes |
| Premiere: | March 28, 1935, Ufa Palast, Berlin |
| 16mm Rental: | Janus Films, New York; Museum of Modern Art, New York; Phoenix Films, New York |

Note:   In 1942 a British film company, i.e., Silver Tone News, produced a two-minute film satirizing *Triumph of the Will.* Calling it "The Lambeth Walk-Nazi Style," its producers took footage from *Triumph of the Will*, reversed it in part, and combined it with jazzed-up music, thus rendering the ominous marching sequences in the original *Triumph of the Will* totally ridiculous.

## TAG DER FREIHEIT: UNSERE WEHRMACHT (DAY OF FREE-DOM: OUR ARMED FORCES); (Leni Riefenstahl Studio Film, 1935)

| | |
|---|---|
| Producer: | Reich Party Congress Film of Leni Riefenstahl Studio Film |
| Photography: | Willy Zielke, Guzzi Lantschner et al. |
| Music: | Peter Kreuder |
| Editor: | Leni Riefenstahl |
| Cast: | German army and officers |
| Running Time: | 21 minutes |
| Premiere: | December 1935. This film was shown as a short feature before a major UFA film screening |
| 16mm Rental: | Kit Parker Films, P.O. Box 227, Carmel Valley, California, 93924 |

## OLYMPIA. Part 1; FEST DER VÖLKER (FESTIVAL OF NATIONS); Part 2; FEST DER SCHÖNHEIT (FESTIVAL OF BEAUTY); (Olympia Film, 1938)

| | |
|---|---|
| Business Manager: | Walter Traut |
| Photography: | Hans Ertl, Walter Frentz, Guzzi Lantschner, Kurt Neubert, Hans Scheib, Willi Zielke, Andor von Barsy, Wilfried Basse, Johannes Dietze, E. Epkens, F. von Friedl, Hans Gottschalk, Richard Groschapp, W. Hameister, Wolf Hart, Hasso Hartnagel, Walter Hege, E. von der Heyden, Albert Höcht, Paul Holzki, W. Hundhausen, Henry Jaworsky. H. von Kaweczynski, H. Kebelmann, S. Ketterer, Albert Kling, Ernst Kunstmann, Leo de Laforgue, A. Lagorio, E. Lambertini, Otto Lantschner, Waldemar Lemke, Georg Lemki, C. A. Linke, E. Nitzschemann, Albert Schattmann, Wilhelm Schmidt, Hugo Schulze, L. Schwedler, Alfred Siegert, W. Siehm, Ernst Sorge, H. von Stwolinski, Karl Vass |
| Set Decoration: | Robert Herlth |
| Music: | Herbert Windt, Walter Gronostay |
| German Narration: | Paul Laven, Rolf Wernicke |
| Sound: | Siegfried Schulz, M. Michel, Hermann Storr, Otto Lantschner, Guzzi Lantschner, J. Lüdke, Arnfried Heyne, W. Brüning |
| Editor: | Leni Riefenstahl |
| Cast: | Olympic contestants, Olympic committee officials, spectators, Nazi officials |

| Running Time: | Part 1, 120 minutes (3,269 meters); Part 2, 105 minutes (2,712 meters) |
|---|---|
| Premiere: | April 20, 1938 (Hitler's Birthday), Ufa Palast, Berlin |
| 16mm Rental: | Janus Films, New York; Museum of Modern Art, New York; Phoenix Films, New York |

Note:   The film was produced in four versions: German, English, French, and Italian. The Italian version was made by Cinecittà. The version distributed in the Federal Republic of Germany after World War II was de-Nazified and is shorter (part 1: 3,138 meters; part 2: 2,710 meters). *Olympia* was shown in West German film theaters with a new title for part 1, i.e., *Die Götter des Stadions* (*The Gods of the Stadium*), which is a translation of the French title of 1938, *Les Dieux du stade.*

**TIEFLAND (LOWLANDS)**; (Leni Riefenstahl Produktion, 1954)

| Assistant Director: | G. W. Pabst |
|---|---|
| Screenplay: | Leni Riefenstahl; based upon opera *Tiefland* by Eugene D'Albert |
| Photographer: | Albert Benitz |
| Set Decoration: | Isabella Ploberger |
| Music: | Eugene D'Albert with new compositions by Herbert Windt |
| Editor: | Leni Riefenstahl |
| Cast: | Leni Riefenstahl, Franz Eichberger, Bernhard Minetti, Aribert Wäscher, Maria Koppenhöfer, Luise Rainer, Frieda Richard, Karl Skramps, Max Holzboer |
| Running Time: | 98 minutes; 2,695 meters |
| Premiere: | February 11, 1954 |
| 16mm Rental: | Janus Films, New York |

# Index

219